M. ckb. Nachlas, Ph. D.

THE POTENTIAL OF WOMAN

MAN AND CIVILIZATION

THE POTENTIAL OF WOMAN

a symposium edited by

Seymour M. Farber   Roger H. L. Wilson

University of California
San Francisco Medical Center

McGRAW-HILL BOOK COMPANY, INC.

New York   San Francisco
Toronto   London

THE POTENTIAL OF WOMAN

This book is a record of the third symposium Man and Civilization, *held at the University of California San Francisco Medical Center January 25, 26, and 27, 1963, produced in collaboration with William J. Brant, Enoch Callaway, III, David Krech, Hilda Krech, and Ester Peterson, members of the program committee. Within the limits of space, it consists of the actual material as it was presented. To preserve spontaneity, the panels in particular have been presented in their original form with only minor editing. Thus we have as true a mirror as possible of this unusual symposium.*

CONTRIBUTORS

Ethel M. Albert, Ph.D., Associate Professor of Speech, University of California, Berkeley, California

J. Ralph Audy, M.B., B.S., Ph.D., Director, Hooper Foundation; Professor of Tropical Medicine and Human Ecology, Department of Medicine, University of California Medical Center, San Francisco, California

Wiliam J. Brandt, Ph.D., Assistant Professor of English, San Jose State College, San Jose, California

Klaus W. Berblinger, M.D., Associate Professor of Psychiatry, University of California School of Medicine, San Francisco, California

Enoch Callaway, III, M.D., Associate Clinical Professor of Psychiatry, Langley Porter Neuropsychiatric Institute, San Francisco, California

Seymour M. Farber, M.D., Assistant Dean, in Charge of Continuing Education in Medicine and the Health Sciences, University of California Medical Center, San Francisco, California

Willard C. Fleming, D.D.S., Vice-Provost, University of California, San Francisco Medical Center; Dean, School of Dentistry; Professor of Operative Dentistry, San Francisco, California

Barbara Bates Gunderson, B.A., Writer, Lecturer, Former U.S. Civil Service Comissioner, Washington, D.C.

Mark Harris, Ph.D., Associate Professor of English, San Francisco State College, San Francisco, California

Catherine C. Hearst, Regent, University of California

Eleanor R. Heller, LL.D., Regent, University of California

Thomas Carr Howe, M.F.A., Director, California Palace of the Legion of Honor, Lincoln Park, San Francisco, California

Morton M. Hunt, A.B., Author, New York, New York

Phyllis C. Jay, M.A., Fellow, Center for Advanced Study in Behavioral Sciences, Stanford, California

v

Clark Kerr, Ph.D., LL.D., President, University of California; Professor of Industrial Relations, Berkeley, California

Adrienne Koch, Ph.D., Professor of History, and Chairman, American Studies, University of California, Berkeley, California

Peter Koestenbaum, Ph.D., Associate Professor of Philosophy, San Jose State College, San Jose, California

David Krech, Ph.D., Professor of Psychology, University of California, Berkeley, California

Hilda Krech, Ph.D., Author, Berkeley, California

Honorable Alice K. Leopold, Former Assistant to Secretary of Labor, Washington, D.C.

Eleanor E. Maccoby, Ph.D., Associate Professor of Psychology, Stanford University, Stanford, California

David G. Mandelbaum, Ph.D., Professor of Anthropology, University of California, Berkeley, California

Marya Mannes, Author, New York, New York

J. Fenton McKenna, J.D., Chairman, Creative Arts Division, Professor of Drama, San Francisco State College, San Francisco, California

John Money, Ph.D., Associate Professor of Medical Psychology and Pediatrics, The Johns Hopkins University, Baltimore, Maryland

Helen E. Nahm, Ph.D., Dean, School of Nursing, Professor of Nursing, University of California School of Medicine, San Francisco, California

Edmund W. Overstreet, M.D., Professor of Obstetrics and Gynecology, University of California School of Medicine, San Francisco, California

Honorable Esther Peterson, Assistant Secretary of Labor and Director, U.S. Department of Labor, Washington, D.C.

Karl H. Pribram, M.D., Professor, Departments of Psychiatry and Psychology, Stanford University, Stanford, California

John B. DeC. M. Saunders, M.B., F.R.C.S. (Edin.) Provost, University of California, San Francisco Medical Center; Dean, School of Medicine; Professor of Anatomy and Chairman, Department of Medical History and Bibliography, San Francisco, California

Albert E. Schwabacher, Jr., Investment Banker, San Francisco, California

Katherine A. Towle, LL.D., Dean of Students, University of California, Berkeley, California

Alan Watts, Author, Philosopher, Sausalito, California

Roger H. L. Wilson, M.D., Assistant Head, Continuing Education in Medicine, University of California Medical Center, San Francisco, California

PREFACE

Whatever problems one may wish to lay at the door of the twentieth century, the substantial emancipation of women that has taken place in these sixty-odd years is surely an example of significant human progress. Never in the history of Western civilization (unless prehistoric Greece was in fact matriarchal, as has sometimes been argued) have women come so near to the real freedom that equality with men implies. This development is as revolutionary as anything this age has seen, and it is already extending very rapidly from the United States and Great Britain to a large part of the European continent and to many non-European countries. By the end of the century it is likely that full equality between men and women will be the normal state of affairs over the whole earth.

The right to vote is only a small part of this new freedom. In the past, women necessarily defined themselves by the relationships they established with men. There was surely some choice available to women in previous periods. They could choose to be complacent or shrewish, domineering or submissive, efficient or burdensome. But their choices were very limited, and they were always made in terms of the masculine figures in their lives. Today great numbers of women can, if they choose, define themselves as independent, self-determining individuals. They can become fully human, since self-definition is the capacity marking human beings off from the rest of the universe.

However, this change has taken place with enormous rapidity; its effects have only become general since about 1920. Predictably, this rapid revolution has produced dislocation and even chaos. For one thing, it is difficult to know the practical limits of equality. The mere biological differences between the sexes imply, in some areas of endeavor, a kind of fundamental inequality, or would seem to. But we do not know what these limits are, even theoretically. Furthermore, our progress toward equality has been very uneven. Any woman today can get an education as good as she has the capacity to absorb; equality in the schoolroom has been almost completely achieved. But economic equality is some distance off. Furthermore, and perhaps most seriously, it has proved much easier to weaken and destroy the old roles which women traditionally filled than to create new ones. It is easy enough to assert that women must be something more than wives and mothers, but it is not easy to define that something, nor is it easy to reconcile the added human stature that equality implies with the old biological roles.

These are not problems that permit easy solutions. Indeed, the more important solutions will be evolutionary ones, to which time and experience and daily adjustments, some trivial in themselves, will contribute very heavily. But this does not mean that earnest thought about these difficulties cannot be finally crucial in determining women's ultimate role in society. These personal and social difficulties are unavailable to the operations of a computer, or human brains trying to behave like computers. But we can put our heads together, so to speak, and perhaps influence those daily solutions which will be decisive. Intelligence plays its role in even the most complex of human affairs, though its operation be involved.

At least, such was the thinking that went into the symposium of which this book is a faithful account. Our intention was to gather together a group of people, from as many professions as possible, to talk about the potentialities of women and the hazards that they confront in their search for that most meaningful of freedoms, the freedom to be oneself. That discussion was, we think, brilliant, informative and, finally, useful.

From the very beginning of this symposium many women expressed their deep interest, and the Program Committee profited from the help and advice of more women than can possibly be enumerated here. But the help of three women in particular cannot be passed by without notice. The Honorable Esther Peterson, Assistant Secretary of Labor, took part in our planning from the very beginning, and her advice and encouragement were indispensable. Mrs. Randolph A. Hearst and Mrs. Edward H. Heller, LL.D., both Regents of the University of California, offered their services to the committee very early in its work, and their contributions to the final shape of the symposium were substantial. The abiding interest that these three charming ladies have in the welfare of women everywhere made this symposium possible, and to them belongs the credit for whatever positive contribution it may have made. And we would be remiss if we failed to acknowledge the wise guidance and contributions of Mrs. John B. deC. M. Saunders, who saved us from many errors. Our experience has proved her wisdom.

The Schering Corporation and the Schering Foundation through President Francis C. Brown contributed generously to the presentation of the original symposium, and we are deeply grateful. As usual, our staff, under the inspired direction of Miss Sadie Kaye, performed in a more-than-human fashion and with a more-than-human efficiency. They, too, were indispensable, and we can only repay their devotion by acknowledging our dependence upon it.

Seymour M. Farber, M.D.
Roger H. L. Wilson, M.D.

INTRODUCTION

Provost John B. deC. M. Saunders

This is the third of the symposia presented under the general title "Man and Civilization," the purpose of which is to explore in multidisciplinary fashion problems of great contemporary importance and interest.

The modern world has become increasingly aware of the ever-deepening chasm which has appeared in our culture because of the advancement of specialization in almost all fields of knowledge. Specialism has become, especially in intellectual affairs, the characteristic feature of the modern age, but unfortunately by its very nature it imposes limitations and restrictions on understanding.

Yet we cannot do without specialization, for out of it has come the technology to provide the great profusion of goods and services enjoyed by so many and envied by so many more. Consequently human desires compel the ever-increasing utilization of special techniques while human aspirations demand that we improve the world of general communication and understanding in the larger affairs of life itself.

To accomplish the latter aims it is important that we learn by means of symposia such as this something of the difficult art of interdisciplinary conversation. We must bring together those, such as the scientist and economist, who play an instrumental rôle in modern life, with those who are deeply engaged in value judgments, such as the philosopher, artist, and man of letters, if we are to see things whole and preserve the best from the two worlds.

It is entirely appropriate that, having explored in the previous symposia the mind of man and its control, and the problems of conflict and creativity, we should now turn to that other half of man and explore the rôle and potentiality of woman in our modern society.

It is also most appropriate that a symposium such as this be held at a medical center, since the first solid blow in support of the emancipation of women came from a physician. The illustrious Mohammedan physician and philosopher Averroes (1126–1198) of Cordova, the great interpreter of Aristotelianism to the Western world, made a remarkable and influential philosophical plea on behalf of women's rights. He contended that women differed from men not in quality but only in degree; that they are apt in all men's occupations though to a lesser degree, and they sometimes surpass them. He gave examples of the aptitudes of women in war, and he could see no impediment to their governance of the state. Some of these ideas were taken up by that curious Gallocentric publicist and reformer Petrus de Bosco (Pierre Dubois) (c. 1250–1321) which were embodied in the visionary appeal of his *De Recuperatione Terrae Sanctae* for the education of women as missionaries trained in the professions, especially in medicine and surgery, to permit the matrimonial penetration and conquest of the Muslim and other infidels where the Crusaders had failed. Likewise de Bosco's younger contemporary, the English logician and Franciscan friar William of Ockham (d.c. 1349) proclaimed the revolutionary doctrine of feminism that since women have souls to save, there is no reason why they should not vote.

These strong opinions of the Middle Ages on emancipation and woman suffrage received practical support with the growth of the towns and the development of borough laws which permitted the woman trader. Despite the restriction of church and custom, middle-class woman with substantial business ability played a considerable rôle in the mercantile life of the medieval city, while her aristocratic sister exhibited that social freedom which developed the romance literature and artistic patronage and bred such strong feminine personalities as Eleanor of Aquitaine and the Countess of Montfort.

With such a rich legacy from the Middle Ages it is astonishing that we should have waited until the twentieth century for the acceptance of women as self-determining and independent individuals. A strong case can be made for the belief that during the intervening period of nearly four hundred years the chains which bound women were those which shackled her to witchcraft. These gruesome beliefs, as exemplified in that astonishing document, the *Malleus Maleficarum* of the Inquisitors

Johann Kraemer and Heinrich Sprenger, expanded to immense proportions during the fifteenth and sixteenth centuries. Women now tottered from the pedestal to the pit. A mass psychosis or endemic persecutory mania affected the whole of the Western world, extending almost to the nineteenth century. How recent were the witch trials at Salem! The many reasons for this extraordinary aberration cannot be gone into now. It is only necessary to point out that the persecutions were directed overwhelmingly against women, and most often against impressionable children of ten to fifteen years of age. Failure to appreciate fundamental physiological and psychological phenomena and their related disorders led to an obliteration of the dividing line between physical or mental illness and heresy or apostasy. The first awakening of scientific skepticism aroused both lay and ecclesiastic authorities to a measure of self-defense signalized by persecution. The healing of this breach has taken centuries of time, and its appalling effects are illustrative of the dangers attending a schizoid culture.

Appropriately, then, Part One of this book takes up some of the biological and behavioral aspects of the female. It is only by the acknowledgment of scientific fact and by an appreciation of the gaps and uncertainties in scientific knowledge that we can hope to derive any holistic concept of human problems. Thus it is astonishing to read recently reported views that democracy will perish unless scientists and the technology they serve are brought under the control of man. This sounds uncommonly like the attitude which led to the repressions of women in the fifteenth century. Since science is concerned with the objective analysis of natural phenomena, there is as much possibility of placing controls upon its development as King Canute was able to exercise on the tides of the sea. The man of letters, the poet, the artist, the statesman, and the everyday citizen can direct the future wisely, in proportion to his understanding of the principles of nature as revealed by science. This knowledge of science and nature he must weave into the spiritual patterns of human creativity and of wisdom.

May I leave you, then, with a wish for a successful and stimulating conference and with my doubts on the opinion expressed by Samuel Butler in his *Hudibras:*·

> Such great achievements cannot fail
> To cast salt on a woman's tail.

CONTENTS

THE CONSEQUENCES OF EQUALITY

Chairman: Katherine A. Towle

THE MALE REVOLT

Chairman: Helen E. Nahm

THE PRIVATE WORLDS OF MR. AND MRS. MITTY

Chairmen: Alice K. Leopold
Enoch Callaway, III

PART ONE

THE EXPERIMENTAL STUDY OF THE FEMALE

Chairman: Esther Peterson

The first session of the symposium was devoted to objective studies of what is known about the basic nature of woman. In the first paper the physical anthropologist presented the studies of the more primitive primate, the langur monkey, and the basic patterns of mother-child relationships seen in this species. This was followed by a paper on the general biologic make-up of woman, in which the impact of biologic factors on her pattern of life at various ages was contrasted with the altogether more primitive situation of the previous presentation. The final paper of this session dealt with psychological studies of girls and women in an attempt to gain insight into the underlying abilities and goals that would be expected. The panel which followed integrated these three separate aspects, expanding upon the limitations of present knowledge and the potentialities for future study.

Phyllis C. Jay

THE FEMALE PRIMATE

With few exceptions the nonhuman female primate is an extremely social animal. Her life is spent with familiar animals in a familiar place acting out a regular daily and annual routine. Novelty is minimal. Her primary focus, a role which occupies more than 70 per cent of her life, is motherhood. Females in some species of monkey which give birth every year may spend one-half of their adult life pregnant. A female raises one infant after another for her entire adult life. Among the Asian langur monkeys some females are very good mothers, while others are much less efficient. Experience handling infants and the personality of the female are two important variables in being a good or poor mother. Sexual activity occurs on fewer than 3 per cent of the days of adult life and only during certain parts of the month when the female is not pregnant or nursing a young infant. The monkey female is the sole initiator of sexual activity. What is "normal" for the nonhuman primate female and for the human female are substantially different ways of life.

The female primate: who is she, what are her social roles, and how like or unlike a human female is the nonhuman primate? Because of the great burst of interest and research on free-ranging primates in the last ten years we are in a good position to begin to answer some of these questions. Since all those who follow me in this conference will discuss the human female primate, I will focus on her closest

3

living female relatives—the perhaps more predictable though not less interesting nonhuman female primates.

First of all, we can say that with very few exceptions the non-human female primate is an extremely social animal. She is born into, raised within, and dies in one social group. All monkeys and apes spend their lives in social groups composed of animals of both sexes and in all ages. These are usually social groups whose membership is stable and whose yearly cycle of activity is unchanging. Her life is spent with familiar animals in a familiar place, acting out a predictable daily and annual routine. Novelty is minimal in the life of the non-human primate.

But, to answer the first of our questions more specifically, who is she? Primates are varied in size, structure, color, and temperament. Depending on the species you wish to consider, the female may be extremely aggressive, or she may be pacific and docile. These are not temperaments found in equal numbers in all species but are instead closely correlated with the way of life to which the species has adapted. There are many basic similarities in behavior among all species; we have just mentioned a few. There are also fundamental patterns of social behavior which are common to all kinds of monkeys and apes but which are emphasized differently in different kinds of primates.

For instance, a ground-living monkey, such as a baboon, may walk miles every day out onto a treeless savannah where the only protection against predators such as lions are the large and powerful adult males of the troop. Dominance among these monkeys is very important, and it is essential to survival that the social group be able to mobilize rapidly when danger threatens (Washburn and DeVore, 1961). These are very different forms of adult behavior from those among a species of monkey which spends its life in the trees. Arboreal monkeys such as the Asian langurs are always within or close to the relative safety of trees. They are adapted behaviorally and morphologically to essentially different ways of life. Dominance, although present, is much less important; adult males and females tend to be of more equal size, and in general the tenor of life is relaxed (Jay, 1963).

Since the female primate normally does not exist apart from a social group, and, indeed, she cannot mature into a normal adult outside this context, I will discuss her activities in a free-ranging social group—the context to which her social behavior is adapted.

The most important, time-consuming role of the nonhuman primate female, and her primary focus as an adult, is motherhood. She raises one infant after another from the time she assumes adult roles at the age of about three to four years, until the time she dies. In other words, more than two-thirds of her life, and probably much more, is spent nurturing and protecting her infants. Her dominance status, associations with adult males, female companions, and daily activities to a large extent are a function of her status as a mother and her phase of the reproductive cycle.

The next most important and time-consuming activity, one which she engages in throughout her life, is mutual relaxed grooming. Grooming cuts across all boundaries formed by social status, dominance, and age. A female has close grooming ties to most of the members of the troop, and by far the majority of her contacts with adult males occur in mutual relaxed grooming.

Dominance interaction is usually minimal in the life of a female. She is invariably subordinate to all the adult males in the group and seldom if ever contests his superior status. In some species the females form a dominance hierarchy among themselves in which some females are very dominant while others are consistently subordinate. In other species dominance is extremely poorly defined, and it is difficult to tell which females are more or less dominant than other females.

Sexual behavior actually plays a very small part in the life of an adult female. A female is sexually receptive only when she is in estrus. This lasts for from five to seven days a month when she is not pregnant or lactating. She is receptive only during the period of her sexual cycle between menstruations when ovulation is most likely to occur. This is in contrast to the human female, who is continually sexually receptive. If the female is pregnant approximately six months, cares for a dependent infant closely for an additional six months, and is not sexually receptive again until the infant is weaned at from ten to twelve months of age, she will not give birth again for another six to eight months. Births in many species such as langurs in India are spaced at approximately two-year intervals. In these species a female is sexually receptive on less than approximately 5 per cent of the days in her adult life, and in reality is sexually active on less than 3 per cent. If we were able to figure out exactly the number of hours during which she was sexually active, it would be far less than 1 per cent. This is an exceedingly small percentage. When she is not in estrus, the adult males show no sexual interest in her. She is the sole initiator of sexual activity, and she is not mounted unless she solicits the attention of the male. In some species such as the rhesus macaque and the baboon, the female undergoes a period during the monthly cycle when the perineal skin swells and becomes bright red. This is a clear indication of sexual receptivity to a male. Many other species such as the Asian langurs and the African colobus show no such swelling, and the female must indicate to the male by her behavior that she is sexually receptive.

Consider then what is "normal" for the primate female. If births are spaced at two-year intervals as in langurs, less than 3 per cent and probably much less than 1 per cent of a female's adult life is spent in sexual relations. She is pregnant approximately one-fourth of the time, or 25 per cent. She lactates and cares for a dependent infant one-third of the time, or 33 per cent of her adult life. Weaning occupies one-fifth, or 20 per cent, of her adult life. Weaning may overlap with the resumption of her estrus cycles, but often it does not. This means that approximately *70 per cent* of her adult life is spent being a mother!

Other species of monkeys such as some of the rhesus macaques give birth every year. Rhesus females spend approximately 50 per cent, or half, of their adult life pregnant, and during the remaining portion of their adult life they are associated with infants. In these species one female is frequently associated with several offspring, since the last is not completely weaned and is not independent of the mother when the next is born. She is sexually active on only approximately 3 to 5 per cent of the days of her adult life. Percentages may differ slightly from species to species, but the overwhelming amount of time the adult female spends being a mother is the same for all monkeys. To the monkey then, "normal" is repeated motherhood, not repeated menstrual cycles as is normal for the human female for so many years of her life.

After this general introduction let us look at the world of the female langur monkey. Langurs are arboreal Asian leaf monkeys with stomachs specially adapted to digest huge quantities of relatively unnutritious mature leaves. The common Indian langur monkey is found throughout India. It spends more time on the ground than any of the closely related langurs in South and Southeast Asia. But, even though the common langur may spend up to 80 per cent of the day on the ground, it is never far from the safety of trees.

In most respects the langur female is a typical monkey female. She is extremely gregarious, devotes most of her time to raising infants, and is active in the grooming relations of the troop. In other respects the langur female is rather unusual and presents strong contrasts to ground-living monkey females whose social behavior is adapted to an essentially different way of life. In addition to the larger differences in behavior among species, there are also smaller variations among the adults of one species. Not all langur females behave in the same way. Unique experiences which occur in the development of each langur produce variations in adult behavior, and variations in the personalities of adult monkeys contribute still more to these differences. Another important factor which increases variations of social behavior are changes from one stage to another in the reproductive cycle—changes which affect every adult female. A female's dominance status is not constant. Instead, it changes as she enters different phases of her reproductive cycle. She rises slightly in dominance status when she is in estrus (sexually receptive) and during the last weeks of pregnancy. When she is with a newborn infant, she is outside the dominance hierarchy altogether and avoids dominance interactions.

The mother—newborn infant relationship is the strongest and most intense social bond in the life of the langur monkey (Jay, in press). At birth the infant langur is dependent on its mother for nourishment and transport, but it is by no means completely helpless. It is a clinging, vocal animal, capable of controlling to a great extent its relations with the mother. The central nervous system of a human infant is not as well developed as that of a newborn monkey until the human infant is approximately six months old. The monkey can cling to its mother with no assistance within a very few days after birth and can secure itself so tightly under her body that she can run on the ground and make long jumps through the air without dislodging it. Although the natal coat color remains dark brown for approximately the first five months of life, the infant is able to move independently of the mother long before that. The mother and other adult females are most intensely interested in an infant only as long as it is dark brown. When its coat color changes to white, active female interest decreases.

The birth of a langur infant is an important event in a langur troop. As soon as the females in the troop, whether adult, subadult, or juvenile, notice the infant, they immediately cluster closely around the mother. All reach out gently and try to be the first to touch, lick, and smell the newborn.

The mother inspects, licks, grooms, and manipulates the infant from the hour of its birth. When the newborn infant is resting quietly, she grooms and strokes it softly without disturbing or waking it. She usually turns her back to the waiting females until the infant is dry— only a few hours after birth. As soon as the infant is dry, she allows several of the waiting females to handle the infant, and within a few minutes one of these females takes the infant from its mother and holds it. As soon as the favored female has the infant in her arms, she inspects it minutely, gently manipulating, nudging, licking, and smelling the infant. Special attention is given to inspecting the infant's head, hands, and genital area. At the first sign of discomfort the newborn struggles or starts to whine and is taken by another of the waiting females. Often, if the mother is sitting nearby, she reaches out and intercepts her infant before another female can take it. The infant may be held by as many as eight females during the first day of its life and may be carried up to 50 feet away from the mother. However, she is able to retrieve her infant from any other female in the troop regardless of the relative dominance status of the females involved.

Although female langurs are intensely interested in newborn infants, there is great variation among mothers in the care of their infants and among females when they are holding the infants of other females. Not all females can keep an infant quiet and content— a few females are awkward and clumsy—but the majority have little or not trouble. The range of ability extends from extremely competent to incompetent. Competent females are casual but firm, apparently unaware of the movement of the often very active infant, while less competent females are uncertain of themselves and constantly readjust the infant to shift it from side to side. A very few females, much less than 1 per cent, are simply inept. They hold the infant too tightly, upside down, or away from their body to inspect it constantly. These females also seem to have trouble making a newborn cling and nurse.

There is also much variation among females as to whether they allow the newborn infant of another female to take a nipple and try to nurse. Some females pull the infant away from their breast each time it succeeds in finding a nipple. Many females let the infant press against their chest and at least take a nipple. Of all the females observed holding the infant of another female, less than one-fourth deliberately helped the infant locate and grasp a nipple.

Older females which have given birth to many infants are, in general, better, more efficient mothers than are very young females. These older and more experienced females are usually more confident with a newborn and need to expend little effort in keeping it calm and quiet. The length of time a female can hold a newborn infant before it is uncomfortable is a measure of her ability to handle it, because whenever a newborn is uncomfortable, it squirms and squeals. Experience appears to be important in caring for an infant. Because langur mothers allow other females to hold their infants, no langur female is completely without some experience in infant care. A baboon mother, on the contrary, does not allow another female even to touch a newborn infant for several weeks.

Another source of considerable variation which influences females in their interest in, and aptitude for, holding infants is the female's temperament or personality. A tense, nervous, and easily irritated female frequently startles the infant with quick or unpredictable motions, whereas a calmer and more relaxed female makes few sudden movements.

In many species the mother's behavior and relationships with other adults are very important, and her social status, or dominance position, may be reflected in the development of her infants. Research workers at the Japan Monkey Center have followed the lives of many Japanese macaque monkeys for over ten years, and it is possible to see the effect of the mother's dominance status on the status of her offspring as they mature. Among the Japanese macaques only infants of the most dominant females grow up in the center of the troop. This area is occupied only by the most dominant males and the most dominant females.

Infants raised here apparently learn the behavioral patterns characteristic of dominant rather than subordinate adults. They learn to dominate animals which are forced by the dominant animals to remain on the periphery of the troop's center of activity. The Japanese workers suggest that infants raised in the troop center learn the roles characteristic of leaders and very dominant monkeys (Imanishi, 1960).

In the case of another primarily ground-living monkey, the baboon, the social status of the mother is also very important for the eventual status of her offspring. The degree of insecurity and frustration of the infant is apparently correlated with the mother's position in the dominance hierarchy. If the mother is dominated frequently, if she is constantly threatened and forced to give way to other adults, her infant's behavior is affected. If the mother is constantly upset, so, too, is her infant. Those baboon mothers which constantly receive attacks and threats appear to be less responsive to their infants and more short-tempered (DeVore, in press).

Dominance is much less important in the daily life of a langur female. The dominance status of an adult female is seldom apparent in her relations with other members of the troop, and as a result it is unlikely that her status has any significant effect on her offspring. Infants of all the females in the troop have free access to other infants in play and can venture into any part of the troop without being threatened by the adults. Some females tend to stay together more than with other females, but these preference groupings are temporary and not exclusive. During the course of a few days all females sit by and groom all other females. In species such as langurs the dominance status of the mother is not as influential on the development of her young as is her temperament.

Results from laboratory experimentation also demonstrate the tremendous importance of mothers. Dr. Harry Harlow at the University of Wisconsin has shown that infants raised in isolation do not develop into normal adults, and further, that more than the addition of a cloth or wire surrogate mother is needed for normal social development. Harlow gave some of his rhesus monkey infants a surrogate mother, ". . . a mother, soft, warm, and tender, a mother with infinite patience, a mother available twenty-four hours a day, a mother that never scolded her infant, and never struck or bit her baby in anger." However, this mother was "biologically adequate but psychologically inept" (Harlow, 1958). More than an available, warm, soft, nourishing object is necessary for normal social development, and if there is a substitute for development in a social group, it must include at least a real mother. He also found that in addition to needing a real mother it is absolutely necessary for the infant monkey to grow up with age-mates. A mother is important and necessary to normal development, but she is not sufficient.

Our view of the female primate has been brief, but we can generalize about some of her universal qualities and roles. As a very gregarious animal she lives her entire life in a social group with others of her species. Over 70 per cent of her life is spent raising young—this is her major role in life. Females of species where births occur every year may spend up to 50 per cent of their adult life pregnant.

If we think of what is normal for a nonhuman primate female, it is caring for young, pregnancy, and lactation. This is not our conception of what is normal for a human female. A human female goes through years of menstrual cycles and is constantly sexually receptive. At a certain age she ceases to be able to reproduce, and menstrual cycles stop altogether. She usually lives many years after this age as a nonreproducing member of her species. This is very unlike the female monkey or ape. No adult female monkey or ape has ever been observed which was too old to go through estrus cycles and reproduce. Very old females have been observed—but all were still bearing young. There appears to be no menopause for the nonhuman primate.

Sexual behavior occupies very little of a female's life, since she is active sexually on less than 3 per cent of the days of her adult life. The female monkey is the sole initiator of sexual activity, and the male monkey is not sexually interested in a female unless she is in estrus and solicits him. This condition is very unlike the constant receptivity of the human female and the soliciting of the human male.

Greater understanding of the basic patterns of behavior which have been modified and built upon in the course of human social evolution will give us insights into the behavior of the human female today. Above all, we must realize that what we consider "normal" behavior for the human female is very different from normal for other primate females. It is probably equally different from "normal" behavior for the female from which the modern human female evolved.

References

DeVore, I. Mother-Infant Relations in Free-ranging Baboons. In *Maternal Care in Mammals*. Ed. by Harriet Rheingold. New York, John Wiley & Sons, Inc. Publication in 1963.

Harlow, Harry. The Nature of Love. *The American Psychologist*, 13(12):673–685, 1958.

Imanishi, Kinji. Social Organization of Subhuman Primates in Their Natural Habitat. *Current Anthropology*, 1(5–6):393–407, 1960.

Jay, Phyllis. The Indian Langur. In *Primate Social Behavior*. Ed. by C. H. Southwick. Princeton, N.J., D. Van Nostrand Company, Inc. Publication in 1963.

Jay, Phyllis. Aspects of Maternal Behavior among Langurs. In *Relatives of Man*. Ed. by J. Buettner-Janusch. *Annals of the New York Academy of Science*. Publication in 1963.

Washburn, S. L., and Irven DeVore. The Social Life of Baboons. *Scientific American*, 204(6):62–71, 1961.

Edmund W. Overstreet

THE BIOLOGICAL MAKE-UP OF WOMAN

The title of this presentation, "The Biological Make-up of Woman," is one which, obviously, covers a very broad field of knowledge. To attempt even to outline woman's entire biological make-up not only would be an impossible task in my allotted time, but it wouldn't serve any real purpose for the symposium that is to follow. For our later discussion we are not really interested in the fact that the human female has a head and extremities, a gastrointestinal tract, a nervous system (sometimes a *very* nervous system), a respiratory system, and so on. In thinking about the potential of woman in civilization what we are really interested in scrutinizing are those biological structures and functions possessed by woman which are different from those possessed by the human male. Presumably these structural and functional differences, by their very nature, produce mentational and emotional behavior in the woman which is different from that of the man. And it is largely these behavioral differences, both individual and social, which will be discussed at some length in the remainder of this symposium. As I review the structural differences I will barely have time to suggest in what ways they might influence woman's behavior. Indeed, there won't even be time to review all the differences which might be significant. So I will have to choose those aspects of the biological make-up of woman which I feel to have the greatest potentialities for producing distinctive female behavior. It will be up to the rest of our speakers to enlarge on these potentialities and on the specifics of the behavior.

The greatest single structural difference of woman is, in a sense, also her most minute. It occurs, of course, at the moment of conception when, as a single cell, she starts out possessing two X chromosomes instead of the male's single X chromosome and single Y chromosome. This single difference is the prime cause of all the later differentiated differences which we will pass in review. It is interesting to note, though, that much of our recent knowledge about this chromosomal difference arises from new discoveries in individuals who have a chromosomal aberration, a chromosomal error. We have tended to think of the X chromosome as the potent determiner of femaleness. In recent years we have discovered women whose genetic constitution is, instead of the normal two X chromosomes, three X chromosomes. These individuals were originally spoken of as "superfemales." They are anything but superfemales. They are very sad examples of womanhood. They are usually mentally defective and sterile, incapable of reproduction. So the X chromosome alone is not the measure of woman. And of course the moral is: don't put too many X's in one basket!

But the normal woman's genetic constitution does produce differences of development in her from the moment of conception throughout pregnancy and intrauterine life. For example, the girl baby is born weighing on the average 100 grams less than the boy baby. At birth, however, by far the most important visible structural difference is seen in the external genitals of the male infant and their absence in the female infant. The fact that this difference is easily visible in the female at birth is tremendously important in relation to behavior—as is attested by the very extensive psychiatric literature dealing with penis envy, castration feelings, and so on. And apparently it is only the visibleness, the easily seen difference, which leads to the differences in behavior—almost exclusively because of sociologic influences. Because the boy and the girl up to about the age of seven are essentially the same in their endocrinologic and physiologic functioning. They produce and excrete the same amounts of estrogens and androgens, the so-called sex hormones; and their metabolic functioning is the same in relation to thyroid hormones, adrenal hormones, and insulin. The functioning of the pituitary hormones is the same—with perhaps one exception. Here there is a subtle endocrinologic and metabolic difference between boys and girls from before birth right on through adulthood. The girl develops faster than the boy, both physically and mentally. By the age of puberty the girl is approximately one year ahead of the boy of the same age. We see this in a behavioral way, perhaps, at the time of puberty, as heterosexual interest becomes more fully aroused; the girl tends to seek male companionship among boys two to three years older than herself. In the boy, however, the growth spurt at puberty so speeds up his development—again both physical and mental—that the developmental gap chronologically between male and female steadily narrows; and it ceases to exist by about the age of eighteen to twenty. All of us who have been parents have found it fascinating to speculate on the behavioral influences inherent in this developmental pattern. And I'm sure that all of us have on occasion looked at the associated behavior with utter bewilderment, sometimes with despair, and once in a while with frustrated rage. Often we are just not hep; and we don't dig our own adolescent offspring.

One of the difficult things to distinguish in the developmental pattern and behavior of the prepuberal woman is how much is due to inherent biological make-up and how much is due to imposed social custom—imposed indeed from the moment of birth. Even exact similarities are made to look different in relation to the sex of the infant. For example, in childhood there is no structural difference between the hair on the head of a boy and that of a girl. And yet from the time of the first haircut, our culture produces an apparent structural difference, the better to identify the potential woman and the potential man. We are still uncertain about any actual difference of general muscular bodily strength between the young boy and the young girl; even now long progressive studies on this are in progress. It seems likely, though, that at any stage of development up to about the age of seven—compensating, that is, for the different rates of development of boys and girls—the bodily strength of both is essentially equal. One wonders then how much the cultural influence of the special tasks and recreations assigned to little girls as compared to little boys gradually produces a difference in muscle strengths and muscle skills.

At about the age of seven, however, there begins to be a divergence of sex endocrine functions. The girl begins to produce definitely more estrogen than does the boy, and this difference steadily increases to puberty. By the age of about ten, this increased estrogen function in the girl is sufficient to produce discernible secondary sex characters. The hips begin to take on a slight feminine rounding, the female subcutaneous fat layer develops, and slight growth of breasts is discernible. Then—at an average age of 13½ in the United States—come the tremendous changes of full puberty and the onset of menstrual periods at menarche. No matter how the girl has been mentally and emotionally prepared for menstruation and its significance, there is no denying the tremendous behavioral impact of the biological event itself. In many cultures the little girl is thoroughly informed almost from infancy that she—and not the little boy—is destined to bear children. Unfortunately, in the American culture the early imparting of this knowledge is often sadly deficient and inept. Nevertheless, I think that most prepuberal girls in this country do know that menstruation will occur and that it signals the onset of childbearing ability. But knowing is not the same thing as experiencing. So when the first menstrual period does take place and the girl first experiences uterine bleeding and its concomitant symptoms, this demonstration of her structural and functional difference from males is a peak of behavioral influence probably unmatched since the time of her birth.

Let us look a moment at menstruation and the menstrual cycle with reference to how they may affect a woman's activities. Their deep psychologic and emotional implications I must leave to the psychiatrists and psychologists. But a simple recital of some of the facts of menstrual function can give us a basis for drawing certain obvious conclusions about its influence on woman's behavior. First of all, the very fact that the woman has approximately a monthly cycle of tremendous hormonal variation constitutes a marked difference from the physiology of the man. Males have no such regular rhythm in hormonal variation or indeed any comparable hormonal changes.

While we gynecologists for various reasons speak of a single menstrual cycle as starting with the first day of a menstrual period, from a behavioral point of view we may do better to approach it just after a menstrual period has ended. At this point estrogen production is about at its lowest level and is having the least influence on other body functions. Estrogen secretion and activity then steadily build up to reach a peak at the time of ovulation, approximately the twelfth to fourteenth day of a twenty-eight-day menstrual cycle. At ovulation many women have slight symptoms. There may be a few hours of slight crampiness similar to menstrual cramps, and in a few women this may be so severe as to imitate, for example, an acute appendicitis. In a fair number of women there may be very slight spotting bleeding from the vagina at the time of ovulation; and microscopic bleeding from the uterus can be demonstrated by smear techniques in approximately 60 per cent of all women. With estrogen production at this peak level, various metabolic effects throughout the body are exerted by it, notably, a growth effect on breast ducts, a growth effect on skin, a stimulating effect on bone turnover, a stimulating effect on the contractility of smooth muscle structures throughout the body, most particularly a growth effect on the endometrial lining of the uterus, and many other general metabolic effects. Some of these produce mild noticeable symptoms, in particular, increased frequency of urination, increased bowel peristalsis leading to abdominal bloating, increasing breast fullness and tenseness with perhaps even slight tenderness, a tendency to headaches, and others. As an example of how widespread are the effects of the hormonal changes of the menstrual cycle, women singers tell us that their voices perform differently at different times of the cycle—a demonstration of the hormonal effects on the vocal cords.

At the time of ovulation the woman's body now begins to be subject also to the influences of a second sex hormone, progesterone, produced by the corpus luteum which forms in the ovary at the spot where the egg broke out of the ovary. Progesterone has very specific effects on the endometrial lining of the uterus, preparing it for implantation of a fertilized egg; but it also has other general bodily effects. It stimulates growth of the glandular secreting structures of the breasts, the acini. This adds to the breast symptomatology already started by estrogen. Fortunately, just after ovulation, estrogen production decreases somewhat for a few days but then begins to rise again to a second peak shortly before the start of the next menstrual period. Both estrogen and progesterone have the ability to produce retention of salt and water by the woman's body; in some women, this effect may be quite marked, giving rise to definitely noticeable swelling of hands, feet, and face, and a weight gain of as much as 5 to 10 pounds in the week before menstruation. We think of this salt and water retention effect as the principal mechanism in producing what is spoken of as the premenstrual tension syndrome—although doubtless there are subtler effects of these hormone levels on the central nervous system, as yet not fully elucidated. At any rate, all menstruating women are aware of at least some slight degree of general bodily symptomatology of a fairly specific nature in the week prior to menstruation; in about 25 per cent of women these symptoms are severe enough to cause them to seek medical relief. But to greater or lesser degree—usually scarcely noticeable—every woman in menstrual life experiences in the two to seven days before a menstrual period fullness and perhaps tenderness of the breasts, some degree of abdominal bloating, perhaps slight tightness of rings and shoes, a tendency to temporary weight gain, and finally and most importantly, specific changes in mental and emotional function. These last changes, of course, are most significant in terms of behavior. In the premenstruum there is a tendency to depression, irritability, emotional instability, hair-trigger emotional response, decreased concentration ability, increased frequency of headaches, and other personality changes. Many women sum it up by saying that they tend to be "ornery" just before a period—and they resentfully add that their husbands often tell them so. Some of these personality changes tend to be quite specific. But something else happens. Whatever minor neurotic traits a woman may possess—and don't we all have them?—these traits tend to be exaggerated by her premenstrual physiology. The implications with regard to the behavior of women are, of course, enormous. For example, the highest suicide rate among women occurs in the premenstrual week. The effect on marital and family relations is obvious and sometimes far-reaching—to put it mildly! The effect on the work performance of woman has been quite objectively measured. Dr. Ernest Page gives the example of a young woman patient of his who was a court reporter. Holding her job depended not only on the speed of her shorthand or stenotyping but also on its accuracy. She had noticed that the number of mistakes which crept into her reporting work tended to increase considerably in the week before a menstrual period. What was more worrisome, her boss had noted this increase in errors—and she was in some fear of losing her job. This was her reason for seeking Dr. Page's therapeutic help, because otherwise her premenstrual symptomatology wasn't especially marked. Fortunately, with adequate therapy as commonly used for the premenstrual tension syndrome, the number of errors in her court reporting work in the week prior to menses dropped off almost to her standard normal level—and her job was saved. One could go on at length citing examples of the effect of woman's premenstrual biology on her behavior and performance, but this is a neat and sufficient one, I think, to indicate how objectively this influence can be measured.

Then, after the premenstruum, comes menstruation itself. Here the woman is subject to a number of symptoms which can clearly influence her behavior. She may have lower abdominal cramps, changes in bowel function, unusual headaches, nausea, changes in appetite, and above all the nuisance of the uterine bleeding itself to be taken care of. The custom structure built up around the physiologic fact of menstruation in various cultures is, of course, huge, quite varied, and constantly changing.

An example of this change is the rather strict prohibition to our grandmothers against going swimming during a menstrual period for fear of dire effects on general physical health. Today that prohibition has been discarded as nonsensical. There is still, in modern American society, the concept that a woman, by menstruation, gets rid of certain toxins and poisons in her blood and body—although medical science can demonstrate no such process. Indeed, many women still, so to speak, feel safer if they regularly have rather heavy menstrual flows. Yet the gynecologist knows that this is one of the commonest causes of secondary anemia in women, simply from the loss of perfectly good, healthy blood. At any rate, the biology of the menstruation process alters and limits woman's activities and behavior in ways too multiple to detail here. Again, her psychic reaction to this function is the subject of a very extensive psychiatric and psychologic literature which will doubtless be called upon in our further discussions.

Once puberty has been passed by the boy and the girl, the differences between them other than the menstrual cycle are obviously visible. Leaving aside such striking secondary sex characters as the male beard, we can mention certain specific female differences. From puberty onward, the woman's general body-muscle strength is never again equal to that of the man's. A good demonstration of this is the game of golf. No matter how expert, how long-trained, a top-flight woman golfer simply can't drive a golf ball as great a distance as a top-flight male golfer; she simply doesn't have the strength to do so. Naturally, this strength difference has manifold implications for the tasks and activities to which the woman will turn—despite certain of the primitive societies where what we think of as the male and female roles are reversed.

It is said that while men have the superior muscular strength, women have greater skill in the tasks requiring fine muscle control. Whether this is truly a biological difference or simply a matter of training in relation to cultural pattern, I frankly don't know. One specific biological difference is definite, however, and not by any means well explained. This is woman's greater resistance to, and lesser susceptibility to, disease in general. In overall mortality figures, the life expectancy of woman becomes increasingly greater than that of man from puberty onward. Some of this resistance to illness is physiologically determined by hormonal function. For example, in the decade before menopausal age, the likelihood of coronary artery heart disease for women is only about one-tenth that for men. But after the menopause, when estrogen function declines in woman, if the menopausal state be untreated, then the rates for coronary artery heart disease for women rise close to those for men. Let us look for a moment at the biological difference between the nature of sex function in men and in women. Here a multitude of behavioral implications swarm up. One of the most striking, perhaps, is that woman is structurally susceptible of rape, whereas man is not. All down the ages and in all cultures this fact has had extensive influence on the daily behavior of woman. The actual biological difference in the nature of the sex act itself, as accomplished by a male as compared with a female, has extremely important influences on the approach to and reaction of each to sex function.

This brings us then to the most significant difference of all between men and women, that is, woman's role in human reproduction. She "can have a baby" while a man cannot. Moreover, man's role in the reproductive process is a very short, transient one, while woman's starts from that episode and stretches out through nine months of gestation. During this time she's subject to all sorts of very extensive changes in body symptoms and functions. She has nausea, her appetite changes, she steadily gains weight, she becomes awkward and ungainly in balance and gait, her capacities for physical work steadily lessen, she becomes increasingly vulnerable to the daily threats of modern life, she becomes increasingly dependent on the labors of others for her own subsistence, and so on. Finally, she has the extraordinary experience, trauma, joy, and threat of the birth process to go through. It seems almost unnecessary to say that the behavioral implications to woman of the gestational and birth processes are so extraordinarily extensive that they will doubtless be the subject of speculation and study as long as mankind exists. And psychiatrists and psychologists would agree, I am sure, that they have scarcely scratched the surface of woman's psychologic reactions to her reproductive function. Certainly this is the major and most overwhelming aspect of woman's biological nature as it affects what she does, how she thinks, and how her emotions impel her. We shall not be able to escape referring to it time and time again as this symposium proceeds.

But after woman's reproductive life is over, she presents another important biological feature uniquely female, that is, the climacteric, the menopause. At this time, an average age of fifty in the United States, the woman goes through a sudden decline of ovarian function which results in extensive bodily changes. The man has no such sudden climacteric, for his testicular function and his reproductive capacity simply decline gradually along with his aging process. He can sire children up into the eighties and nineties. The woman, by contrast, when her menstruation ceases at approximately fifty, can no longer bear children. Simply her knowledge of this biological fact has tremendous impact on her behavior and personality, and there is an extensive psychologic literature which attempts to elucidate this reaction. In addition, as menstrual periods cease, the woman's body undergoes a very considerable physiologic upheaval. With the ovarian production of estrogen dropping to low levels, not only is the menstrual cycle lost, but all the general body metabolic influences maintained by estrogen action during reproductive life now decline as well. This would include the growth effect of estrogen on the reproductive tract, on the breasts, on the skin, on bone, and so on. At this time the pituitary gland seems to engage in a frantic effort to stimulate continued estrogen function of the ovary, greatly increasing the production of certain pituitary hormones. In addition, the delicate balance of end-organ effects throughout the body between estrogens and other glandular hormonal secretions is upset. Thus the adrenal gland goes right on functioning at its usual level of activity; it goes right on producing androgenic, male-type hormones in the woman's body as it has done all her life. As the feminizing influence of estrogen is withdrawn, the woman experiences increase in facial hair growth, a resurgence of acne, a loss of feminine skin softness, a loss of feminine body contours, a regression of breasts, occasionally even a tendency to baldness. Depending upon the degree of ovarian estrogen decline, some women develop certain specific menopausal symptoms. Best known are the hot flashes and night sweats—which are so thoroughly documented over women's bridge tables that it is almost unfashionable not to have them. Along with these come variable degrees of emotional instability, irritability, depression, lack of concentration, weepiness, headaches, and the like. Disturbances of bladder and bowel function, changes in libido, vaginal irritation, dizziness, are not uncommon. And especially striking at this time may be an aggravation of the neurotic components of a woman's personality.

Finally, if postmenopausal ovarian function declines to certain deficiency levels, then the woman sooner or later develops serious metabolic illnesses: coronary artery heart disease, more rapid hardening of the arteries, weakening of bones by osteoporosis. And, especially significant to our discussion, there is good evidence that postmenopausal estrogen deficiency hastens the usual senile mental deterioration to which we are all subject.

When you come right down to it, perhaps women just live too long! Maybe when they get through having babies they have outlived their usefulness—especially now that they outlive men by so many years. That is a rather shocking way of pointing up a question which many gynecologists are asking today, namely, "Is a woman's postmenopausal status a normal, physiologic condition, or is it actually a pathologic, disease state?" Take note of what obtains in the rest of the animal kingdom. Rarely is there found among the higher animals in nature a female surviving much beyond the age of reproductive life. In this sense, some gynecologists conceive that modern civilization and modern medical science have pushed woman's longevity far beyond her natural biological span—and that it is now up to medical science to make her extra years more comparable to her earlier ones by appropriate substitution therapy for her hormonal deficiencies. Others of us at present feel that in general the menopausal involutional process is a normal physiologic one. But all of us recognize that at least 25 per cent of postmenopausal women have a true estrogen-deficiency disease. This group requires estrogen-supplementation therapy the rest of their lives to protect them against the excessive metabolic changes I have mentioned. Knowledge about this whole business is still very fragmentary, yet its implications for the behavior pattern and potentialities of the older woman are critical. We are hopeful that studies now going forward in this area will give us a much better answer, before too long, to this aspect of the biological make-up of woman.

Eleanor E. Maccoby

WOMAN'S INTELLECT

Not many years ago, families took it for granted that an intelligent son would be sent to college and an intelligent daughter would not. It is only during a brief span of thirty to forty years that large numbers of women have had opportunities for higher education opened to them, but the period has been long enough so that we are in a position to begin to appraise the results. To those who had hoped that equal educational opportunities for women would yield equal intellectual achievements, an appraisal must be disappointing. A Madame Curie is conspicuous by her very rarity. Even in the field of letters, where many of women's special talents are presumed to lie, we have more men than women who are productive, creative writers. When it comes to achievement in science, the imbalance is much greater. Our colleges produce very few women who become intellectually excited by, and immersed in, a scientific research problem or who organize large bodies of diverse data into a new theoretical statement. And even though creative scientists must have moments of almost intuitive insight, woman's famous intuition does not appear to have helped her much in making a contribution to scientific thought.

Taking publication as an index of productivity (and although it is not an entirely satisfactory index, it is difficult to find a better one!) we find, from a study of 400 Radcliffe Ph.D.s (1956) that women published substantially less than men of comparable jobs and rank. Half of these women Ph.D.s had published little or nothing since earning their advanced degrees. So even with first-rate advanced graduate training, the difference between the sexes in intellectual achievement appears not to be erased.

It is evident that women have many other things they often choose to do with their lives, over and beyond pursuit of their intellectual interests. It is reasonable to believe that the other demands upon women are more incompatible with the life of an intellectual than would be the case for men. It is difficult to continue in the single-minded pursuit of a set of ideas while being a competent wife and mother—more difficult than for a man to do so while being a competent husband and father. These matters of conflicting interests and responsibilities will be discussed by others in this conference, and they are not our primary concern today. It is necessary to ask, however, whether they constitute the entire explanation for women's lack of signal accomplishment in the intellectual sphere. I am inclined to think they do not. One bit of evidence comes from the study of Radcliffe Ph.D.s already cited; the ones who had married had published as much as those who had not, and this would appear to indicate that even an unmarried professional women (who presumably is more comparable to men with respect to the other demands on her time) is either under some special restraints affecting her intellectual productivity or lacks in some degree the positive motivation that would optimally affect her work.

If we examine woman's intellectual performance through a large range of her life cycle, we find other reasons for suspecting that it is not just the conflicting demands upon her time created by marriage and children that interfere with her achievement. There are not very good facts available on the subject, but I suspect careful studies would reveal that the educated woman does not behave as an intellectual during her college years, nor "go underground" during the period of life when she is raising young children and then emerge again as an intellectual when the children are grown and no longer require so much of her time. Rather, it appears that some of the restraints upon her intellectuality make themselves felt long before marriage and continue to be present during those long years from thirty-five to sixty-five when the most demanding phase of child rearing is over—the period when many men are at the peak of their productive careers. It seems possible that there may be some relevant early-formed personality traits, or even some early-established basic qualities of mind, that characterize women and that bear upon intellectual performance, and it is these factors that I would like to explore today.

Let us first review what is known concerning the development of intellectual abilities in girls. In attempting to determine what are the special intellectual qualities of females (if indeed such special qualities exist), we must stress the ways in which girls differ from boys in their performance. In doing so, we may give insufficient attention to the ways in which the two sexes are alike intellectually, or to the great variations among individuals of the same sex. But bearing this danger in mind, let us attempt to draw a quick picture of some of the reliably established sex differences in intellectual functioning.

The Stanford-Binet intelligence test, which was for many years the most widely used individual test, revealed few differences between boys and girls in total "intelligence" as this test measured it. From this fact it was widely assumed that the sexes might differ in interests and in temperament but not in underlying mental abilities. It was not widely known or understood that during the early phases of work on the Stanford-Binet test, when many items were being tried out for possible inclusion in the test, items which consistently revealed sex differences were discarded from the test whenever possible. The test builders hoped in this way to create a test on which the scores for boys and the scores for girls could be evaluated against the same norms. And for the most part they succeeded, although girls did come out slightly ahead in the early years and boys in the middle and later school years (McNemar, 1942). But it is clearly not possible to use a test standardized in this way to investigate the magnitude of the sex differences that do exist or at what ages they make their appearance.

Relying now on test materials which were not standardized so as to eliminate a portion of existing sex differences, we find the following facts: Girls get off to a very good start. Insofar as it is possible to measure abilities which we would be willing to call intellectual abilities during the first three or four years of life, girls seem to be slightly ahead of boys. They articulate more clearly than boys; they say their first word at a slightly younger age on the average; they begin to combine words into sentences slightly sooner; they count accurately sooner (Oetzel, 1962). In interpreting these facts we should remember that performance on the sorts of tests we have been able to devise for very young children does not predict very well what intellectual level the individual will ultimately reach. Furthermore, we know that girls are on a somewhat faster developmental timetable than boys from the standpoint of physical growth; this same slightly advanced timetable may apply to the maturation of certain motor and perceptual abilities that underlie intellectual performance, and again, this rate of maturation doesn't necessarily imply anything concerning the ultimate level to be reached.

But to continue with the description of sex differences in abilities. Upon entrance into school, girls learn to read a little more easily, and there are more boys who have reading problems severe enough to call for special remedial reading programs. But the differential between the sexes on some aspects of verbal skill soon begins to disappear. During the school years, there are no consistent differences to be found in vocabulary; and after about the fifth or sixth grade, most studies show the boys to be doing as well as the girls in reading comprehension. The girls do continue to excel in "language" skills such as spelling, punctuation, and diagraming sentences. They also excel in measures of "verbal fluency"; for example, they write longer themes, they can think of more words with certain characteristics in a short time, and they can tell longer stories in response to stimulus pictures. So the stereotype that women talk more than men appears to have some basis in fact, but it does not imply a general superiority of the female in all aspects of verbal skill.

How about mathematical skills? It is commonly supposed that men have a consistent edge over women in this respect. It came as a surprise to us, therefore, when we recently reviewed the test results bearing upon mathematical abilities (see Oetzel, 1962), to discover that the sexes do not differ consistently in the early and middle school years. Of course, during much of this time, it may be a misnomer to say that we are dealing with *mathematical* abilities. It would be more accurate to say that the skill usually measured between the ages of seven and eleven or twelve is skill at arithmetical computation. Children are also given some of the so-called arithmetical reasoning problems at these ages— questions about how long would it take three men to dig a basement if seven men can do it in 2½ days, or how long it would take a bullet to travel from one train to another if the speeds of the two trains and the time since starting are given—and girls appear to be able to handle these questions about as well as boys. It is not until high school that we begin to get quite consistent sex differences, with the boys forging ahead when they come to analytic geometry, trigonometry, and algebra and doing considerably better in tests involving quantitative reasoning. By the time the Scholastic Aptitude tests are administered for admission to college, we find that boys score on the average as much as 50 points higher on the mathematical portion of the test, while girls are scoring only 8 to 10 points higher on the verbal, or "language," segment. Of course, girls do not as frequently elect to take the more advanced math courses in high school, and it is difficult to know whether this is true because they lack the ability to handle the material or whether their interests lie elsewhere. The career fields which will require training in math—engineering, and the natural sciences—are primarily masculine fields, and girls may stop taking math simply because they are preparing themselves for more feminine occupations. But another possible explanation exists: that girls may indeed more often lack certain abstract or analytical qualities of mind that are not called into play during the learning of square root, decimals, etc., in the earlier grades, and that it is not until mathematics becomes more abstract (as it does in geometry and algebra) that this particular deficiency becomes a handicap to them.

At the moment, we lack definitive data that would make it possible to choose between these alternatives. But girls' characteristic difficulty with geometry does probably relate to a fairly consistent sex difference that may be detected at a considerably earlier age. Throughout the grade school years, boys do better than girls on tests of "spatial" ability. Some of you may have taken tests which include items for space ability: such tests require the subject, for example, to say how many surfaces there would be on the opposite side of a pile of cubes—the side the viewer cannot see—or to select from an array of jigsaw drawings those that would fit together to form a designated pattern. Another element in spatial ability involves finding a simple figure which is embedded in a more complex one. Newspapers sometimes carry drawings of landscapes in which one can find animals or human faces involving the same lines that are first perceived as parts of clouds, leaves, or tree trunks; the trick in finding these hidden figures is to be able to break away from the set that is established by the entire drawing of the landscape—to respond to only an isolated segment of the drawing and avoid being influenced by the momentarily irrelevant parts. There are formal tests of the ability to perceive parts of a visual field analytically, and the results very consistently show that boys can perceive more analytically, while the girls are more global, more influenced by all the elements of the field together.

The sex differences, to the extent of being bound by the field as a whole, are well illustrated by the performance of the two sexes on the so-called rod and frame test, a test used extensively by Witkin in his studies of individual differences in underlying modes of perceiving (Witkin, 1954). In this test, the subject is seated in a darkened room. He looks at an illuminated frame that looks like a picture frame; and within this frame is an illuminated rod, which can be adjusted through various degrees of tilt to an upright position. The subject's task is to adjust the rod so that it looks straight up and down. Sometimes he is required to do this when the frame itself is tilted. Girls are consistently more influenced by the tilt of the frame; if it is tilted, they think the rod is upright when it is tilted to correspond to the tilt of the frame rather than when it is truly upright. Boys, on the other hand, are more able to ignore the frame and adjust the rod to the true upright. It is on the basis of tests of this kind, as well as the embedded-figures test, that girls have been labeled more "field dependent" (Witkin, 1954; Witkin, Dyk, Faterson, Goodenough, and Karp, 1962), and it is interesting to note that the greater field dependence of women and girls has been found in studies of people in a variety of cultures, from Western Europe to Hong Kong. It appears entirely possible that some of the difficulty many girls have with the kinds of analytical processes required in high school math could be traced to this earlier-established difference in their mode of dealing with a stimulus field.

Related to the greater field dependence of women is their greater difficulty in breaking an established set. Let me illustrate what is meant by set. Suppose you were asked to solve some number series—to say what would come next in a series of numbers. We would begin with some easy series. For example, we would ask what comes next after 2, 4, 6, 8—and you could easily say 10. Or what comes next after 2, 4, 8, 16, 32—and you would say 64. Now try this one: 14, 23, 34, 42, 50, 59,

72, 81–. Even if you knew New York very well, you would have difficulty recognizing these as the stops on the Eighth Avenue subway, because you were set for an entirely different kind of number series. If
you had not had the other series first, you might recognize this series
immediately and be able to continue it. There are special test problems
which are designed to test an individual's ability to break away from
an established set, to restructure a situation for a fresh attack on it, and
men do better on such tests than women (Guetzkow, 1951; Sweeney,
1953).

Another kind of task that illustrates the difference between the
sexes in their mode of dealing with problem materials is a task developed by Kagan et al. (1963). Subjects are given an array of pictures
or drawings showing a variety of objects and people with a variety of
postures, modes of dress, and states of activity. The subjects are simply
asked to group together the pictures that seem to belong together. Girls
are more likely to form what Kagan calls "functional" groupings. For
example, they will group together the picture of a doctor, a nurse, and a
wheel chair, because they are all associated with the care of sick people.
Boys, on the other hand, will be more likely to form groups by select-
ing out some detail they have in common—they will, for example, group
together all the pictures of people who have their right arms raised.
This kind of grouping Kagan calls "analytic" grouping, and the fact
that boys do this kind of grouping more may be regarded as another
instance of their tendency to break down a percept—to deal with detailed elements rather than the whole.

I would like to suggest, then, that the difficulty girls have with
doing high-level work in math and science is only partly a result of
the fact that these subjects are required for preparation for engineering
and other distinctly masculine occupations; I suggest that girls on the
average develop a somewhat different way of handling incoming information—that their thinking is less analytic, more global, and more per-
severative—and that this kind of thinking may serve them very well
for many kinds of functioning but that it is not the kind of thinking
most conducive to high-level intellectual productivity, especially in
science. Let me hasten to add that in trying to make this point I may
have produced an exaggerated impression of the magnitude of the sex
differences that exist. There are many women who think analytically,

and many men who do not, but there are consistent differences in the average performance of the two sexes, and by concentrating on the differences we may be able to find some clues as to what underlies the development of intellectual processes in women.

Why do some people develop more analytic modes of thought than others? So far, we are only beginning to make a research attack upon this question. But there do seem to be some consistent trends in the work that has been done so far. The key to the matter seems to lie in whether, and how soon, a child is encouraged to assume initiative, to take responsibility for himself, and to solve problems by himself, rather than rely upon others for the direction of his activities. An early study by David Levy (1943) was among the first to suggest the importance of independence training for certain intellectual functions. He studied a group of boys whom he labeled "overprotected." The behavior of the mothers of these boys was extreme in the direction of "babying" them at a late age—for example, some of the boys, at age ten or eleven, were still being led to school by the hand by their mothers, and their mothers were still dressing them each morning. These overprotected boys were quite good in their language work at school—they were good readers, for example. But they were notably poor at math.

Recently, Dr. Rau and I at Stanford studied a group of children who were good at verbal tasks but poor at math or space tasks and contrasted them with children who were good at math or space but relatively poor at verbal tasks. Dr. Elizabeth Bing observed these children in interaction with their mothers. She asked the mothers to give the children some problems to work on and noted how much the mother became involved as the child worked on the problems. To speak now only about the girls in the study, it was evident from Dr. Bing's reports (Bing, 1963) that the mothers of the highly verbal girls were intrusive: they offered suggestions, praised the child for performing well, and criticized her for performing poorly. The mothers of the girls who were best at math or spatial tasks, however, more often left their daughters alone to solve the problems by themselves.

Still another piece of evidence comes from some recent exploratory work of Witkin, Dyk, Faterson, Goodenough, and Karp (1962), who wished to discover what conditions of a child's life were associated with his being field-dependent versus field-independent on the rod-and-frame test and the embedded-figures test. Witkin interviewed mothers to ascertain their attitudes about child rearing and the methods they had used to raise the particular child whose modes of perceiving Witkin had measured. The mothers of the children who were analytic in their perceptions had given their children quite a bit of freedom to explore the environment at an early age and had tried to encourage them to do things on their own initiative; by contrast, the mothers of the children who were "field-dependent" in their perceptions had kept their children quite closely tied to the maternal apron strings, had talked to them a good deal about the dangerous aspects of the environment, and had been in general unwilling to tolerate self-assertiveness in their children. There were many other things that characterized these two groups of mothers, as well, and it is difficult to sort out the factors that were most crucial in the home lives of the children with different modes of perceiving. But the relationships that I have selected to report here are consistent with our own findings and those of Levy in suggesting that activities of parents which are designed to foster the independence of their children and encourage them to take initiative will be associated with analytic thinking in the children and good ability in the math-science area, while continued close control and restriction of the child will be associated with the more field-dependent, or global, modes of thinking in the child and *poor* ability in math.

If this is true, we must ask ourselves whether girls are allowed less independence, less self-assertiveness in early childhood than is allowed to boys. We have very little evidence indeed on this point. I know of no evidence that would show that boys are allowed to play outside alone or cross streets earlier than girls, for example, but it may very well be true that they are. At the moment we will simply have to consider it an unanswered question whether parents treat daughters differently from sons with respect to training for independence, and whether they do so to a sufficient degree to account for the differences between the sexes in their modes of perceiving and their differential skill at tasks, such as mathematics, which seem to require an especially high degree of analytical thinking.

I think we can begin to see, however, from what has been said so far, that when we begin to try to understand the intellectual performance of women and girls, we cannot understand them by studying

these kinds of performance alone; we will find that intellectual development does not occur as a kind of isolated "unfolding" process obeying
its own inner laws, but rather that it is responsive, in some degree, to
the nature of the network of interpersonal relations in which the child
is involved, and that certain modes of thought may depend on the development of certain aspects of the person that we have previously
thought of as "personality" rather than as qualities of intellect.

Let me take another approach to illustrate this point. As you may
know, the "intelligence" of an individual child as it is measured by
standard intelligence tests is not constant over the period of his growth
from birth to maturity. Some children show progressive increases in IQ
as they grow older; others show a progressive decline. There are a few
centers of child development research in this country which have studied
groups of children longitudinally; that is, they have followed the same
children from very early childhood into adulthood, and it is possible to
determine from their data what some of the factors are which are associated with progressive changes in children's intelligence test scores.
Sontag et al. at Fels Research Institute (1958) have selected from
their files a group of cases of children whose intelligence test scores
consistently improved from preschool years through age ten and contrasted them with a group whose scores consistently declined during
this period. They asked these questions: What kinds of children show
increases or decreases in IQ? Can one predict, from knowing something
about the personality characteristics of young children, which ones will
have rising, and which falling, IQs? The answer to the second question is clearly yes. Here is what a child is like at age six if he or she is
among those whose IQs will increase during the next four years: he
or she is competitive, self-assertive, independent, and dominant in interaction with other children. And the children who will show declining
IQs during the next four years are children who are passive, shy, and
dependent.

I'm sure it will already have struck you that the characteristics
associated with a rising IQ are not very feminine characteristics. One
of the people working on the Fels study I have just described was
asked about what kind of developmental history was necessary to make
a girl into an intellectual person; he replied, "The simplest way to put
it is that she must be a tomboy at some point in her childhood."

Does this seem bizarre? Before we consider the implications for the raising of girls, let us see whether there is any other evidence, beyond the Fels study, for an association between the sorts of analytic thinking we have been discussing and the possession of nonfeminine traits by girls. First of all, if we may consider high ability in arithmetic and math as indicative of analytic skill [and it is know, for example, that skill in math is correlated with ability to find embedded figures while verbal skill is not (see Bieri, 1958)], then it is relevant to refer to a study of the autobiographies of a few famous women mathematicians, done by Plank and Plank (1954). This study revealed that women mathematicians had one important element in common: they all described an unusually close relationship with their fathers, rather than their mothers, as they were growing up, and they attempted to pattern themselves on their fathers. Related to this is the finding of Bieri and his colleagues (1960), who devised measures to determine the degree to which a group of college women had identified with, or patterned themselves upon, each of their parents. They found that women who were especially good at finding the hidden figures in the embedded-figures test were more strongly identified with their fathers than their mothers, while the reverse was true of the women who were relatively poor at solving embedded figures. The women in this study were also given a test designed to measure their acceptance of authority, and the women who were good at solving the embedded-figures problems tended to be *low* in acceptance of authority—another indication of the importance of autonomy in the development of this particular kind of analytic thinking. In still another study (Milton, 1957), college students were given problems to solve, many of which required breaking of set, or "restructuring." For both sexes, the students who were most skillful at problem solving were those who scored at the more masculine end of personality tests designed to measure masculine versus feminine traits.

And finally, our own work at Stanford, in which we selected groups of fifth-grade girls who were especially good at arithmetical or spatial tasks, revealed the following characteristics of these girls: The girls who did better on spatial problems than other kinds of problems were somewhat more masculine and aggressive than other girls with similar total IQs and rather withdrawn from social contact with their age-mates. The girls whose area of greatest competence was numerical tasks were popular with their classmates, largely because they were seen as girls with high competence in planning and organizing. According to their own report, these girls were also less likely than others of similar IQ to ask their parents for help when they encountered difficulty in solving a problem. When the girls were observed in interaction with their mothers, it was the girls who were especially good at verbal tasks who most often asked their mothers for help; the girls who were best at either math or space tasks tended to work on their own. Thus we see that these girls not only were characterized by greater independence while working on problems but also possessed some traits we think of as being more characteristic of boys: aggression in the case of the high-space girls, dominance in the case of the high-number girls.

It would appear, then, that what evidence we have indicates that girls who do well at the various kinds of analytic thinking we have been discussing are not very feminine creatures, at least not according to the standards our present society sets for feminine behavior. It has been repeatedly shown, in studies of girls, that they early develop a greater interest in other people, and in what other people think of them, than do boys; they tend to be more influenced by the opinions of others, and they are more conforming to what they perceive to be the social demands of the situations they are in. It is probably these conformist tendencies that help them to excel at spelling and punctuation —the kinds of performance for which there is only one socially prescribed, right answer. But for higher-level intellectual productivity, it is independence of mind that is required—the ability to turn one's back on others at least for a time, while working alone on a problem—and it is this which girls, from an early age, appear to find so difficult to do.

But of course, not all girls find it difficult. And it is interesting to consider for a moment the situation of a little girl who at preschool age does have the qualities that could make her into an analytic thinker. She is full of curiosity, likes to explore things, is dominant and independent, probably likes to play with boys and wear blue jeans, and isn't especially interested in dolls. Assuming that her parents have been tolerant of her temperament, what happens when she enters school? One of the first blows is that the boys won't play with her any more—they form their own exclusive play groups, and she must fall back upon the company of girls. In many ways she begins to discover that she is not behaving as girls are expected to behave, and the disapproval she encounters generates a certain amount of anxiety. This may sound like pure speculation, but there is some evidence that this is the course that development does take in girls who start out as tomboys. Sears, in a recent study (1961), traced the development of aggression, and anxiety about aggression, between the ages of five and twelve. The boys who were most anxious about aggression at age twelve were the ones whose parents had not allowed fighting when they were younger, and at the age of five they had already become fairly unaggressive children. The girls who showed most anxiety about aggression at age twelve, however, were the ones who had been fairly aggressive at kindergarten age. But more importantly for our present discussion, the ones who showed the most of this kind of anxiety in middle childhood were the ones who had been trained in ways inappropriate to their sex in preschool years. For example, in most American homes, there is a certain amount of division of labor between the parents such that mothers assume a larger role in the discipline and caretaking of daughters, fathers of sons. But the girls with high aggression anxiety levels in middle childhood had received an unusually high amount of both discipline and caretaking from their *fathers*. Furthermore, they had been encouraged to fight back when attacked by other children in the neighborhood—an encouragement which is more often reserved for boys in our culture. We see, then, that these girls were being to some degree masculinized in early childhood, and we can only assume that it was at least partly the social disapproval they encountered over their unfeminine behavior that produced the anxiety they manifested at a later time.

Let me make a leap from these findings to our present concerns with woman's intellect. Suppose a girl does succeed in maintaining, throughout her childhood years, the qualities of dominance, independence, and active striving that appear to be requisites for good analytic thinking. In so doing, she is defying the conventions concerning what is appropriate behavior for her sex. She may do this successfully, in many ways, but I suggest that it is a rare intellectual woman who will not have paid a price for it: a price in anxiety. And I hazard the guess that it is this anxiety which helps to account for the lack of productivity among those women who do make intellectual careers. We are beginning to know a good deal about the effects of anxiety on thinking: it is especially damaging to creative thinking, for it narrows the range of solution efforts, interferes with breaking set, and prevents scanning of the whole range of elements open to perception. When anxiety facilitates performance, as it sometimes does, it facilitates already well-learned tasks; it does not contribute to breaking new ground.

From the standpoint of those who want women to become intellectuals, this is something of a horror story. It would appear that even when a women is suitably endowed intellectually and develops the right temperament and habits of thought to make use of her endowment, she must be fleet of foot indeed to scale the hurdles society has erected for her and to remain a whole and happy person while continuing to follow her intellectual bent.

From the standpoint of parents and educators who are charged with the responsibility of raising and training girls, the requisites for intellectual development in girls appear to pose something of a dilemma. Shall mothers encourage whatever tomboy tendencies they find in their young daughters? Shall teachers attempt to free girls from the emotional involvement with others that helps to make them so tractable in the classroom? I do not mean to imply that the concerted efforts of parents and teachers together would necessarily serve to make girls just like boys intellectually. I think it is quite possible that there are genetic factors that differentiate the two sexes and bear upon their intellectual performance other than what we have thought of as innate "intelligence." For example, there is good reason to believe that boys are innately more aggressive than girls—and I mean aggressive in the broader sense, not just as it implies fighting, but as it implies dominance and initiative as well—and if this quality is one which underlies the later growth of analytic thinking, then boys have an advantage which girls who are endowed with more passive qualities will find difficult to overcome. But it also appears likely that the way children are dealt with by the adults responsible for their care, and the social roles girls know they are preparing themselves for, have a bearing also on whether they will develop the characteristics that will be conducive to the growth of higher-level intellectual skills. And insofar as child training does have an influence, parents and educators have some difficult value judgments to make. What kinds of women do they want to produce? Do we want to encourage intellectuality in women if it must be done at the expense of femininity?

As always, when faced with this kind of devil-and-deep-blue-sea dilemma, it is wise to inquire whether there may not be some other alternative. I wonder whether our current social definition of the feminine woman and girl could not undergo some revisions without any damage to the essential functions of woman. Does a woman really need to be passive and dependent in order to be sexually attractive to men, or in order to be a good mother? Could we not accept and encourage the active, dominant, independent qualities of the intellectual girl without labeling her as masculine, and encourage in her whatever aspects of femininity *are* compatible with an analytic quality of mind? I recognize that I am raising some controversial and intricate issues here, for the social and economic role of woman is by very necessity a dependent one during her childbearing years. But these years have become a much smaller segment of her life span than they once were, and I ask whether our whole definition of femininity should be such as to prepare her for this segment of her life and no other. I hope that the remainder of this symposium will help to elucidate this issue.

References

Bieri, J. Paternal Identification, Acceptance of Authority, and Within-sex Differences in Cognitive Behavior. *J. abnorm. soc. Psychol.,* 60:76–79, 1960.

Bieri, J., Wendy M. Bradburn, and M. D. Galinsky. Sex Differences in Perceptual Behavior. *J. Pers.,* 26:1–12, 1958.

Bing, Elizabeth. The Effect of Child Rearing Practices on Development of Differential Cognitive Abilities. *Child Develpm.,* 1963 (in press).

Guetzkow, H. An Analysis of the Operation of Set in Problem-solving Behavior. *J. genet. Psychol.,* 45:219–244, 1951.

Kagan, Jerome, Howard A. Moss., and Irving E. Siegel. The Psychological Significance of Styles of Conceptualization. In J. C. Wright and J. Kagan (Eds.), Basic Cognitive Processes in Children, *Monogr. Soc. Res. Child Develpm.* 23:No. 86, 1963.

Levy, D. M. *Maternal Overprotection.* New York, Columbia University Press, 1943.

Maccoby, Eleanor E., and Lucy Rau. *Differential Cognitive Abilities.* Final report, Cooperative Research Project No. 1040. Stanford, Calif., Owen House, Stanford University, 1962.

McNemar, Quinn. *The Revision of the Stanford-Binet Scale: An Analysis of the Standardization Data.* Boston, Houghton Mifflin, 1942.

Milton, G. A. The Effects of Sex-role Identification upon Problem-solving Skill. *J. abnorm. soc. Psychol.,* 55:208–212, 1957.

Oetzel, Roberta. *Selected Bibliography on Sex Differences.* Mimeographed, prepared for Social Science Research Council. Stanford, Calif., Owen House, Stanford University, 1962.

Plank, Emma H., and R. Plank. Emotional Components in Arithmetic Learning, as Seen through Autobiographies. *The Psychoanalytic Study of the Child,* Vol. IX. New York, International Universities Press, 1954.

Radcliffe Committee on Graduate Education for Women. *Graduate Education for Women.* Cambridge, Mass., Harvard University Press, 1956.

Sears, R. R. Relation of Early Socialization Experiences to Aggression in Middle Childhood. *J. abnorm. soc. Psychol.,* 63:466–492, 1961.

Sontag, I. W., C. T. Baker, and Virginia A. Nelson. Mental Growth and Personality Development: A Longitudinal Study. *Monogr. Soc. Res. Child Develpm.,* 23:No. 68, 1958.

Sweeney, E. J. Sex Differences in Problem-solving. Dissertation submitted to Stanford University, 1953.

Witkin, H. A., Helen B. Lewis, M. Herzman, Karen Machover, Pearl B. Meissner, and S. Wapner. *Personality through Perception.* New York, Harper & Row, 1954.

Witkin, H. A., R. B. Dyk, H. E. Faterson, D. R. Goodenough, and S. A. Karp. *Psychological Differentiation.* New York, Wiley, 1962.

RESEARCH ON THE NATURE OF WOMAN

> *This is an actual transcription of the formal but spontaneous panel discussion of the papers immediately preceding. Only minor editing has been done where continuity and clarity required it. The editors feel that the spontaneity of the actual discussion gives a particular value to the panel in this form, since it amplifies questions arising from the formal presentations of the participants as well as answering questions from the audience.*

Moderator: J. Ralph Audy
Panel Members: Phyllis C. Jay,
Eleanor E. Maccoby,
Edmund W. Overstreet

Dr. Audy Mrs. Jay has considered woman as if she might be a sort of ape in sheep's clothing. She has stressed the fact that in the nonhuman primate society the female has a very clear-cut role, that of bearing infants and rearing them in their earlier years. One clearly obvious factor is that the dependence of the infant for its whole future proper development in the group on its mother is not severed at the umbilical cord. Firstly, the future development of the infant depends upon mother relationships which are always most intimate, and secondly, the mother's experiences, pushed around and upset by members of the group, influence the infant's future behavior and development.

Next, Dr. Overstreet, as an obstetrician and gynecologist, sees women as a string of endocrine glands, controlling two ovaries in charge of a uterus, whereas Mrs. Jay gives us some glimpses into what may be biological and appropriate in the female human, judging from nonhuman primates. He is concerned with how woman differs from man biologically and very rightly stresses that the many differences which we find between males and females are, in fact, products of culture. They act from the moment an infant is born and are terribly difficult to distinguish from things which have a genetic origin, and are therefore part of female human basic make-up.

Unlike other primates, the human female is a very complex creature in her whims, whimsicality, and sophistication. One point about this is that she may resent something which is in fact absolutely natural. Also, social strictures against her sex may force her to hold back from ambitions and desires of a sort which no langurs, macaques, or other apes have ever dreamed about.

Dr. Maccoby looks her sex squarely in the eye and focuses on intelligence, intellect, attitude, and aptitudes. She can judge those only, of course, by comparing those with similar features in the opposite sex—man. She finds an enormous number of very interesting and fundamental differences, one of them being that females tend to see wholes, especially functional wholes, rather than the component parts which make them up. This is in contrast to males, who usually tend to be able to isolate the component parts; therefore they are more analytically minded. It seems that this gives the male some tremendous advantages, so that this difference and other feminine attributes tend to make females less good at mathematics and various intellectual pursuits, which may be measured by such yardsticks as rising intelligence quotients in one's earlier years or perhaps numbers of papers per girl per year among the Ph.D.s. But she pulls the rug out from under our feet by pointing out that in actual fact most of the things she has been talking about seem to be due, not to the female genetical make-up, but to cultural influences and person-to-person interactions, starting from the time the child is born. It seems that we must quite clearly distinguish between what is female and what is feminine.

Let us say that the differences between males and females are of three fundamental kinds, the first two being genetic and therefore really being in the female make-up. First of all, we have the perfectly obvious physical and physiological differences between the two, of which you might say, *"Vive la différence!"* Then there are the rather more subtle differences of attitudes and potentialities which are very difficult to separate from the third lot: those differences between males and females which are culturally imposed, are very important, and are therefore much more presumably under some sort of control by us.

To be provocative, I would like to put man in his proper perspective here. James O'Connor wrote a story called "The Genius" about a little boy in a tiny, sleepy Irish village, who was always asking questions. You will remember that the little boy's respect for his mother as a woman surged upward after she had given him a long, rambling talk about where babies came from. It took her the whole afternoon. During all this talk about bees, pollen, and flowers, this little boy grasped the basic principles, that mothers had a wonderful engine inside them which, once started, would manufacture babies, and all that man had was a starting handle. Human society has grown up with the feeling that the male is dominant and being dominant must be the superior sex. We have evidence for that in the way man behaves. We already know that cultural beliefs can decide how society decides feminine and masculine roles. Also among the larger animals, we find large, hefty baboons guarding the tribe, obviously dominant, even if only amongst themselves; and among other big animals the male is obviously something very strong. However, people who study natural history are constantly surprised to find crazy animals where the male is not dominant. Biologists have been surprised to find that you find no real evidence in the animal world that the male is necessarily the dominant or superior sex. Everybody knows about the male spider, and the mantis is always eaten while he is actually mating. There are several creatures, such as worms, where the female carries around the male as a little sort of internal microscopic parasite, just to be safe.

Therefore, although we have grown up with the idea that the male is a dominant and superior sex, the situation is this: once a female evolves beyond the state of laying eggs and just leaving them, she is obliged to go through periods in her life when she is at a biological disadvantage. She may be heavy with young, or while bringing them up she may find them just as dependent as if the umbilical cord still were there. During these stages she is obviously at a disadvantage, compared with herself in intervening periods or with males that don't have these troubles. Under those conditions it is necessary for nature to devise some kind of compensating mechanism. There are only two avenues open to nature, both of which have been exploited. One is to have the female more aggressive, cryptic, and tougher in some way during the time that she is pregnant or caring for the infant. The second is to develop groups in which a male accepts a defensive and protective role; so you get partners, or little groups like the monkey societies where all the males are protective and are stronger.

I would like to suggest that since we know that most of the differences between the sexes do seem to be cultural in origin and since presumably our culture is something we can do research work on and even ultimately manipulate, this is the field where we should try to determine, first of all, what is woman's real genetic potentiality. Then we can develop her normally instead of forcing her to do things for which she is not properly fitted, like geometry. Perhaps this is the greatest field for research, and since the title of the panel discussion is "Research on the Nature of Woman," we should start paying serious attention to the cultural aspects which decide differences between the sexes, to see whether we cannot perhaps restore woman to some dominant role. She is, after all, the person who both bears and rears children, so against my sex I would like to suggest that this is something really important. For one thing, among animals, the infant depends upon its mother completely for its proper development. If that development is not there, you get defective youngsters; if there are too many defective youngsters, they can't make good parents, and therefore there is an element of perpetuation which is terribly serious and which you see in our own society.

In animals, the father has developed along his own lines and is not sufficiently adaptable to take over some of the roles of the female. We presumably are—so one of the questions I would like to ask first of the panel is: do you think that the human father, or other males, can take over in any way some of the roles for the essential proper development of our infants and youngsters, roles which can no longer be taken over by females because of the fix she got herself into in our modern society?

Another very important point, illustrated by Harlow's work, is that play between infants can to some extent compensate for deficiencies in the mother, which suggests the second question: is it possible that we can also, by encouraging play at the earliest stages among different infants, compensate again for some of the deficiencies which we detect in modern woman?

Dr. Maccoby Actually, when I try to think about the question to what extent child-rearing and child-training functions can be performed by other people than the mother, I have to add another question that I don't know the answer to. Mrs. Jay and others interested in primatology have told us quite a lot about the importance to the infant of being mothered. But what about the importance to the mother of doing that mothering? I am wondering whether Mrs. Jay has ever observed a female adult primate who did not have infants to mother and whether there is any evidence that this produced a sort of neurosis in her, or that there was a deficiency, perhaps. We don't know what the biological underpinnings of maternal behavior are, but if you try to divide child training among males and females, we might find out that females need to do it and that males don't.

Mrs. Jay On several occasions, I have had an opportunity to see a female who had a dead infant or one who had died. The intense interest of the female langur monkey actually continues long after the death of an infant, if she is lucky enough to have given birth that year. Often females may not become pregnant or may not have a live birth in a year, and there are well-documented cases of females which are so upset by this that they kidnap infants of other females, which leads to a great deal of disruption within the troop. When you watch these females, it is obvious that they are under a great deal of stress, to say nothing of the physiological stress of their body preparing for nursing and caring of an infant. These females which had the most difficulty in becoming pregnant are generally those who have very severe antisocial and social problems as well, and the normal mother always is a mother.

The effect on a female of having an infant is something that has not been well studied among primates. We know a great deal about what it means to an infant to have a mother, and there is plenty of evidence that it is extremely important for a mother, too, to have the infant. Probably all primate females are equally interested in infants, but culturally this in its expression may be inhibited in some societies, while it is really encouraged in others. This is true of species of monkeys as well. A baboon mother will not let another female touch her infant, but I would be willing to bet that all mother baboons love infant baboons.

Dr. Overstreet   Turing back into the human realm, we have at the present time among humans about a 15 per cent rate of involuntary infertility. Do you have any evidence that the women who are involuntarily infertile turn more to vigorous, dominant, or intellectual pursuits because of their nonchildbearing?

Dr. Maccoby   I know of no such evidence, and judging from what else I know about the so-called law of compensation in human behavior, it does not apply. We have found that women who, before they begin to have children, are most taken up and bound up in their jobs are the ones who are most enthusiastic and committed as mothers when they do have children. We expected that being cut off from profession and all their work activities might have frustrated these women when they started having children, but the reverse was true; so that I suspect you don't find compensation but rather a feeding in from one facility to another.

Dr. Overstreet   We do have one example, in modern obstetrics, of the male not so much taking over some female functions as participating in the reproductive function. This is the matter of "natural childbirth," which has taken the view that it is natural (and this is still a wide open question) for the father to participate more in the reproductive process from an emotional and psychologic point of view. There are many who question this as really being natural and who feel that perhaps it is a passing fad and fancy which is not solidly based biologically. This remains open to proof in the future, but it is one example of the male going farther into the female role in reproduction.

Dr. Audy   It would seem that this is not culturally generally accepted; if it were, it would probably be a very good thing, but when it is not, it would mean that some males would suffer trauma of a deleterious sort and others would find this a necessary experience between husband, wife, and child together.

From the Floor   In view of the fact that if we encourage our female children to strive for intellectual achievement, this creates anxiety and tension for them, is it fair to lead them in this direction and thus assure an adult life full of conflict?

Dr. Maccoby   I see some parallels in this to current problems with desegregation. Is it fair to encourage minority groups to try to strive for something when to do so is to create conflict? My answer is yes. I would not encourage all girls to strive for an intellectual career, since not all are suited to it; but when one detects the potential that goes with it, then I personally would be willing to encourage the child in the hope that if we get good intellectual performance from women who can also be feminine in essential ways, then we can change the stereotype that makes life difficult for them. Let them challenge this difficult situation, but they will have to meet conflicts.

From the Floor   Should not more facts be available to men on the biological make-up of women to better their understanding and smooth the path for many a marriage?

Dr. Overstreet   There is a good amen answer to that, I am sure. I have the impression that in the imparting to children of knowledge about the biological functioning of women, especially menstrual functioning and childbirth functioning, we are still under the cloud of our Puritan heritage, so that to a very large extent parents, to whom it properly belongs, abdicate the job of really informing children as they grow up in early years as to what the biological functioning is like.

This does two bad things in my experience as a gynecologist: it makes going through the biological changes much more difficult than it should be in the first place, such as onset of menstruation, and it tells men, who will have to live with women, far too little of what they're going to be like and how they will have to be lived with.

Mrs. Jay   I think you can see one pit into which we must not fall: Man has an exceedingly complex society greatly differing from the langur monkey. I study monkeys, not in the sense of direct application of the information obtained to the situations of human societies, but rather in the search for biological fundamentals which may cast light upon very basic human affairs. I would like to close this panel with a delightful piece of doggerel, taken from the Congressional Record of March 13, 1961:

Monkeys

Three monkeys sat in a coconut tree,
Discussing things as they're to be;
Said one to the other, "Now listen you two,
There's a certain rumor that can't be true:

That man descended from our noble race!
The very idea is a disgrace!
No monkey ever deserted his wife,
Starved her babies and ruined her life;

And you've knever known a mother monk
To leave her babies with others to bunk,
Or pass them on from one to another
Till they scarcely know who is their mother.

And another thing, you will never see
A monk build a fence 'round a coconut tree,
And let the coconuts go to waste,
Forbidding all other monks to taste.

Why, if I'd put a fence around a tree,
Starvation would force you to steal from me!
Here's another thing a monk won't do:
Go out at night and get in a stew;

Or use a gun, a club or knife,
To take some other monkey's life;
Yes, man descended, the ornery cuss.
But, brother, he didn't descend from us!"

PART TWO

THE SPECTRUM OF FEMININITY

Chairman: Mrs. Randolph A. Hearst

The first paper dealt with the development of femininity in the human child, emphasizing both biological and cultural factors which come to underlie the adult female personality. The paper which followed concerned the relationship of women to the whole field of art, both in the Renaissance and today. It emphasized duality of the creative aspect: actual painting and the support and development of painters by patrons. The third paper emphasized the importance of the person in the dual roles of masculinity and femininity common to both sexes. The panel which followed elaborated upon biologic and psychologic aspects of women in relation to her goals.

John Money

DEVELOPMENTAL DIFFERENTIATION
OF FEMININITY AND MASCULINITY
COMPARED

The simple dichotomy of innate versus acquired is conceptually outdated in analysis of the developmental differentiation of femininity and masculinity, which is not to say that one should obliterate the distinction between genetics and environment. Rather, one needs the concept of a genetic norm of reaction that defines limits within which genetics may interact with environment and, vice versa, of an environmental norm of reaction that defines limits within which environment may interact with genetics. Then one would speak of a norm of interaction when genetics and environment are in conjunction under optimal circumstances. Abnormality, or deviation from the norm of interaction, may be engendered by alteration of either a genetic or an environmental factor to be other than optimal.

In the sexual differentiation of the human embryo, the norm is ordinarily male when the sex chromosomes are X and Y, and female when they are a pair of X's. Nonetheless, in some lower species, the environment of the chromosomes may be so manipulated experimentally

Note: The author is supported in research by a USPHS Research Career Development Award, #MH-K3-18,635. Research drawn on for this paper was done under Grant #M-1557, the National Institute of Mental Health, The U.S. Public Health Service; and under an earlier grant from the Josiah Macy, Jr., Foundation.

as to reverse the norm. In amphibian experiments, complete reversal of phenotypic sex has been achieved. Thus, an egg of the Mexican salamander, or axolotl, fertilized as a genetic female can be forced to develop as a morphologic and fertile male, under the influence of an embryonic testicular graft. This phenotypic male, which is genotypically female, is then capable of mating with a regular female. The only tell-tale sign of their both being genetic females is in the faulty sex ratio of the offspring: 25 per cent of the offspring that should have been males are females with an abnormal sex-chromosome complement (25 per cent of the offspring are genetically normal males, 50 per cent normal females, and 25 per cent abnormally homozygous females [Humphrey, quoted in Jones and Scott, 1958, p. 17]).

In human beings, complete phenotypic reversal of genotypic sex is not known either experimentally or in spontaneous occurrence; but in the phenomena of hermaphroditism there are some quite remarkable partial reversals or incongruities of differentiation. Striking incongruity is found in the female-simulant type of male hermaphroditism known as the syndrome of testicular feminization. In this condition, a baby is born who is morphologically a normal female in appearance and who eventually matures spontaneously into a perfectly normal feminine puberty except for absence of menstruation. There is no uterus from which to menstruate. The tubes and ovaries also are lacking. The internal structures which are present are paradoxically male. The two gonads, one in each groin, are microscopically testicular, but they secrete estrogen lavishly. They are sterile. The chromosome count is 46, XY, as normally expected for the male. Psychosexually these people invariably develop as feminine.

Cases of the testicular feminizing syndrome illustrate a fundamental principal in embryonic sexual differentiation, namely, that irrespective of the sex chromosomes, the norm of reaction in the absence of gonads is to differentiate as a morphologic female, unless a masculinizing principle is added. Jost, in France, proved this point with exceptional clarity (Jost, chap. 2 in Jones and Scott, 1958).

Jost succeeded with the very delicate task of castrating fetal rabbits *in utero* without fatally interrupting pregnancy. If castrated early enough, namely, before the twenty-first day, all the fetuses differentiated as females, internally and externally. No more than three days later, on the twenty-fourth fetal day, castration did not interfere with the proper continuance of masculine differentiation already begun. On the twenty-third day, castration arrested masculine differentiation and resulted in incompletion of the masculine organs, so that they looked hermaphroditically ambiguous.

It was possible to reverse the effects of castration by implanting testosterone pellets where the gonads had been. An implant on one side only had a specific localized action, producing lateral hermaphroditism, that is, masculine internal differentiation on one side and feminine on the other. Lateral hermaphroditism sometimes occurs spontaneously in human beings.

Jost's demonstration appears to be but one example of a broadly applicable principle of female precedence. Nature herself apparently takes cognizance of the greater hazard of being a male and prepares for the greater mortality of the male by decreeing that more male babies will be born than female.

The sex ratio of births is 106 males to 100 females (Stern, 1960, chap. 21). Though not absolute, this birth ratio holds widely in countries where accurate birth statistics are kept. The ratio of male to female conceptions has not, for obvious reasons, been ascertained, but sex-chromatin surveys of early abortions have yielded findings of male-female arbortus ratios of 160:100 (Tricomi, Serr, and Solish, 1960) and of 122:100 (Szontágh, Jakobovits, and Méhes, 1961).

The initial surplus of males at birth is progressively diminished by a higher death rate for males. It is higher at all ages (Figure 1), even when female vulnerability is enhanced by the mortality of the childbearing period. With variations dependent on local conditions, males still outnumber females during the marrying ages. Numerical equality of the sexes is reached around the age of fifty. Thereafter the males die off more rapidly—leaving a sellers' market for geriatric male escort service!

The greater vulnerability of the male shows up in more than mortality tables. There are diseases also to which the male is more prone. Those of special interest here are the psychosexual and sex-behavioral pathologies. Inevitably, the epidemiology of sex pathologies is not accurately known, owing to the population's legal and moral fears of self-incrimination in disclosing personal data. It is part of the

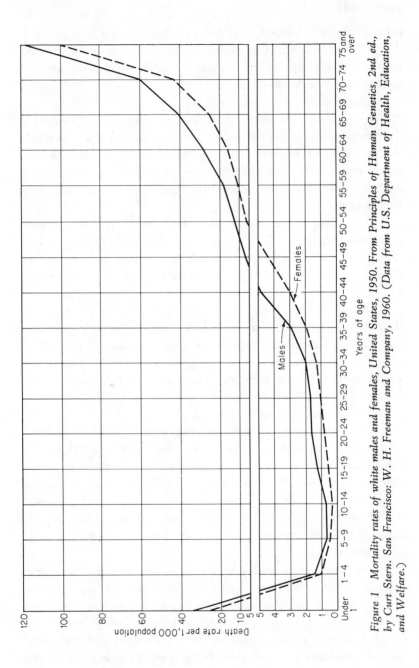

Figure 1 *Mortality rates of white males and females, United States, 1950. From Principles of Human Genetics, 2nd ed., by Curt Stern. San Francisco: W. H. Freeman and Company, 1960. (Data from U.S. Department of Health, Education, and Welfare.)*

clinical lore of psychiatry and sexology that male far exceeds female incidence of the more rare sexual anomalies, especially those in which erotic arousal becomes linked visually to some incongruous or incomplete object or image. Kinsey, Pomeroy, Martin, and Gebhard (1953, chap. 16) reviewed relevant data on exhibitionism, peeping and voyeurism, fetishism and transvestism, as well as other nonpathological preferences in visual stimulation.

The Kinsey surveys furnish incidence figures which show an excess of male over female with respect to both homosexual and animal contacts (Kinsey, Pomeroy, Martin, and Gebhard, 1953, chaps. 11 and 12; Kinsey, Pomeroy, and Martin, 1948, chaps. 21 and 22).

The figures for homosexuality are as follows: the accumulative incidences of overt contacts to the point of orgasm in the female sample reached 13 per cent, whereas in the males the figure was 37 per cent. Further, it was estimated that 4 per cent of white males are exclusively homosexual throughout life, whereas the corresponding figure for females is only a half to one-third as many. A similar ratio of 8 men to 3.6 women was found in the accumulative percentages for animal contacts. For the majority of individuals, contacts with animals were sporadic and transient; exact figures are missing, but men outnumbered women in repeating the experience and in becoming habituated for a period of years.

There is no ready explanation of why psychosexual differentiation as a male may, like embryonic differentiation, be more complex and open to error than differentiation as a female. It is necessary to know a great deal more about the entire process of psychosexual differentiation. One inroad into this problem has been made by the study of human hermaphrodites (Money, Hampson, and Hampson, 1955; Money, Hampson, and Hampson, 1957; Hampson and Hampson, 1961; Money, 1961b; Money, 1962).

In the annals of hermaphroditism and the related congenital sexual deformity of penile agenesis, it has happened that individuals of the same anatomical and physiological diagnosis have been raised, some as girls, some as boys. The appropriate surgical corrections are undertaken, and at teenage the congruous hormonal therapy is given. Then it is usual to discover that the gender role and psychosexual identity agree with the sex of assignment and rearing. The importance of these cases is that they show a complete overriding of sex-chromosomal constitution and of gonadal status in the establishment of gender role and identity.

There are other cases that demonstrate the ascendancy of assigned sex over hormonal sex also, notably female hermaphrodites with the adrenogenital syndrome raised and living as women. Before the advent of cortisone therapy in 1950, to suppress adrenal androgens, these women were exceptionally heavily virilized and totally lacking in female secondary sexual characteristics. The subordination of their hormonal sex to their assigned sex in psychosexual differentiation is, therefore, all the more remarkable.

Unquestionably, it is difficult to establish and maintain a feminine gender role and erotic identity when the body is heavily virilized, and harder still if the sexual organs are hermaphroditically masculinized with gross enlargement of the clitoris and partial fusion of the labia as in a scrotum (or homologously vice versa, for boys). Yet even this contradiction in external genital appearance, surprisingly enough, can be tolerated and a feminine identity established at variance with it.

Hermaphroditically ambiguous external genitals may, however, tell a lie to their owner, as well as to other people, so that it is therapeutically highly desirable to have them surgically corrected at an early age. The internal organs, by contrast, being hidden, do not appear to have any effect on the differentiation of gender role and identity.

The evidence of hermaphroditism, then, shows that it is possible for psychosexual differentiation to be contradictory of chromosomal sex, gonadal sex, hormonal sex, external genital sex, and internal genital sex, and to agree instead with assigned sex.

One is confronted with the conclusion, perhaps surprising to some, that there is no primary genetic or other innate mechanism to preordain the masculinity or femininity of psychosexual differentiation. Factors of innate origin may exert influence as secondary determinants, however. The obvious example is the anatomy of the external genitalia which, in the normal course of embryonic events, is determined by biochemical organizer substances which in turn are regulated by chromosomal sex. Postnatally, the anatomy of the genitals determines the sex of assignment, the gender-specific reactions of other people to the growing child, and the proof to the child through his own body image that other people are correct.

In psychosexual differentiation, the analogy is with language. Genetics and innate determinants ordain only that language can develop and differentiate, provided that the sensory and motor capacities are intact and that communicational stimulation is adequate, but not whether the language will be Nahuatl, Arabic, English, or any other. Psychosexually, also, genetics and innate determinants ordain only that a gender role and identity shall differentiate, without directly dictating whether the direction shall be male or female. In fact, the expected norm of reaction may be completely reversed by factors that come into play after birth.

As gender role and identity become fully differentiated, they become permanently indelible and imprinted, and subsequently as irreversible and powerful in influencing behavior as if innately preordained *in toto*. This idea of the indelibility of the products of the interaction of heredity with experience and learning is rather novel in psychology, but profoundly important. The evidence from hermaphroditic cases of sex reassignment is that the critical period for gender imprinting is in early childhood, beginning with the onset of mastery of language. The die is cast, pretty well, by the age of six, after which major realignment of gender role and identity is rare.

It is not for a moment claimed that psychosexual differentiation as male or female is a simple-minded matter of environmental determinism. Rather, the environment is viewed as an integral and essential constituent of that differentiation, more profoundly contributory than has often been allowed.

Nonetheless, for all the psychosexual differences that can be regarded as environmentally conditioned, in the sense of culturally learned, there are some psychosexual differences that go deeper. Their roots lie, obscure still to the scientific gaze, apparently in the endocrine and nervous systems.

It is an unsolved question as to whether some sex-different hormonal factory may, by originally affecting the organization of the nervous system itself, eventually affect sex-different behavior. Phoenix, Goy, Gerall, and Young (1959) ventured such a hypothesis after studying the behavior of female guinea pigs some of which had been rendered visibly hermaphroditic, others not, by injecting the pregnant mother with androgen. The guinea pigs exposed to androgen *in utero* subsequently exhibited, in a complex series of tests, mating behavior which, though not absent in normal females, had an arousal threshold and frequency of occurrence approaching that of the normal male. The behavior was not sex specific; rather, its threshold and frequency was.

Irrespective of neuroanatomy and fetal androgens, it is quite possible that the sex hormones, represented in different ratios in the two sexes, have different threshold effects on the nervous system, both receptor and effector. Smell acuity, for example, at least for some compounds, appears to be regulated by estrogen level. Women generally have greater acuity than men. Though Elsberg, Brewer, and Levy (1936) reported three cases to the contrary, acuity is at its peak for most women when they are not in their progesterone (menstruating) phase of the menstrual cycle (Schneider and Wolf, 1955). Their acuity is lost after ovariectomy, but regained if they are given estrogen (Le Magnen, 1952). Hypophysectomy, which suppresses ovarian function, also brings about loss of the sense of smell (Schon, 1958).

Another sex difference that appears to be hormonally regulated is the intensity or urgency of libido, or sexual desire. In this case, there is considerable evidence that androgen is the libido hormone for both men and women (Money, 1961a, c). When men are given estrogen, as in the treatment of prostatic cancer, they usually report loss of sexual desire and of potency. Excessive androgens of adrenal origin in women with the adrenogenital syndrome are accompanied usually by a low threshold for erotic arousal and for clitoral tumescence, both of which are somewhat increased when androgen is suppressed by cortisone therapy. Normal women deprived of their normal adrenal androgens by either adrenalectomy or hypophysectomy, as part of the treatment of breast cancer also experienced a lessening or total loss of libido, which was not the case when they were deprived only of estrogens by ovariectomy (Waxenberg, Drellich, and Sutherland, 1959; Schon and Sutherland, 1960). Conversely, normal women given androgen treatment for various gynecological reasons many times find their libidinal intensity increased, perhaps to unfamiliarly high levels. The androgens of eroticism in normal, untreated women may be of adrenal origin or may derive from the closely related progestins. They may also be exogenous. A typist of one of my recent manuscripts disclosed that young men about town who wish to put the make on their young women have learned to spike the girl friend's Martini with testosterone one weekend in advance.

Closely connected with libidinal threshold is yet another sex difference, namely, in responsiveness to visual and pictorial images and to erotic narrative material. Men, in general, are much more responsive to this type of stimulation than are women, and they are responsive in a different way. For example, the strip-tease girl at a show or the pin-up girl on a calendar becomes the object of a male's desire. If these same stimuli arouse a women, as they often do, it is because she projects herself into the position of the seductive one. Then, significantly enough, her desire is not for anyone and everyone in the admiring herd but for the one special person, even though he may be many miles absent, who is the object of her long-term romantic affection.

The other side of the woman's coin is that it is rare for her to be erotically aroused—romantically alerted, yes, but not erotically aroused—by the perceptual or pictorial image of a male. For the male, the other side of the coin is that, unless he be homosexual, he will not be able to project himself into the image of another male on erotic display. Thus, in exhibitions and stag movies of sex and copulation, a male is quite likely to be more aroused by the reiteration of the female image when two women are shown in Lesbian play than when a man and a woman are shown together. Herein may lie an element of the explanation of why, in man-made laws, male homosexuality is a crime and Lesbianism is unmentioned.

It can, of course, be argued that these perceptual-arousal differences between men and women are culturally determined and perpetuated—there are no sex shows, commercially, for women. The counter argument is that culture is built on biology which it may never totally defy. It is anecdotal evidence, but nonetheless pertinent, that women who have, in my professional experience, reported a capacity to be aroused to erotic action by sexy pictures of men or by narrative erotic material have been women who have or once had elevated androgen levels secondary to the adrenogenital syndrome. The significant thing, be it noted, in these cases, is that masculinism applies only to the level of arousal threshold, not its content. The arousing image was heterosexual and perfectly appropriate for a woman. Thus, hormonal influences may have the power to regulate erotic threshold, but apparently not erotic content.

To explain what determines the content of the image that will have erotic arousal power, one turns to the concept of imprinting as discovered and expanded by the school of animal ethologists. In imprinting theory, one postulates an innate releasing mechanism (IRM) in the nervous system. An IRM requires a perceptual stimulus to trigger it into action. The physical dimensions—color, size, shape, shading, contour—of the stimulus may vary, but only within limits phylogenetically determined. Thus, a parakeet may get imprinted to make love to another bird, to a wobbly celluloid toy, or to a human finger. A phylogenetically acceptable stimulus presented at the critical time in the life cycle becomes imprinted rather easily and then possesses a remarkable quality of persistence and preeminence over competitor stimuli. Imprinting could account for the remarkable specificity and persistence of the most preferred and most potent type of erotic stimulus, in both healthy and abnormal psychosexual functioning. Imprinting, in fact, is a way of explaining the very existence of aberrancy in psychosexual imagery and perceptual arousal.

Perception plays a part in another sex difference, namely, in relation to distractibility. More than the female, the male is in his erotic pursuits fairly promiscuously distracted from one love object to another, especially over a period of time, except perhaps when he is in the vortex of having just fallen desperately in love. The female is more steadfastly tied to a single romantic object or concept. In the act of copulation, by contrast, it is the male who has a singleness of purpose, perhaps oblivious even to noxious stimuli, and likely to be unable to continue if successfully distracted by a competing stimulus. This sex difference appears to hold widely in the animal kingdom (Beach, 1947, p. 264). Horsley Gantt (1949, p. 37), director of the well-known Pavlovian Laboratories at Johns Hopkins, wrote:

A marked difference between the male and female cat is that the female's interest in food is not inhibited by the sexual excitation of copulation, for she, as well as a bitch, will accept food not only after coitus but even during the act! . . . The female is however much more strongly oriented about the offspring than about the sexual act; she undergoes a great inhibition of conditional reflexes and of some unconditional reflexes post-partum, a fact which has been demonstrated several times in my laboratory with dogs.

The male's ready arousal by perceiving a new erotic stimulus perhaps relates to his greater expenditure of energy in the service of sexual searching, pursuit, and consummation. Expenditure extends also to adventurous, exploratory roaming, to assertiveness and aggression, and to the defence of territorial rights. Of course the male does not have exclusive prerogative, in these respects, but there does indeed seem to be a sex difference in the frequency with which these patterns of energy expenditure are manifest.

Table 1 Accidental deaths in children according to the five principal types in the continental United States, 1956, and in Venezuela, 1954, by sex and age group *

Type of accident	Continental United States		Venezuela	
	Males	Females	Males	Females
	1–4 years			
Motor vehicle	800	638	28	22
Drowning	463	191	47	38
Fire and explosion of combustible material	443	472	–	–
Poisonings, solid or liquid	196	140	28	19
Falls	155	99	–	7
Burns	–	–	26	27
Poisonous bites by venomous animals	–	–	6	–
	5–14 years			
Motor vehicle	1,785	855	44	28
Drowning	981	204	55	15
Firearms	357	72	–	–
Fire and explosion of combustible material	263	404	–	–
Falls	138	50	19	4
Poisonous bites by venomous animals	–	–	39	6
Burns	–	–	15	31

* Reproduced from Goddard (1959), courtesy of Public Health Reports.

The difference becomes apparent even in childhood. When boys are out staking territory claims, constructing hideouts, forts, or camps, and fending off rival intruder gangs, girls are expending somewhat less energy, usually closer to home, making lairs and homes for the young and raising doll babies.

A striking demonstration of the sex difference, during childhood, in types and variety of energy expenditure is provided by the figures for accidental deaths in children. Table 1 compares statistics for males and females, under and over four years of age, in the United States and in Venezuela, for five principal types of accident. Inspection of the table shows that the deaths of boys exceeded those of girls chiefly in those situations in which the boys had gotten in harm's way or had inaugurated some dangerous activity. In brief, the boys went further to meet death than the girls did.

Evidence to supplement the various findings on the human species may be found in the observations of Harlow (1962) on the macaque monkey during childhood. Harlow found that male monkey children make many more threats toward other monkeys, boys or girls, than do female monkey children, whose threats, moreover, are reserved primarily for other girls. The young females retreat more often than the males, specifically by adopting the female sexual posture. The male youngsters initiate more play contacts, with playmates of either sex, than do female. In addition, rough-and-tumble play is strictly for the boys! With increasing age, male infants show increasing frequency of the male mounting position in their copulatory play. The males show practically no grooming behavior which, in adults, is specifically feminine sexual behavior.

It would be going too far, on the basis of this kind of evidence, to equate masculinity with aggressiveness and femininity with passivity, as has sometimes been fashionable. It is rather that the sexes differ with regard to the types of behavior pattern that they initiate and persist in, versus those that they discontinue most frequently.

It is not possible, in the present state of knowledge, to relate the foregoing types of male-female difference in patterns of energy expenditure and sexual play either to genetic mechanisms, to fetal hormonal effects on the central nervous system, or to hormonal functioning in childhood. Harlow's own studies do show, however, that proper exercise of patterns of energy expenditure in childhood play are essential to the final emergence of adult sexual patterns. Monkeys, male and female, raised in individual cages and deprived of play with their agemates failed to develop normal sexual behavior and were hopelessly unable to master the art of copulation even under the tutelage of a cooperative, experienced mate.

Parenthetically, one may raise the question of whether the suppression, in our own human society, of childhood sexual play may adversely affect sexual behavior in adulthood and perhaps promote the occurrence of sexual aberration.

A few of Harlow's female monkeys did, he reports, after heroic efforts of animal husbandry, become pregnant. They had known no real, live monkey mothers of their own, since they had been raised in individual cages with experimental surrogate objects for mothers. When they had their own babies, they were totally inept at motherhood—as liable to crush and kill their babies on the floor as to pick them up gently.

Motherhood itself, then, is yet another instance of behavior in which genetic patterns and environmental patterns in interaction with one another are equally important to the mature coordination and emergence of the final product.

My wheel has done a full turn, all the way from X and Y chromosomes to motherhood. I close with a witticism attributed to Oscar Wilde on the occasion of his being asked to explain the difference between the sexes. He paused epigrammatically and replied: "Madam, I can't conceive."

References

Beach, F. A. 1947. A review of physiological and psychological studies of sexual behavior in mammals. *Physiological Reviews*, 27:240–307.

Elsberg, C. A., Brewer, E. D., and Levy, I. 1936. The sense of smell. IV. Concerning conditions which may temporarily alter normal olfactory acuity. *Bulletin of the Neurological Institute of New York*, 4:31–34.

Gantt, W. H. 1949. Psychosexuality in animals. In *Psychosexual Development in Health and Disease* (P. H. Hoch and J. Zubin, eds.). New York, Grune & Stratton.

Goddard, J. L. 1959. Accident prevention in childhood. *Public Health Reports*, 74:523–534.

Hampson, J. L., and Hampson, J. G. 1961. The ontogenesis of sexual behavior in man. Ch. 23 in *Sex and Internal Secretions* (3rd ed., W. C. Young, ed.). Baltimore, Williams & Wilkins.

Harlow, H. F. 1962. The heterosexual affectional system in monkeys. *American Psychologist*, 17:1-9.

Jones, H. W., Jr., and Scott, W. W. 1958. *Hermaphroditism, Genital Anomalies and Related Endocrine Disorders*. Baltimore, Williams & Wilkins.

Kinsey, A. C., Pomeroy, W. B., and Martin, C. E. 1948. *Sexual Behavior in the Human Male*. Philadelphia, Saunders.

Kinsey, A. C., Pomeroy, W. B., Martin, C. F., and Gebhard, P. H. 1953. *Sexual Behavior in the Human Female*. Philadelphia, Saunders.

Le Magnen, J. 1952. Les phénomènes olfactosexuels chez l'homme. *Archives des Sciences Physiologiques*, 6:125-160.

Money, J. 1961a. Components of eroticism in man: 1. The hormones in relation to sexual morphology and sexual desire. *Journal of Nervous and Mental Disease*, 132:239-248.

Money, J. 1961b. Hermaphroditism. In *The Encyclopedia of Sexual Behavior* (Albert Ellis and Albert Abarbanel, eds.). New York, Hawthorn.

Money, J. 1961c. Sex hormones and other variables in human eroticism. Ch. 22 in *Sex and Internal Secretions* (3rd ed., W. C. Young, ed.). Baltimore, Williams & Wilkins.

Money, J. 1962. Cytogenetic and psychosexual incongruities with a note on space-form blindness. *American Journal of Psychiatry*. In press.

Money, J., Hampson, J. G., and Hampson, J. L. 1955. An examination of some basic sexual concepts: The evidence of human hermaphroditism. *Bulletin of The Johns Hopkins Hospital*, 97:301-319.

Money, J., Hampson, J. G., and Hampson, J. L. 1957. Imprinting and the establishment of gender role. *Archives of Neurology and Psychiatry*, 77:333-336.

Phoenix, C. H., Goy, R. W., Gerall, A. A., and Young, W. C. 1959. Organizing action of prenatally administered testosterone propionate on the tissues mediating mating behavior in the female guinea pig. *Endocrinology*, 65:369-382.

Schneider, R. A., and Wolf, S. 1955. Olfactory perception thresholds for citral utilizing a new type olfactorium. *Journal of Applied Physiology*, 8:337-342.

Schon, M. 1958. Psychological effects of hypophysectomy in women with metastatic breast cancer. *Cancer*, 11:95-98.

Schon, M., and Sutherland, A. M. 1960. The role of hormones in human behavior. III. Changes in female sexuality after hypophysectomy. *Journal of Clinical Endocrinology and Metabolism*, 20:833-841.

Stern, C. 1960. *Principles of Human Genetics*. 2nd edition. San Francisco, Freeman.

Szontágh, F. E., Jakobovits, A., and Méhes, Ch. 1961. Primary embryonal sex ratio in normal pregnancies determined by the nuclear chromatin. *Nature,* 192:476.

Tricomi, V., Serr, D., and Solish, G. 1960. The ratio of male to female embryos as determined by the sex chromatin. *American Journal of Obstetrics and Gynecology,* 79:504–509.

Waxenberg, S. E., Drellich, M. G., and Sutherland, A. M. 1959. The role of hormones in human behavior. I. Changes in female sexuality after adrenalectomy. *Journal of Clinical Endocrinology,* 19:193–202.

Thomas Carr Howe

WOMEN IN THE FIELD OF ART

The subject, "Women in the Field of Art," suggests a wealth of material that is both provocatively and bewilderingly abundant. Virtually every one of the fascinating personalities I have selected for consideration today is worthy of a serious study of volume length. In fact, quite a number of them have been. It is, therefore, something of an impertinence to take so fleeting a look at so glittering a roster of distinguished ladies as I have assembled from the pages of history. For the sake of variety and contrast, it has been a random selection. I offer no apologia for the nature of the selection—that is my privilege and my risk—but I do regret that individual comment must of necessity be so brief. It is appropriate to point out at the beginning that, with a single exception, the women who figure in this discussion have been chosen for the roles they have played in the promotion and appreciation of art—either as patroness or collector, or both—rather than as creative artists.

One is tempted to hark back to the twelfth century, to that fabulous personality Eleanor of Aquitaine, mother of Richard Cœur de Lion and other kings and queens, for a venerable, first example of feminine patronage of the arts in the Middle Ages. But, on second thought, this ex-

Note: In April, 1960, Miss Agnes Mongan of the Fogg Art Museum, Harvard University, delivered a lecture entitled "Lady Collectors" at the California Palace of the Legion of Honor. I am indebted to Miss Mongan for certain illustrative material which I have incorporated in this discussion, "Women in the Field of Art."

traordinary woman is more to be remembered for her sage statesmanship than for her encouragement of the gentler, visual arts, notwithstanding her concern with the beautification of Poitiers and other historic cities within her vast domains. For our purposes, it is more to the point to skip to the period of the high Renaissance in Italy and begin with two celebrated sisters who made such a lasting imprint on the cultural development of the region of their origin: I refer to Isabella and Beatrice d'Este. The daughters of Ercole I of Este, the ruling family of Ferrara, and Leonora of Naples, Isabella was born in 1474, Beatrice in 1475. Isabella became the wife of Francesco Gonzaga, Marquis of Mantua; her sister, Beatrice, married Lodovico Sforza, duke of Milan, known— because of his swarthy complexion—as "Ludovico il Moro." Both were women of extraordinary beauty and great cultivation, who numbered Leonardo da Vinci and Raphael among their friends. To their circle belonged Elizabetta Gonzaga, wife of Guidobaldo da Montefeltro, son of the great Federigo, duke of Urbino, and Lucrezia Borgia, the dazzling daughter of Pope Alexander VI, who was married to Alfonso d'Este. Two other remarkable women of the same period frequented the lavish courts of Isabella and Beatrice. These were the vigorous Caterina Sforza from Forli and the celebrated Vittoria Colonna, Roman wife of the Marquis of Pescara, the devoted patroness of Michelangelo in the closing years of his life. Still another brilliant woman of this period was Caterina Cornaro, former Queen of Cyprus and called the "daughter of the Republic of Venice," to whose court came the cultivated Cardinal Bembo, secretary to Pope Leo X, better remembered as the lover of Lucrezia Borgia. As Francis Taylor has observed in his *Taste of Angels* (1948), Florence in the last quarter of the fifteenth century was the New York of its day, the envied if noisy financial center of the time. Rome he has likened to our Washington, the seat of the government, and Milan he has termed ". . . the crude Chicago of the Renaissance, while Venice stood at the Golden Gate to the Orient." Through the Este family, referred to above, Urbino, Naples, Milan, and Modena were all connected with Mantua by blood or by marriage. All the noble ladies here mentioned shared one bond in common: they were passionately devoted to art and the superb collections with which they filled their palaces and villas. Their husbands, for the most part, were content to leave to their wives the business of embellishing the family name with a reputation for devotion to the finer things of life. Taylor goes on to say that perhaps the true secret of the Renaissance woman was her inclination to be attentive to the artist attached to the household, to heed his counsel, and to be guided by his taste. Thus, it is not surprising that the collections accumulated in this way evenually formed the basis for family "museums" that have come down to us today more or less intact, if not always preserved on the original premises.

Turning to Northern Europe, one of the most indefatigable collectors of the early sixteenth century was Margaret of Austria, daughter of the Emperor Maximilian and his wife, Mary of Burgundy. Her life was a singularly unhappy one. Married to the Dauphin of France—the future Charles VIII—at the age of three, she grew up at the French court. When cast aside by Charles for Anne of Brittany, her father arranged for her marriage, at the age of seventeen, to Don Carlos, the Prince of the Asturias and son of Ferdinand and Isabella. At his death in less than a year, she married Philibert, Duke of Savoy, who was killed in a hunting accident a few years later. In 1504, at the age of twenty-four, Margaret was a beautiful, grief-stricken widow. Her nephew, the future Emperor Charles V, was entrusted to her care, and it is generally conceded that she was responsible for his discriminating taste for art. Aside from supervising Charles's education, she devoted herself exclusively to art collecting and writing. The inventory of her palace at Malines revealed her to be a collector of formidable proportions. Aside from a fabulous collection of tapestries, there were statuettes, objects of gold and silver, mirrors, ivories, jewels of rare workmanship and a library of manuscripts that was the finest outside Italy. Most of the manuscripts are preserved today in the Bibliothèque Royale at Brussels. Margaret, however, had apparently no taste for German art. In his *Letters,* Albrecht Dürer made the following comment, in 1521, after a visit to Malines: "And I went to Lady Margaret's and showed her my Emperor [his portrait of Maximilian, Margaret's father, which is today in Vienna] and would have presented it to her but she so disliked it that I took it away with me. . . . And on Friday Lady Margaret showed me all her beautiful things; amongst them I saw about 40 oil pictures, the like of which for precision and excellence I have never beheld." Dürer went on to say that they included works by Mabuse and Jacopo dei Barbari and that he asked her for the Jacopo sketchbook but that she had promised it to someone else. He also mentions having seen at Malines the treasure of Montezuma, brought back from Mexico by Cortes—the first reference to pre-Columbian art by a European. This treasure, it is interesting to note, lay neglected in the basement of the Kunsthistorisches Museum in Vienna until a few years ago. But it was Margaret's picture gallery which was one of the wonders of the day. It included more than a hundred masterpieces—among them the celebrated Van Eyck "Portrait of Jean Arnolfini and His Wife" which is today one of the glories of London's National Gallery. It was listed in Margaret's catalog of the year 1516.

The dominant part played by François I as a lavish patron of the arts in France during the first half of the sixteenth century has understandably overshadowed that of his daughter-in-law, Catherine de' Medici (1519–1582), the wife of his son, Henri II, and the mother of three kings of France, François II, Charles IX, and Henri III. To her, a daughter of the great banking house of Florence, the love of beautiful things came naturally, though the indulgence of this taste was in part political. Humiliated by her husband's neglect of her in favor of his mistress, Diane de Poitiers—noted for her devotion to *French* artists and craftsmen, especially in the decoration of the Château d'Anet—Catherine dedicated herself to demonstrating the superiority of the *Italian* artistic genius. Her Paris residence, the Hotel de Soissons (which stood on the site of the present Bourse), provided her with an ideal setting. Her collection of tapestries—some 130 pieces in all—of Flemish, French, and Italian manufacture was too numerous to be shown at one time, so they were displayed in rotation. Rich oriental carpets covered the floors. Superb Limoges enamels and Italian mirrors adorned the walls of various cabinets. All in all, the house was a tribute to the cabinet-maker's art, with richly inlaid furniture and mantels of onyx and marble. The draperies were of the finest velvets and brocades. Though she cared more for *bibelots* and miniatures than for monumental canvases, her collection of paintings numbered nearly five hundred. More than two-thirds of these were portraits—many of them by Clouet and Corneille de Lyon, the nucleus of the Louvre's great collection today. Catherine had a great fondness for porcelain and *objects de vertu* as the superb collection in the Galerie d'Apollon at the Louvre bears witness. In addition she owned a vast collection of Venetian glass, ivories, and bronzes and no less than 140 examples of the ware of Bernard Palissy. Her taste tended understandably to be rather baroque.

Some thirty years after the death of Catherine, another Medici, Marie, the widow of Henri IV and mother of Louis XIII, made her one great contribution to the cultural patrimony of France and, incidentally, thereby established her single claim to patronage of the arts. This was in 1622 when, as Queen Mother, she summoned Rubens to Paris to decorate her favorite residence, the Palais du Luxembourg. These decorations consisted of the most brilliant episodes in her life and that of Henri IV, the famous series which is presently preserved in the Louvre and constitutes one of its principal treasures. If not herself a great collector or patron of the arts, her daughter Henrietta Maria was to become the wife of one of the most voracious of collectors—Charles I of England.

Later in the seventeenth century we encounter in the person of Christina of Sweden one of the most enigmatic personalities in the field of the arts. Daughter of the famed Gustavus Adolphus, she succeeded to the throne in 1644 at the age of eighteen. Having received an education befitting a monarch, she gave serious attention to affairs of state during the first years of her reign. Soon thereafter she gave way to great extravagance and a frenzied social life. Through lavish patronage of art, science, and literature, she attracted many foreign scholars—Descartes among them—to the Swedish court. She collected Italian and Flemish paintings on a grand scale and bought from Mazarin an entire library which she added to the many volumes that her father had appropriated during his conquests years before. Furthermore, she is said to have read them all! Then in 1650, after ruling for six years, she abruptly decided to abdicate. In this attempt she was not successful. It was not until 1654 that she achieved her wish, designating her cousin Charles as her successor. Dressed as a man, she set out for Innsbruck, where she was baptized a Catholic and later established herself in Rome. Running out of funds, she lived on the bounty of the Pope. At the death of her cousin, Charles X, in 1660, she considered attempting to regain her throne. In this she was unsuccessful. She made a second attempt, equally fruitless, in 1667. Thereafter she settled again in Rome, where she died penniless in 1689. Christina is indeed one of the most puzzling of royal products.

Two dominant figures in the eighteenth century—one royal, the other regal to the point of royalty—claim our attention. When Catherine the Great became Empress of Russia in 1764 at the age of thirty-three, one of her first acts was to make her court the equal of those in Western Europe. Aside from relatively modest collecting on the part of Peter the Great, the rulers of Russia had paid little attention to the artistic activities of the French and German monarchs. Catherine was determined to change all that, and it soon became apparent that she was as predatory when it came to works of art as she was about men. Describing her feeling about collecting, she said: *"Ce n'est pas l'amour de l'art; c'est la voracité. Je ne suis pas amatrice, je suis gloutonne."* In 1765 she ordered the French architect, de Lamot, to construct a pavilion—a hermitage patterned after that of Jean Jacques Rousseau—connected with the Winter Palace to house her collections. At this stage of the game they consisted of a group of pictures which had been assembled by a German merchant for Frederick the Great. It included three Rembrandts, one of which, "Joseph and Potiphar's Wife," is now in the Mellon collection at the National Gallery in Washington. In 1768, she acquired the collection of Louis XV's secretary, Gaignat, and in 1769 that of Count Brühl of Dresden. The Brühl collection, one of her wisest acquisitions, greatly enriched the treasures of the Hermitage—among them, two Rembrandts, five Ruysdaels, works by van Mieris, Ter Borch, Rubens, and numerous important Italian masters. In 1771 she bought *in toto* the noted collection of François Tronchin, which Voltaire and Diderot had urged her to acquire. The following year 400 pictures from the Crozat collection were added. Among these were Titian's "Danaë," his portrait of "Cardinal Pallavacini," the great Poussin today in the Philadelphia Museum, Raphael's famous "Saint George" and several Rembrandts. But her greatest achievement in collecting was her purchase in London, through her ambassador—for the sum of 40,000 pounds—of the vast Walpole collection at Houghton Hall, sold regretfully by Horace Walpole to settle the debts of the second and third Earls of Oxford. This fabulous group of 198 pictures comprised 79 Italian works, 75 Flemish and Netherlandish paintings, 7 Spanish, 22 French, and 5 English paintings. Despite her constant complaint that she was poor as a church mouse, it seemed that Catherine's agents turned up everywhere in Europe with unlimited funds. So, in a few short years of frenzied buying, Catherine the Great formed the great bulk of the magnificent collections which make the Hermitage one of the greatest galleries of the world.

Catherine's somewhat younger but scarcely less imperious contemporary in France was Mme. de Pompadour. Born Jeanne Antoinette Poisson in 1720, she married at an early age M. Le Normant d'Étioles, nephew of the Fermier-Général. Although little is known of her education, she is said to have had instruction in engraving, singing, and playing the harpsichord. Shortly after her marriage to the wealthy aristocrat she formed a circle of interesting literary, artistic, and musical personalities which included Voltaire, Boucher, and Rameau. By 1745, when she was turning twenty-five, she had met and captivated Louis XV, and she maintained her ascendancy over him until her death nearly twenty years later. She was virtually the ruler of France, which, politically speaking, was unfortunate; but in the arts her supremacy resulted in the flowering of creative activity unparalleled since the days of the Italian Renaissance. The King bestowed on her the title of Marquise de Pompadour in 1746 and, ever since, the name has been synonymous with an age of brilliant and luxurious artistic production. Boucher was her principal court painter and designer. Incidentally, he is said to have had a genuine admiration for Pompadour's own talents as an etcher and engraver. These talents as a practicing artist doubtless served to sharpen her critical faculties. Mme. de Pompadour had an insatiable appetite for building. For example, she built the Ermitage in the park at Versailles in 1746 and three years later the Château de la Celle at the Porte de Versailles and also a villa at Fontainebleau. The Hôtel d'Évreux in Paris was remodeled for her at fantastic cost. She also had establishments at Crécy, Aunay, and Ménars. However, her special favorite was Bellevue, on the Seine between Sèvres and Meudon. It was built in 1750 and in six years she spent over three million livres on it. Boucher was the supervising decorator, Caffieri did the plaster ornamentations, and the furnishings were created only by the leading *ébénistes*. Coustou and other leading sculptors and painters of the day were engaged by Boucher to create this show place of an epoch. (It is of interest to note in passing that four panels executed by Carle Vanloo for Bellevue are today in the collection of the California Palace of the Legion of Honor—likewise two superb serving tables by Carlin which were designed for Mme. de Pompadour.) Despite the incredible range of her interests and projects,

Pompadour remains one of the very greatest of art patrons and collectors of her time. She was a woman of indomitable spirit and inexhaustible energy—even in the last years when she no longer held the King's love. Trenchard Cox (1933) relates an appealing story of Pompadour's last moments: "When the priest, who had given her a hurried viaticum, made a movement as if to depart, Pompadour, the courtesan, prematurely old at 42, said with her accustomed imperiousness, defiance, courtesy and wit: 'One moment, please, M. le Curé, we will go out together.'"

Bridging the eighteenth and nineteenth centuries and serving more as an artist-ambassadress than as a patroness of the arts is the fascinating French portrait painter, Marie-Louise Élizabeth Vigée-Lebrun. Born in Paris in 1755, she was the pupil of her father. She won membership in the Academy in 1783 with an allegorical piece called "Peace Bringing Back Plenty." But before that she had already made a name for herself as a popular society painter. Marie Antoinette was a great admirer of Mme. Vigée-Lebrun and was painted by her no less than twenty-five times. During the revolution, the artist wisely and gracefully worked in Italy. Later she visited Vienna, Berlin, and St. Petersburg and traveled extensively in Switzerland, Holland, and England. Her charm and her talents were equally acclaimed, and she was received everywhere as a kind of ambassadress without portfolio, much as Rubens was lavishly welcomed on his travels about Europe—though he, of course, was on occasion an accredited diplomat. Mme. Vigée-Lebrun was made a member of all the leading academies and painted an infinite number of portraits of distinguished persons in the course of her travels. In her later years she reestablished herself in Paris, where her salon became a center of art and fashion. She died in 1842 at the age of eighty-seven.

By way of seriocomic contrast, I should like to introduce the name of a slightly younger contemporary of the dashing Vigée-Lebrun, but one with whom she had nothing whatever in common, namely, Marie Gresholtz, rather better known as Madame Tussaud. This remarkable woman, of Swiss birth, learned the art of modeling in wax from her uncle, J. C. Curtius, the proprietor of a wax portrait gallery in the Palais Royale in Paris. By the year 1780, when she was twenty years old, she and her uncle were already well known, and during the revolution they became famous for their portraits of leading political figures of the time. In 1802, she took her waxworks to London where she established "Madame Tussaud's Exhibition." With its famed Chamber of Horrors, it became enormously popular. In 1833 she moved to the long-celebrated Baker Street address. After her death in 1860 the display was moved to larger quarters in the Marylebone Road, where it continued to be one of the "institutions" of London. In 1925, a fire destroyed the building, and some of its valuable Napoleonic relics—but happily the portrait and other casts were salvaged, and in 1928 the exhibition was reopened to the accompaniment of great fanfare by the press.

Coming now to our own shores—more specifically to Boston at the close of the Civil War, we find a high-spirited young New Yorker, Isabella Stewart, as the bride of John Lowell Gardner, a Brahmin of Brahmins. In a very proper house on Beacon Street, the young Mrs. Gardner set about creating a center for brilliant social affairs and more particularly a gathering place for painters, musicians, and literary figures. At first her husband's family and their conservative friends looked upon the quixotic "Mrs. Jack" with disapproval and were openly critical of her. This did not in the least disturb her or her husband, who looked upon her often whimsical and occasionally outrageous behavior with amused and understanding tolerance. Mrs. Gardner's lifelong interest in art led her to acquire many works by celebrated artists both past and present. In due course, with her husband's assent, she began to make plans for the creation of an art museum. During many years of her collecting, Mrs. Gardner enjoyed the advice and assistance of the late Bernard Berenson. She conceived of a Venetian palace to be built on the Fenway near the Museum of Fine Arts. Finished during the last years of her life, it was opened to the public only on certain days of the year. At her death in 1924 it became, as she had wished, a public art gallery. One of the most personal and fascinating of collections, Fenway Court houses many very great treasures—one of which has been termed the greatest single masterpiece in the United States. I refer to Titian's magnificent "Rape of Europa," which is certainly one of the principal glories of Fenway Court.

While Mrs. Gardner was making startling headlines in the Boston papers about the mammoth and mysterious *palazzo* she was building in the marshy fens of the city, two retiring sisters named Cone were quietly making art history in Baltimore. During the early years of this century, these sisters, Dr. Claribel and Miss Etta Cone, daughters of a wealthy cotton merchant, were gradually filling to overflowing their labyrinthine and adjoining apartments of some seventeen rooms, with works by the great masters of the late nineteenth- and twentieth-century French School. In these activities they were joined by a brother who predeceased his sisters. Dr. Claribel, one of the earliest women graduates of the Johns Hopkins Medical School, went to Paris in 1905 to do further medical research. Her younger sister Etta accompanied her. There, through Gertrude Stein (a distant cousin who had also attended, but not graduated from, Johns Hopkins) they met Matisse and Picasso. Although they acquired works by both of these artists, their great love was for Matisse, and their collection constitutes the greatest single assemblage of his works in this country—forty-two oils dating from 1892 to 1947 and eighteen bronzes. As the Cone sisters proceeded with their omnivorous collecting, museum people all over the country sought permission to see the amazing collection, which was eventually to number more than 350 paintings—works by Renoir, Van Gogh, Manet, Gauguin, Cézanne, and Degas, in addition to the Picassos and Matisses—50 sculptures, over 700 textiles, rugs, laces, and pieces of jewelry, and a fine library. Alfred Barr of the Museum of Modern Art is reported to have remarked, not altogether in jest, that the collection was "far too good for Baltimore." Dr. Claribel, who died in 1929, herself shared the view at one time, for when she bequeathed her share of the collection to her sister, she stipulated that it should go to Baltimore only if ". . . the spirit and appreciation of modern art in Baltimore" improved before Miss Etta died. That it *had* became apparent when the demure but strong-minded Miss Etta not only left the entire collection to the Baltimore Museum at her death in 1949 but provided $400,000 for properly housing it. Today the Cone Wing of the museum, which was completed in 1957, constitutes a collection rivalled only by those of the Museum of Modern Art in New York, the Barnes Foundation at Merion, Pennsylvania, and the Art Institute of Chicago.

An equally arresting figure among American women collectors of the present century was the late Mrs. L. L. Coburn of Chicago. She lived for many years in two small rooms at the Blackstone Hotel which were jammed with works by Degas, Manet, and Renoir. As with the Cone sisters, even her bathroom walls were studded with masterpieces.

At her death in the thirties she bequeathed them to the Art Institute of Chicago and the Fogg Museum at Harvard.

In the summer of 1929 three rich and public-spirited American women, in the course of crossing the Atlantic on the same steamer, decided it was high time for the city of New York to have a museum dedicated to contemporary art. They were Abby Aldrich Rockefeller, Miss Lillie Bliss, and Mrs. Cornelius J. Sullivan—all of them formidable collectors with powerful connections. On their return to the United States in the autumn of that year, they enlisted the advice of Paul J. Sachs of Harvard and A. Conger Goodyear of New York. It was through their combined efforts and a group of people in the East who shared their enthusiasm for the project that the Museum of Modern Art was born. It opened its doors the following year in quarters in the Heckscher Building which the new museum rapidly outgrew. Everyone is aware of what has happened since. Some years later the present Museum of Modern Art was opened on West Fifty-third Street and today continues to expand. Be he a proponent or not of contemporary art, there is hardly a person in the civilized world today who is not aware of the existence and activity of this great institution.

Another colorful and vital personality in the American art world is Mary Woodward Lasker. Following graduation from Radcliffe (with honors in Fine Arts) in the twenties, Mary Woodward became the wife of Paul Reinhardt, well-known New York art dealer. She shared operation of the Reinhardt Gallery with him for several years. Later she married Albert Lasker and guided him in the formation of a very great collection of nineteenth- and twentieth-century French painting. For so impressive a collection to have been assembled in the decade between 1940 and 1950 is an amazing achievement, regardless of the fact that Mr. and Mrs. Lasker had virtually unlimited funds at their disposal. Following Mr. Lasker's death in 1952, Mrs. Lasker took over active management of the Lasker Foundation, one of the principal aims of which is to further medical research, especially in the field of cancer research. The great collection adorns the walls of Mrs. Lasker's handsome house in Beekman Place in New York. It belongs to the Lasker Foundation, and one hazards the guess that it may be dispersed for the benefit of the Foundation at Mrs. Lasker's death. Meanwhile she has on occasion lent it to museums to raise funds for the American Cancer

Society. Some of you may recall its having been shown at the California Palace of the Legion of Honor for this purpose a few years ago.

Lack of time prevents my doing more than touching briefly on three gifted women who have made an enviable place for themselves in the field of museum administration in this country. One was the late Belle da Costa Greene, High Priestess of the Morgan Library for many years; another was the unforgettable, husky-voiced and outspoken Julianna Force, who presided so effectively over the destinies of the Whitney Museum of American Art. No one who had the good fortune to be exposed to her caustic yet kindly wit in the apartment atop the old Whitney Museum on Eighth Street in New York will ever forget this dynamic personality. A third, who is fortunately still very much with us, is the distinguished Adelyn Breeskin, until recently the director of the Baltimore Museum. She, more than any other single individual, gently but firmly emphasized to a not always receptive public the importance of modern art—thereby winning for Baltimore the prized Cone collection. In 1961 she became the director of the Washington Gallery of Modern Art, the first gallery in our national capital to be dedicated solely to contemporary art. The gallery opened its doors to the public in October of 1962.

No account of women who have made their mark in the field of art would be complete without reference to San Francisco's Alma de Bretteville Spreckels, to whom the city owes its beautiful Palace of the Legion of Honor. Impressed by the beauty of the French Government's pavilion at the Panama Pacific International Exposition of 1915—it was a replica of the Palais de la Legion d'Honneur in Paris—she and her late husband reproduced a free replica of the building in permanent materials atop the hill in Lincoln Park. In addition to providing it with numerous important collections, notably the great representation of Rodin, of whom she was an early admirer in this country, she has, over the years, since its founding in 1924, been one of its most generous supporters. Not content with having established one of the handsomest museums in America, Mrs. Spreckels was the moving force in creating San Francisco's Maritime Museum, and a third cultural project to which she is currently devoting her boundless energy is a Museum of the Dance, the growing collections of which are temporarily housed in the California Palace of the Legion of Honor. I want here to tender her a grateful salute for what she has done—and continues to do—for the arts in San Francisco.

To sum up, from what we know of the energetic and gifted women just passed in review, it is apparent that the truly dedicated collector and art patron is the victim of a curious but enjoyable virus. Once afflicted with it, she cannot resist collecting. The women whom we have discussed were by no means all equally gifted, nor equally just and/or virtuous. All of them had some training in art if not in actual craft. All were certainly endowed with an ability to judge *performance* in the field of their interests. All were, or are, outstandingly intelligent patrons either intuitively or by training. However, only the Americans in the group here considered felt a deep sense of responsibility beyond their own collections and, in demonstration thereof, have willed or intend to will them to the public.

References

Art Digest. New York, Oct. 1, 1949.

Art Digest. New York, Jan. 15, 1950.

Baltimore Museum News. Baltimore, Oct., 1949.

Baltimore Museum News. Baltimore, Jan., 1950.

Columbia Encyclopedia. New York, 1940.

Conway, William M.—*Literary Remains of Albrecht Dürer*. Cambridge, 1889.

Cox, Trenchard—*A General Guide to the Wallace Collection*. London, 1933.

Dashkov, Princess—*Memoirs Written by Herself, Comprising Letters of the Empress Catherine II*. Edited by Mrs. W. Bradford, London, 1840, 2 vols.

Fizelière, A. de la—"Mme. de Pompadour," in *Gazette des Beaux-Arts*, 1859 (3), pp. 129, 210, 292.

Granberg, Olaf—*La galerie de tableaux de la reine Christine de Suède*. Recherches historiques et critiques. Stockholm, 1897.

Grot, K. Y.—*Lettres de Catherine II à Grimm (1774–1796)*. St. Petersburg, 1878.

Hare, Christopher—*The Most Illustrious Ladies of the Italian Renaissance*. New York, 1911.

Taylor, Francis H.—*The Taste of Angels*. Little, Brown and Company, Boston, 1948.

Waliszewski, K.—*Le Roman d'une Impératrice, Catherine II de Russie*. Paris, 1894.

Who's Who in America, Vol. 32. Chicago, 1962.

Alan Watts

THE WOMAN IN MAN

If I am asked, "What is woman?" I must reply, "I know, but when you ask me, I don't." As soon as we become analytical and definite about things, familiar objects tend to disappear. Under the microscope, human flesh seems to disintegrate into an unfamiliar arabesque of cells. This is why scientific investigation seems so often to be a debunking of popularly held notions, for when we examine things closely and carefully, we realize that the world is a lot less easily categorizable than we might imagine.

Attention has been drawn to the unsoundness of hard and fast distinctions between male and female, masculine and feminine, based upon a bifurcation of the innate and the acquired. In the past the physiologist and biologist were expected to tell us what a woman *really* is; that is to say, how she was made by nature. Then came the anthropologist and the historian, and later the psychologist and psychoanalyst, to tell us how she has been distorted by culture, as if there were some fundamental difference between what man is biologically and physically, and what he becomes through cultural or self-conditioning. This would argue a basic distinction between nature and culture, between natural and artificial, and between the biological and animal on the one hand, and the human on the other. I think that this is a distinction from which our culture is actually suffering, and one to be made only with great care, realizing that it is entirely for purposes of discussion.

We make distinctions between things in order to be able to talk about them. The human body is, after all, a unity; it goes continuously all the way from top to bottom. It has some interesting parts in it, and if I want to talk about those, I describe it in the digital system of language; I have to cut the body into bits. I have to say it has a head, a neck, and shoulders, and speak about these things almost as though they were parts of a machine, which as a matter of fact they are not. This is because we have to cut things up in order to digest them, in the same way that you get a cut-up fryer in the store but you don't get cut-up fryers ready chopped out of eggs.

The differences, then, between what is masculine and what is feminine must be thought of from many points of view. There are things that are typically masculine and typically feminine, using the word "typically" in a very strict and special sense, since things that are typically masculine or typically feminine have no necessary connection with biologically identifiable males and females.

For example, in psychoanalytic symbolism all long things are male and all round things are female. Aggressiveness is typically male; passivity is typically female. But we are only speaking here in a kind of symbolism which is highly useful, so long as we don't confuse it with actual individuals, and what they are supposed to be and how they are supposed to behave. I want then to draw attention to a strong tendency in the Anglo-Saxon subculture of the United States to identify all value with certain stereotypes of the male and to put down and devaluate certain stereotypes of the female. This is quite a different matter from exalting men and debasing women.

I want to talk about things, attitudes, and ways of thinking that are *typically* male or female rather than biologically male or female.

It seems that the human mind, whatever that is—I would prefer perhaps to say the human organism—is equipped with two modes of sensitivity, which I will compare respectively to the spotlight and the floodlight or to something like central and peripheral vision in the eye. According to our system of typical symbols, the spotlight, being a pinpoint sort of thing, will be male, and the floodlight, being diffused, will be female. This is interesting, since our culture puts these two kinds of knowing in a hierarchy of values whereby the spotlight is considered much more important than the floodlight.

To be specific, the spotlight mode of consciousness is what we call conscious attention. It is the kind of attention that we use when we read or when we notice things. For example, a husband can come home from a committee meeting and his wife will say, "Well, what was Mrs. Smith wearing?" And he will say, "I didn't notice," even though she happened to be sitting right opposite him at the conference table. He indeed saw, his eyes registered optically what the dress was, and what its color was, but it was not noticed.

All knowledge upon which science is based, and upon which the careful description, study, and organization of the world is based, depends on noticing, or "spotlight knowledge," and it is characteristic of this that it focuses on certain areas of experience. To the degree that it illuminates those areas brightly and comprehends them, it ignores what lies outside.

Conversely, there is the method of knowing like the floodlight. This is a way of understanding which does not notice but somehow manages to take in a whole variety of things simultaneously. In other words you can drive your car into town without even thinking about it, using that kind of knowledge. You regulate your breathing, the secretions of your glands, the circulation of your blood, and all the homeostatic balances of the organism by this kind of diffused sensitivity. It is a curious thing that there is really no scientific name for this mode of knowing. It has been called the preconscious, the subconscious, the unconscious, the superconscious, but these are all very vague terms, lacking in precision. Yet there is quite definitely underneath the spotlight kind of attention this diffused knowledge, or awareness of all that is going on, without which we should be completely and totally lost.

However, in a culture which underestimates the value of this mode of knowledge, the academic world does almost nothing to develop it. Lynn Whyte pointed out some years ago that the academic world values only three kinds of intelligence: mnemonic intelligence, that is, good memory; computational intelligence, being able to figure; and verbal intelligence, being able to read and write. It does not, he said, develop social intelligence or kinesthetic intelligence.

Social intelligence is something that is exceedingly difficult to teach by any system of verbal instruction; you have to get it by osmosis. But the scientific temper as we have known it undervalues that sort of knowledge, because of its vagueness and uncontrollability. Therefore, we tend instead to value conceptual knowledge, and through that we get a wholly conceptual orientation toward life.

I would like to discuss what seem to me to be four principal symptoms of this one-sided orientation. Firstly, there is a tendency for symbols to be valued more highly than what they represent. For example, money becomes more important than wealth. In other words, the symbol, or notation, for goods becomes more valuable than the goods themselves, and the *reporting* of things that happen becomes more valuable than the events themselves. It is a byword in the academic world today that how you are recorded in the registrar's office is much more important than anything that you did by way of study, because it is your record that counts. If you present yourself in a government office and say, "Here I am," they say you do not exist unless you produce a piece of paper such as a birth certificate to prove that you do exist, and in the same way a lot of people don't feel that they are really alive unless they can read about it in the newspaper.

I believe that is the basis for a great deal of juvenile delinquency. Because you can read all about it, you can be a hero and see that you really do exist, because the record of history has put you down as being really there. So in this sense, we come to what somebody has recently called pseudo-events: the arrangement of meetings, of parties, of all sorts of affairs simply for the purpose of being written about in the newspapers or shown on television.

I am not quite sure this symposium is a pseudo-event at the moment or not, but I want to point out that the style of evaluating things so that what is on the label is more important than what is in the bottle, that the skinny cover of one's automobile is more important than what is under the hood—that whole feeling of the symbol having primacy over what the symbol signifies—is the result of giving an excessive valuation to noticing. In this way it is characteristic of our culture that when you get a menu in a restaurant it is far more interesting to read it than actually to eat what it stands for. This is the difference between our menus and other people's: a French menu just gives the bare name of the dish. But here we go on to say "garnished with crispy toasted slivers of fresh farmhouse potatoes"—a long, long mouth-watering description of something that may well turn up cooked in rancid axle grease.

Secondly, we tend to notice *things* and ignore their contexts or backgrounds. Often with a group I draw a circle on the blackboard and ask, "What have I drawn?" In the vast majority of cases people will say I have drawn a circle or a ball or something like that; very few will ever suggest that I have drawn a wall with a hole in it, because again we tend to notice a small figure enclosed and to ignore the background. While this gives us enormous power of description, it also is a serious disadvantage for human survival in that it makes us blind to the environmental factors of all things and events. We regard what is inside the boundary of one's skin as being much more important than what is outside. This is a familiar problem to architects, because they know that most of their clients think of a house in terms of a person rattling around in a space. But the architect sees the space and the person as an integrated unit and therefore does something more than just provide him with a cubic box to rattle around in; he wants the house related to all that that particular person does within the house, because he sees the house and the person as one activity, a single process.

When human beings do not notice this, and regard the earth that surrounds them, the hills, the forests, the vegetables, the birds, and the waters as a kind of grocery store where you simply expect things to be on the shelves to be exploited and plundered, they become unaware of the solid fact that the earth around them is an integral part of their own body. It is just as much *you* as your hands and your feet, and as soon as you neglect that, you begin to get deteriorated products in the soil, you begin to get problems of water shortage, air pollution, imbalances of insect life, epidemics, and God knows only what. This comes as an exaggeration of this typically masculine way of thinking, which notices the figure and ignores the ground.

The third thing is rather intimately related to that—a conception of the human personality as something *inhabiting* the body, so that each one of us senses himself as a center of consciousness in a bag of skin, confronting an alien world of more or less stupid mechanisms. The primitive science of the nineteenth century has become twentieth-century common sense, and thus it seems generally plausible that value, love, and intelligence exist only within man, within the human organism, and that therefore outside in the world of nature there is an impersonal, mechanical process which has absolutely nothing in common with human values. That estrangement is again a result of noticing only one-half of one's own existence, to notice the half inside the skin and ignore the "better-half" outside.

A fourth way in which this kind of valuation appears in our culture, is that the male tends to become mistrustful of all within him that is feminine, and tends therefore to insist on his masculinity in extremely exaggerated ways and to identify with stereotypes of what it is to be a man, which are quite absurd.

You will notice in current magazines an advertisement sponsored by the United States Marine Corps. It shows enormous phallic rockets standing at Cape Canaveral and a boy in a helmet talking anxiously on the telephone, and the caption says, "What does it take to feel like a man?" Now I don't want to discourage the Marine Corps, but that is not the way to go about it; you won't get real men in the Marine Corps that way. If you want to get real men to join the Marine Corps, there is a very, very simple formula—I leave it to your imagination. But phallic rockets are going to attract the man who is afraid that he is not a male and therefore compensates by identifying himself with exaggerated male stereotypes. As a result of this we get the general feeling that there is something weak about feminine characteristics and the fear that it would be "sissy" for a man to incorporate within his personality elements of grace and charm. To be uncharming, to be gruff, grubby, and tough has been considered the quintessence of maleness.

I was recently reading an anecdote about that great pirate and admiral, Sir Francis Drake, entertaining a Spanish nobleman for dinner aboard his ship. He had actually captured the Spanish nobleman and was negotiating for a fat ransom, but he did it in a gentlemanly way. Here was this tough old sea captain entertaining at dinner, dressed in lavish silks, with gold plate on the table and a trio with violins and flutes. As a parting gift Sir Francis presented the Spaniard with several bottles of fine perfume. Imagine being entertained in such style aboard a United States aircraft carrier.

The person who has no reason to doubt his masculine potency can really afford feminine graciousness, but in this culture he may be thought homosexual or sissy because he does so. But this exaggerated worship of the male gives itself away.

These are four symptoms which show, in various ways, how something that we might call feminine in the typical sense is neglected, undeveloped, unused.

Let me repeat them: Firstly, the symbol has more value than the thing, and Logos more value than Eros.

Secondly, the seed is valued more than the soil and the word more valued than the context.

Thirdly, the individual is more valued than the individual's own extended body, which is his whole natural environment.

Fourthly, a special form of the symbol being more important than the fact, the symbols of maleness are confused with genuine maleness.

It is an ancient tradition that man is completed only by developing the feminine within himself. This underlies such forms of oriental self-development—Tantra in India and Taoism in China. Lao-Tse, great philosopher of Taoism, in his classic, the *Tao Te Ching,* the book of the way and its power, says, "While being a male one should cleave to the female, and in so doing one will become a universal channel and be possessed of a power which one will never call upon in vain." Taoism is the whole art of completing the masculine by the feminine. He says elsewhere, "Man at his birth is supple and tender, but in death he is rigid and hard. Therefore suppleness and tenderness are the marks of life, but rigidity and hardness are the marks of death." This is illustrated by the parable of the willow and the pine. Under the weight of snow the springy branches of the willow give way and the snow falls off them, but the pine stands there with tough strong branches, and as the weight of the snow increases they finally crack. Every engineer knows, in building a bridge, that it must sway in the wind and be flexible; a rigid bridge is a collapsed bridge. This is equally true of psychological and cultural rigidity, and thus symbolic overmaleness is profoundly weak and unsound.

It is not, then, without reason that in old theological writings the soul is always "she," the anima, the *ewig Weiblichkeit,* the muse, the feminine source of inspiration. You don't hear much about that today because souls are out of fashion. We think of the soul as some kind of anthropoid or maybe gynecoid spook, whereas the soul is precisely what I called our generalized sensitivity, our floodlight awareness, as distinct from our spotlight awareness. It is our innate, natural intelligence, complexly structured like our bodies, which are at root a form of thinking, of unbelievably subtle intelligence. The academic fallacy is that what cannot be described in words is neither intelligent nor intelligible. Yet the neurologist is unable to figure out the complexity of the very brain with which he thinks, and such a man tends to become humble through realizing that he is more intelligent than he knows! He is more intelligent than he can explain himself as being, in flat contradiction to the erstwhile scientific fashion of considering rational intelligence more intelligent than subconscious intelligence.

To value and use this hidden feminine aspect is peculiarly important in the problem of bringing about constructive change in human behavior. If history has one monotonous lesson, it is this: that human behavior has never been changed by preaching. Violence, whether physical or moral, does not truly move the human being. Even so great an apostle of nonviolence as Gandhi was still a violent man, because his appeal was a serious and earnest call to duty. Why is it that nobody has yet tried to change human behavior by the force of enchantment? Would you, as a woman, get very far by saying to some man, "It is your duty to raise children and bring up a family; you *must* love me! Come on now, get to work!"

You go about it in an entirely different way, on the principle that you catch flies with honey. In the same way, educators, ministers, legislators, or whoever is interested in changing human conduct must realize that they need to go to charm school and to be like the musician Orpheus, who was supposed to tame the wild beasts and calm the winds by playing on his lyre. He is the archetyped symbol of the man who developed his feminine aspect and became a universal enchanter, commanding the obedience of the world because it just loved to follow. That is the secret power of the feminine. I don't think I am "giving the show away" about the secret of feminine power. Nor am I trying to advocate a greater respect for, and use of, this power by warnings of doom—that we are going to be annihilated by atomic bombs, overpopulation, and ecologic imbalances if we don't pay attention to this principle. The point is rather that it is a way of living which is a delight, not a duty. For it will never be worth surviving if we *must* survive, but only if continuing to live is an expression of joy.

WHAT IS A WOMAN?

> *This is an actual transcription of the formal but spon-
> taneous panel discussion of the papers immediately pre-
> ceding. Only minor editing has been done where con-
> tinuity and clarity required it. The editors feel that the
> spontaneity of the actual discussion gives a particular
> value to the panel in this form, since it amplifies ques-
> tions arising from the formal presentations of the par-
> ticipants as well as answering questions from the audi-
> ence.*

Moderator: Karl H. Pribram
*Panel Members: Thomas Carr Howe, John
Money, Alan Watts*

Dr. Pribram   I think that we are left with an issue, and it is an
old one. The subhuman primate, at least, is considerably determined
genetically, as far as the difference between male and female is concerned. But perhaps in man this determination is not as rigid; as a
multiple determination, we have a more complex organism to start with.
If I may use an analogy, this complexity is somewhat like that of a
general-purpose computer, as opposed to a special-purpose computer.
Special-purpose computers can do only certain specific jobs, but the
general-purpose computer can be programmed to do any of these, or
perhaps even something quite separate.

The question raised by Mr. Watts really is: do we have to come
through life to become this general-purpose machine in quite the difficult way that he and many of us have experienced, and come out to

be finally a more unified whole, or can something be done from the beginning to allow us to be general-purpose computers to start with?

Mr. Watts   I would say it is something like this: I don't think it is a matter quite of the order in which it happens; that is to say that we have to become specialized computers first and then later generalized computers. I feel rather it is a question of educating the human being parallel on both levels, just as he has to learn to walk on two legs, so he proceeds with his analytic way of thinking, simultaneously with his nonanalytic, for which there really is no scientific word.

Dr. Money   The evidence in any studies with the hermaphroditic children shows that we are pretty generalized computers to begin with, and then become specialized, since it is possible to do such amazing things just on the basis of sex assignment, and what is thereby entailed. So one has to look to other aspects of being human to find out why in a particular culture some emphasis on behavior is being masculine versus other behavior being feminine, whereas in another culture, it may all be reversed.

Dr. Pribram   The women Mr. Howe mentioned all, in a way, had men to spotlight the issue for them; the painters who did the actual spotlighting in each case were the men. The women gathered this, husbanded it, and nurtured it. Was this the meaning?

Mr. Howe   I think we have countless instances of that, particularly in the field of fine arts, and it seems to be that the man is inclined in most instances to go along because he seems to feel that his wife or some woman who has influence on him has a distinctive feeling of the rightness of these things. Of course, everyone knows how important it is for a politician to have an attractive and pretty wife; that is equally true when it comes to a man like some of the Renaissance figures. They left the gentle handling of situations to their wives; this was particularly revealed during the Renaissance and again notably in the eighteenth century. It seems to me that Renaissance women were particularly gifted in what Mr. Watts said about how a woman gets hold of the man she especially wants without the blunt approach of suggesting paternity and all that but, in contrast, through gentle suggestion.

Dr. Pribram   I still see an issue here. This was all very nice and polite but I do think that Dr. Money in essence is telling us we do have a general-purpose computer here and that we can program him or her in whatever way we want to, given the cultural norm.

Mr. Watts is telling us to program two ways at once. If we do that to a computer, it might give some trouble.

Mr. Watts But the human being is not as simple as a computer. Here is the difficulty: suppose we are at that point of development in genetics where we know how to breed any kind of human being we want by a combination of genetic means and educating means. Rene Dubos pointed out recently that this is all very well: you may know how to breed any type of human being that you want, but what you never know is what type of human being you're going to need according to changing circumstances. So it seems to me that every situation has to have in it a double element which in a way corresponds to these two ways of thinking. We have to allow enough whimsicality and randomness into our order for it to produce a novelty.

Mr. Howe I wondered if what Dr. Money discussed could result in some magnificent and wonderful genius-type person being produced at will instead of being regarded as a great rarity that comes along in a very great while?

Dr. Money This really raises a particular question in my mind as applied to the field of art: why has it been so conspicuous that women have been the great collectors of art rather than the great creators of it, with relatively few exceptions?

Mr. Howe Don't you think it is possible that the opportunities for independent development of a great talent did not prevail to the extent that they have in the last hundred years?

Dr. Money I think that is part of the reason, but I am puzzled about this on the whole. I am not quite sure that what I shall dare to call Mr. Watts's method of enchantment is either an exclusively female prerogative or a particularly basic one. We might further discuss how much this is an American and Western phenomenon in our women here rather than in other parts of the world.

Mr. Watts That is a very big subject. There is an enormous amount of literature developed in India and China, and also in Japan, on how to be charming, and it is very interesting reading. It is studied also by males.

Mr. Howe Hasn't charm been regarded for a long time as the commodity about which "It doesn't matter whether you know what charm is, because you either have it or you have not"?

Mr. Watts That is the puzzle we're up against. You say of certain children that they seem to have innate intelligence and are educable, but some don't have the marbles. So, naturally, every scientist and psychologist is immediately interested in trying to control the situation. Is there any way we can make things happen?

What we want from human beings in so many cases is spontaneous behavior. We want you to be naturally intelligent; we don't like it so very much when your intelligence is so artificial that it creaks. In the same way we want a person's kindness and love to be somehow natural; therefore we are in a bind when we have to say to each other, "You must be natural!" How can we force you to be natural? But what we must think of is the fact that we don't know enough but at least know a great deal about how people work and are faced with this problem.

Dr. Money I would like to connect this up with the idea of territory defense rights. I am interested to see this behavior in some form or another in human beings, although I don't pretend to understand where it comes from, and I am not at all sure that it is simply a matter of cultural learning. Certainly in some of the other mammalian species that show territorial defense rights, it does not seem to be a matter of learning. Therefore I have to raise the question of whether there is an extremely basic difference between males and females of the human species, or at least some of them in this respect. This leads to the question about the whole issue of belligerent aggressiveness and the matter of taking leadership, particularly leadership of the masses, because there may be very basic differences here between behavior of the aggressive, domineering leader and the slow, insidious enchanter.

Mr. Howe Certainly we have all encountered people who are deceptively gentle and almost tentative in their approach to so many problems and subjects, a kind of—I am sure it is false—helplessness and modesty. But then you find you are doing all the work that they wanted you to do to start with.

Women seem to possess this quality, in my experience, but I have known quite a number of men who are pretty slick at it, too.

Dr. Pribram An anthropologist once said to me that culture is a caricature of biological differences. It could be that there is a direction indicated from the primate studies to those of Dr. Money's, and the direction is one of a more general-purpose instrument, the human body and its environment. But could it be that his particular experiments show within a limiting situation that there is still something to the idea that our culture, which does enhance the masculine and the feminine, much as brought out by Mr. Watts, is still a core problem, which is biologically given? And if so, we cannot take a woman or a girl child and make a man of her, a real man in the sense of all that is best about being a man, without an extremely long period of agony. This would be true, even in the normal: that to achieve this general-purpose machine that we have been talking about is almost impossible.

Dr. Money I think that is a good point to make, because it is certainly an extremely laborious process with these individuals I have spoken of. It is laborious not only in terms of surgery, or hormonal medication, and the only time that I have known it not to be laborious is in those still completely unfathomed cases of extremely severe transvestism or perhaps homosexuality, where you have a naturally appearing disease which is a partial reversal of the gender role in psychosexual identity. But even these cases show up the point Dr. Pribram makes, that it is an extremely laborious thing.

In a somewhat more facetious vein, does Mr. Watts think that one gets the best marines by having their kinds of advertisements enticing the ones that are not quite sure?

Mr. Watts I don't have access to the statistics. What I feel is, though, this discussion has an implicit direction to it; why are we discussing, for example, what is a woman? Because surely the point of discussing this question in a scientific environment is to be able to have control of the situation and mold it nearer to the heart's desire.

What I am suggesting is that the more we control it, the nearer we approach a point of diminishing returns; the more we can control it, the closer we are to some point at which it is less and less worth controlling. Therefore all signs and control mechanisms have to be leveled with sort of intervals for nonsense and randomness.

Dr. Pribram In that same vein is the statement that a woman is made beautiful only to the eyes of the beholder, which leads me to Mr. Watts's statement about charm and enchantment. In order to have charm and enchantment, one has to have a culture in which this particular behavior is charming. As he said, the skin is a sack, but we don't recognize it as such.

From the Floor Some very devilish and evil ends have been brought about by charm; where would you limit this secret weapon? Where does it become razzle-dazzle?

Mr. Watts You know, it used to be said in the early days of the history of the Christian Church in Europe that the devil had all the good tunes; in other words, all the favorite carols we sing and all the favorite hymns were originally bawdy folk songs. What the church did was to borrow them with immense success.

The same thing applies here, of course: charm or any other power can be used for any sort of moral purpose, and the point of it is for people of good will to use it instead of being so boring.

Mr. Howe That recalls the other old saying: we are not always certain that we do want to go (if we *are* going some place hereafter), because nearly all the entertaining and delightful companions of this life are most certainly destined to go to hell and wouldn't we be awfully lonesome somewhere else.

Mr. Watts The beautiful flower may be poisonous—or the most exciting mushrooms are probably quite deadly; some of the most exotic looking mushrooms are quite edible, but there is a kind of sense that the monster attracts its prey by being charming, just as much as the creative act is led up to.

From the Floor I think it has probably been lack of opportunity; look what Catherine the Great did when she had the opportunity.

Mr. Howe The position of women to date seems to have been namely that of nursing rather than creativity. Is this lack of opportunity, drive, or what?

Dr. Pribram My answer to that is yes, look at it. So far the members of the panel have not convinced me that men and women are the same.

Mr. Watts I think we are confused as to the difference between male and female ideas, or stereotypes, and specific male and female human organisms.

After all, to encourage women and not put them down, not repress them, isn't necessarily advancing femininity at all. It is merely saying,

"Hooray, women are, after all, so very little different from men that they ought to be given equal rights." That is a terrible thing, because I think we should enjoy the difference between men and women, and make it as different as possible.

I have been asked, "If man should incorporate in himself some of his feminine characteristics, should woman in turn try to cultivate the spotlight along with the floodlight?" It seems to me that obviously we can be different on the basis of still having something in common. There is a disadvantage in the exaggerated male stereotype, which you see so often in a gathering such as a dinner party, where the husbands and the wives come together and before you know it, the wives are at one end of the room discussing children and the men are at the other end of the room discussing business. Nobody seems to like each other very much, because the cultivation of these stereotypes gives them less and less in common with each other to talk about and to play with.

From the Floor Many create because they cannot procreate. All masculine creations are artificial syntheses, a substitution for creation of a human being. A woman has a synthetizing influence on that which is coming to exist, and her subconscious is different and more complex.

Dr. Money This states the issue rather than asks the question.

I presume that in a general sort of way there is a relationship between the creativity of man and the creativity of reproduction in the female. But one has to look quite widely in these matters of multiple determinism. Woman, under noncivilized circumstances, has usually been obliged to have a large family and quite literally had no time or energy left for being creative in other ways, so that she has for a longer time in the history of civilization been caught in that circumstance that I presume primitive men were so often caught in, namely, that there wasn't time to be creative, that the sheer exhausting business of keeping alive and protected was enough in itself.

I have often speculated myself on how it may have happened that women who could theoretically manage to get along quite well without men, except for brief mating contacts, managed to let themselves get maneuvered into the position in which patriarchy dominated over matriarchy—but that also is another question, isn't it?

Mr. Howe In this context, I have been asked, "Haven't you proved that art collecting is a specialized form of housekeeping?"

I think this is what you might call the apotheosis and rather a splendid kind of housekeeping. I might add, that keeping a museum in order is very definitely a specialized kind of housekeeping, too, whether it is done by a man or a woman. I was asked why I had not mentioned Peggy Guggenheim as one of the patronesses of the arts. This was purely a matter of the arbitrary manner in which one has to select examples.

Dr. Pribram I would like to make one more comment on the spotlight versus the floodlight. It is perfectly well to say that the flood-light way, which is woman's way, would charm and so can lead the world. This would be discounting the spotlight activity which, of course, is closely attendant; it is only that spotlight activity is the major activity of the world these days and in that sense perhaps oversteps its bounds. The important thing that I want to know is whether it is possible to have spotlight and spotlight activity at the same time that the flood-light is on? By spotlight activity in its various forms, I mean looking deep, the creative acts, often a very painful and unhappy state of af-fairs. To turn on the floodlight might destroy that very creative act. These things can alternate, but I wonder if they can coexist quite in the simple way that Mr. Watts has wanted us to train our new human beings for?

Mr. Howe Dr. Money spoke about the incidence of mortality in males versus the mortality of females. Are there any statistics that might indicate how, in general, the division between the woman who wants to be passive balances out against the woman who seeks to be the reverse? It seems to me that it might be misleading to judge by what we encounter in our reading, our daily news. The woman, let us say, who does not elect to be a passive, housekeeping type is likely to attract much more attention, and the spotlight of publicity and notoriety is focused on her, where there may be to her one type thousands who are perfectly content not to put themselves forward.

Dr. Pribram This may be so, but so far the insurance companies have not bought it. A teenage boy still has to pay more for driving a car, for whatever the reason, and again I am reminded of the fact that a culture may be a caricature. When one watches his own children grow up, these differences begin so early, and as Dr. Money has pointed out, they begin because of our attitudes toward the child, but perhaps this is only in part. There must be some soil on which this is falling, because otherwise the caricature just couldn't flower in this rather ribald fashion.

Mr. Watts Going back to the question of whether the two kinds of intelligence can coexist, I think contrapuntal music one of the most striking examples of their coexistence. When you have one line of dominant theme and it changes its place on the staff, you listen to all the others going along with it at the same time. If you play an instrument like the organ, each limb is doing something different, and perhaps in a different rhythm. That is to me an example of the fusion of the two types of intelligence.

From the Floor It has been suggested that abstract creative intelligence may relate to a sex-linked, recessive gene similar to color blindless, hemophilia, etc.

Dr. Money I don't know of any clear and authoritative studies of this kind of relationship, and I think it remains only a suggestion for one very good reason. That is that nobody really knows how to test for, or measure, creative intelligence; perhaps even to describe it leaves it still in an unsatisfactory state. However, color blindness is clearly related to the chromosome, and I have another piece of recent information from the girls I have been studying in my clinic who have a missing chromosome. These are girls who have a 45 chromosome count and have one X chromosome missing, so they are 45 X 0. They have a congenital condition which is known by the name of Turner syndrome. I tested a large number of these patients (forty is a large number for this kind of rarity) and found that on an ordinary Wechsler intelligence scale, they have a very strong tendency, in some cases extremely exaggerated, to have a low score for their nonverbal intelligence but a much better score for their verbal intelligence. When one does a more detailed analysis of their score pattern, it becomes possible to put forward the idea that they have a disability for which, I think, the best name is "space-form blindness." They are relatively mechanically inept and unable to handle things that require the logical relationship of spaces and shapes together, as compared to their ability in solving the relationship between words. This is an interesting sort of thing to find, because it is one of the very few things in mental function that can be related to the genetic pattern. I am not able, however, to give anything too definite about creative intelligence.

From the Floor Isn't it impossible to be creative without having a general floodlight or intuitive background of knowledge available at some level of awareness? Doesn't creativeness require a strong grasp on the reality, i.e., spotlight, while obtaining energy or drive from the general or floodlight areas of awareness?

Mr. Watts All these things always go together, because in a certain way you can't be creative at all unless you have both working. We can go backward and say however creative the male may be, he can't produce without women, and in the same way, looking at it in the sort of reverse sense, however creative one's unconscious may be, it cannot have effective results without the specific disciplines of notation and the study of particular ways of manifesting it, such as language, musical notation, or mathematical notation. The point is that technical dexterity without the other aspect is like being able to talk awfully well but having nothing to say. One may be a master of counterpoint and yet have absolutely no inspiration whatsoever. So these things always go together; they are like flesh and bones.

Dr. Pribram Would you say that maybe the difficulty in current society that you pointed out, with the overemphasis on the notational, might not be rather that there is a confusion between the notational and the other which we have no direct word for; that once each one is made clear, each has its strength, and each is in appropriate relation between the two, then there is no overemphasis, because almost the same point could be made that the existential, the intuitive, is also overemphasized, and only when the distinction becomes clear can one deemphasize, or can the whole thing become clear?

Mr. Watts That is what we're doing at one and the same time, emphasizing the differences, whether they be male or female, structural or gooey, whatever they may be; by emphasizing the difference you get them working together. All philosophical debates fundamentally come down to those who take the side of structure and those who take the side of goo, that is the very basis of human differences of opinion. Often you will see men and women having a discussion together, and the man wants to say, "Look here now, it is really quite definite, this is the way it is, it is simply this." The woman says, "Oh no, just a minute, it is much more complicated than you think, but I am not as articulate as you are and I can't describe it."

Mr. Howe I have been asked, are there more or less male art patrons than female?

In answer, I would think there is a remarkable balance, at least as we have encountered it in this country. It is true, according to actuarial statistics, that women seem to outlive men and perhaps a little later on in life they may start collecting art; they haven't got anything else to do; at least we find a good deal of that. However, as far as the local scene is concerned (and I find this a very interesting commentary on what is happening in the contemporary art world here), periodically we put on exhibitions which include pictures that mostly are for sale. They are bought to a surprising degree by young professional people who frankly can ill afford them. They are chosen not because they will become more valuable—as so many of our worthy collectors always seem to hope—but principally because they would rather have an original work of art as it is than Mr. Van Gogh's invariable "Sunflowers" in reproduction. We know firsthand of many people, not only young, but people of middle age, who are buying pictures and other art works on the installment plan; they are not rich in the sense of a Mellon, a Frick, or some great nationally known collector.

From the Floor Isn't it socially acceptable to have babies, socially inacceptable to create anything new? For example, an idea or a machine, or both?

Mr. Watts It is socially unacceptable to create something new when it oversteps certain bounds of novelty. When you create something new, such as a new word or style of talking, you are in danger the moment you are not able to explain that you are doing today in terms of what you did yesterday. For example, the new meaning of "dig" that has come into use in American life during the past ten years is now generally used. Soon the lexicographer will be able to look up the word "dig" and be able to explain in respectable words what it means—a special kind of appreciation—and thus keep us in touch with the novelty. But sometimes the artist or the creative thinker goes way out and can't explain in old terms what he means by a new thing. This has been the problem with modern poetry and a great deal of abstract painting. He is in difficulty, but he is in less difficulty if people would be willing to soak it up rather than require it explained to them.

How do you learn to dance? There are two ways: there is the way of having a diagram of the steps drawn for you, and the other way, in which you kind of watch the feel of the music for a while and seem to get it. Now you are always going to have difficulty in absorbing the new if you have not got this latter capacity.

From the Floor   Would understanding woman necessarily lead to control?

Mr. Watts   Why not to smoother relationships? It is interesting that this meeting was originally going to be called "The Control of Woman" in pattern with the other ones on "The Control of the Mind." I understand from Dr. Farber that as a result of great protest it was called "The Potential of Woman." It seems to me that smoother relationships is another way of talking about control. In other words, when an artist makes a control line, he says something smooth about it in a certain sense, that it isn't shaky and undisciplined; smoother relationship is a greater control.

Dr. Pribram   In other words, there is considerable misunderstanding of the word "control." There is another question very similar to this.

The members of the panel and other speakers today have all touched upon, and then backed away from, as though touching a flame, the subject of why women are not creative. Can you discuss it, or is it a question which cannot be answered?

Mr. Howe   Can we make some reference to the possible influence that economic conditions under which women live, or have lived, have had something to do with that?

Dr. Pribram   Before we go on to that, I would say let us be sure we define the word "creative," and as I understand it, women obviously create children. As I understand the question, it is the spotlight kind of creativity that is referred to here.

Mr. Watts   Creation such as you notice.

Dr. Pribram   Such as you notice: spotlight effects creativity. Why are women less creative in that sense than men up to now?

Dr. Money   I think, in the first place, one has to allow that women are creative. In my mind, anyway, the real question is, why are there not so many names of women in the ranks of the Hall of Fame of greatness in creativity. In my own mind, the best answer is that historical precedent and causative factors have been against allowing women the kind of circumstances under which they might become creative. It is as if history is conspiring with biology in this respect. Why, since it is known that in the early Mediterranean civilization there were matrilocal and matriarchal societies, did women lose their preeminence in the control of men? They could have taught the men to be baby-sitters, couldn't they?

Mr. Howe That has continued to a certain degree to this day and age.

Dr. Money It is making a renaissance.

But if this particular course of history resulted in the subjugation of women because of less free time, one can understand that historically men were the ones who became the organizers of religion. In the history of our culture, the emergence of artistic, musical, scientific, and mathematical creativity seems to have been very closely related with the emergence and development of a priestly class in religion.

However, let me leave the historical approach and mention something that I came across in a manuscript that was sent to me a few months ago. Here the speculation was made that little girls get their gender role by identification with the mother with whom they are in close contact day by day, whereas little boys also in the position of being in close contact with the mother as the model figure with whom to identify have to reject her feminine behavior and her identification and work in a sort of abstract principle on what they remember father was like last night or last Saturday, since he is not always about. The speculation consequent to this observation was that herein lies the basis for the greater abstract thinking capacity of men and their greater creativity.

From the Floor What is the reason for the distractibility in the objective love of men, and what is its influence on the marital life?

Dr. Money I don't know what the reason for it is. I mentioned it in my paper, because I considered that it is a fairly basic thing, especially as one sees it quite widespread in the mammalian species. I have a hint, without enough experimental evidence to substantiate it yet, that it is closely related to the hormonal functioning, to the androgen level, and it may also, perhaps, be related to the influence of androgens on the developing embryo, but that is all very speculative. But what is the influence on the marital life?

I think in brief one can say that the influence on marital life depends upon the particular pair of people involved. These range all the way from those who are mightily distressed if there is any deviation at all from total fidelity, to the opposite extreme, the pair who more or less willingly, as I learned from the editor of a lonely-hearts column a couple of years ago, decide to join the merry-go-round of a marriage club in suburbia, so that they can have their cake and eat it, too.

Mr. Watts I would like to make a final observation about this problem of creativity. It is true that people have called attention several times to the fact that the names of women in the Hall of Fame—painters, philosophers, mathematicians, and scientists—are much fewer than names of men, and this has been attributed very largely to the kind of economic disadvantage. While this is true, there is another way it might be looked at. There are circumstances under which the spotlight consciousness can be opened up; these are moments that are sometimes called "mystical vision." I would like to call it ecological awareness, because that is more respectable. At such moments, one becomes aware of something ordinarily neglected. That is that the world in which one is living is of the passing and magical beauty, so that in a way there is less necessity for works of art, and thus you see the production of a baby or a pair of blue eyes or of hair as a divine activity. It happens all the time; everybody does it, and therefore it is undervalued. But in our fascination with the problems of conscious attention, we neglect the value of the incredible perfection of our organism, the environment, and things that are going on all the time, and we become blind to them. Perhaps the part of the role of woman is to say, "Is it really so important that you create something of sufficient novelty to call attention to yourself? Are you not maybe neglecting the riches that surround you every day?

Dr. Pribram "Happiness is a warm puppy."

From the Floor Could creativity be linked to an act of aggressive expression? In this case, the feminine lack of aggression might explain the lack of major creativity?

Dr. Money That is a question for a lot of semantic unraveling as to how much aggressiveness and assault and belligerence are all the same thing. It perhaps would be much safer to say that creativity can be linked to an act of energy expenditure and that aggressiveness, fighting, assault, and cruelty also can be defined as acts of energy expenditure. In that case it certainly does appear to be true that for many of the people who have been successfully creative there is a tremendous burning up of energy and complete absorption, consciously and intellectually, with the act of what they are involved in, so that much else is completely blotted out while they are in the turmoils of the moment of creation, waiting for the puzzle to solve itself.

Dr. Pribram   War and birth are influences in the lives of men and women and the diversification of roles. The biological has a function here, and the social or cultural aspect we see is a caricature of the biological foundation. Man is at war and able to fight with weapons; woman is less able to do so and has played a role. This becomes a caricature then in succeeding generations. I think these things have been mentioned but not specifically pointed out, and it is worth doing.

Do any of you have anything to add? We have not solved many problems here.

Mr. Watts   I don't think, you know, that the purpose of these meetings is to solve problems—it is more to have fun discussing.

Dr. Pribram   One astute thing Mr. Watts said was that by pointing out differences we can then bring them together and make our unified whole. I think this goes on in every individual also, and the maleness and femaleness of each individual needs to be pointed out. Let us hope this discussion has not lessened the difference, because that would never do.

So I come to our final question, and I turn to each of the panelists to answer it.

"What is a woman?"

Mr. Howe   I think she is a man's wife.

Dr. Money   Shall I follow that by saying she is also a man's mother.

Mr. Watts   And she is also a man's mistress.

PART THREE

THE ROLES OF WOMEN

Chairman: Mrs. Edward H. Heller

The intracultural aspect was the first topic of discussion, particularly emphasizing the parallels between primitive societies and Western civilization today. A more searching look at Western civilization followed, with particular stress on the problems of creative women. The final paper of this session was a more philosophic approach in which the existentialist view of a person was contrasted with the two preceding approaches. In the panel, the speakers correlated their points of view with the philosophic concept of the person.

Ethel M. Albert

THE ROLES OF WOMEN:
QUESTION OF VALUES

Objectivity is one of the first requirements of scientific study. But who is qualified to make an objective investigation of women? Merely being a woman is not in itself a promising qualification. First, nobody seems quite sure what a woman really is. Second, any favorable statement about women by a woman is suspect as either wishful thinking or blind loyalty to her sex. But any negative statement about women by a woman is suspect as cattiness or sick self-hatred. On the other hand, merely being a man, that is, not being a woman, is hardly a more likely qualification. If a man speaks well of women, he is suspect as uxorious. But if he speaks out against them, he is neurotic or worse. Not being female, moreover, men are necessarily excluded from direct access to some of the primary data. Yet, every investigator is either a man or a woman, whatever these terms designate.

Objectivity in the study of women will then be, at best, difficult to achieve. In this, however, the study of women is not essentially different from any study of human beings by human beings. The dilemma is the same: How can we be objective about our own kind? How can we really understand those from whom we are very different? The resolution is in the selection of a suitable frame of reference and suitable objectives and methods of inquiry. The necessary degree of objectivity can be achieved by attending to the object studied. Making explicit the assumptions of inquiry is prerequisite to clarity, and cross verification by different investigators neutralizes the distorting effects of the personal equation. Sufficient progress in the study of humanity has now been made to justify optimism as to the possibility of objective studies of women. Despite the expression of misgivings and doubts by some, women are human, and the study of women is part of the study of human behavior and human nature. The same techniques can be and are being used. Qualified observers *may* be either male or female; they *must* be well trained in the methods and theory of their specialization.

Approaching the study of women through the social-behavioral sciences is, of course, only one of many ways of dealing with the topic. In no small part, objectivity requires keeping a safe distance from such other approaches as those of the poet lamenting the perfidy of a lost love; of politicians seeking the women's vote; of legislators debating the issue of equal pay for equal work; of a particular woman coming to terms with the problems generated by the particular society she lives in; to say nothing of the husband and wife discussing—if that is the correct word—the relative merits of a trip to Europe or a quiet spell at a hunting lodge for this year's vacation. There is no necessary incompatibility among the different ways of dealing with the character, nature, and roles of women. Each is surely legitimate, but all are different in goal and method. We are far from clarity about the possible interrelations of the esthetic, practical, legal, political, personal, and scientific approaches to this or to any other human subject. Here, the concern is entirely with the social-behavioral-science study of women and with the data and theory of anthropology in particular, as they affect the scientific quest for reliable information and theory about human behavior, including woman's behavior.

Instead of attempting to relate the different ways of approaching the question of woman's nature, let us attempt to relate the investigation of woman as such to other inquiries that have started from some biological characteristic as the basis for the description and prediction of behavior. Perhaps "pseudobiological" is the better term in the present context. For, biology as science is very different from traditional notions associated with simplistic theories of biological determinism. Specifically, we are confronted by an ancient and honorable but naïve and unscientific way of classifying human beings according to easily visible differences and with a causal theory that such visible differences as those of gender, or skin color, or height of forehead, or other physical traits are a reliable index to intelligence, artistic ability, mechanical aptitude, emotional stability, leadership skills, and other critical characteristics of persons.

Some categories are less useful than others for scientific purposes, when we mean by scientific purposes adequate description and prediction, and when the utility of a category is defined as follows: the characteristic chosen to define the category is a good predictive index of other shared characteristics. We can be quite sure that red hair is not a reliable index to ill temper; that fatness does not predict jollity; that skin color, while it is a useful index to probable color of eyes and hair, proportion of limbs to body, and the like, has no predictive value for intelligence, skills, or any other personal or behavioral characteristics. A study of woman, conducted on the assumption that gender predicts significantly no non-sex-linked phenomena is almost certain to be a scientific failure. What do we know about a human being, when we know the gender? We can assert with confidence that if any person is a mother, that person is surely a woman, or, at least, is surely female. The same certainty attaches to statements about individuals designated as wife, sister, daughter, aunt, mother-in-law, daughter-in-law. They are bound to be female—though a few seem to have arrived at this enviable status via Copenhagen and the surgeon's knife. But we cannot judge whether any of them are intelligent or stupid, mentally well or ill, tenderhearted or tough as nails, industrious or lazy, attractive or ugly, happy or wretched. And if we do not know these things, we do not know much of value. With femaleness, as with skin color or height of forehead or other external signs, we cannot learn about persons from appearances.

Let me hasten to offer this reassurance. I am not at all asserting, as did overzealous egalitarians of a generation ago, that there is no difference between male and female. This is rather to overstate the case. I am unconditionally on the side of those who say, *"Vive la différence."* That males and females are different from each other at least physiologically is one of the few relatively clear and simple facts of life. But the male-female difference is *a* difference, not *the* difference. What remains problematic is this: for any physical-biological difference, what difference does the difference make? This is the crucial question for interpreting the behavioral significance of any physiological characteristic singled out for special study. And it is here that the simplistic pseudobiological categories fail.

The rejection of broad, obvious categories like race or sex or body type is perfectly compatible with the view that physiological factors are indispensable elements in the description and prediction of human nature and behavior. Long-standing arguments about biological determinism as opposed to some sort of antibiological or nonphysical determinism only get in the way of clarity. All human behavior is biological; but it is never only that. Mankind is a sociocultural being. Biological variations and sociocultural variations, not simplified stereotypes, are the object of serious, scientific inquiry. What any individual becomes depends in part on nature and in part on sociocultural values and ideal role-models, as these are worked out in the specific circumstances of each individual life history. For the study of sex differences, we may say that nature—biology, if you will—makes us male or female; the values and norms of the society in which we develop make us men or women; and the interrelations of these factors with the other biological, sociological, and situational components of experience make us the kinds of persons we become. No single factor explains the complex totality of any individual personality or of the human species.

A sampling of anthropological data will help us to judge what behavioral difference the biological male-female difference makes. The relevant data are scattered throughout the voluminous monographic literature of anthropology, for the description of any society must include a description of its women as well as its men. A systematic assembling of data and some illuminating interpretations may be found in Margaret Mead's study, *Male and Female* (1949). Even a very small selection of the ideas and ideals of the feminine found in other societies than our own is illuminating, and so too is an examination, however cursory, of the curious interrelations of cultural ideals with situational and behavioral realities. Such data are useful for developing theory, but they may also suggest the kinds of information to look for when we face the hard task of studying the place of woman in our own culture.

No human society overlooks so patent a biological contrast as that between male and female. But we find cross-cultural differences of great magnitude in what various societies think is female nature, as distinct from male nature; in what different societies construct as the ideal woman and the ideal man; and, if that were not diversity enough, we find that everywhere actual behavior is permitted to diverge to a greater or lesser degree from society's ideals and role-models.

First things first. Let us start with this question: is the male or the female by nature the more sexually aggressive? As every nice girl in Western culture knows, it is the male who is the aggressor, while the passive female submits with good or bad grace. But if we ask this question of Africans or of American Indians, we do not get the same reply. Obviously, they tell us, women are more driven by sex than men. Among the Zuni Indians as among ourselves, there are stories of fearful newlyweds facing up to the terrors of the first night of marriage. But the Zuni stories feature the groom, not the bride, in a state of fear. I suspect that not a few males from other societies, possibly even our own, understand the Zuni groom's sentiments very well, but unlike the Zuni, they have been brought up to believe that the male is the fearless aggressor and that any display or feeling of fear is unmasculine. Now, I do not know which version is "biologically" true. Perhaps social expectations work on nature's endowment, which is probably variable to begin with, so that some grow up hot, some grow up cold, and those fare best whose biology is in harmony with the prevailing sociocultural notion about what is natural.

Next question: which of the sexes is by nature better fitted for heavy manual labor? In the madonna-and-child value system of middle- and upper-class European and American culture, it is plain that women are the more delicate, the weaker sex. Heavy work is for men, in fact, for he-men, who are more muscular, stronger, and generally coarser. But if we change the social stratum or continent or historical era, the pale, delicate, weaker sex disappears from view. In the not so remote American past, pioneer women were and had to be strong, quick on the trigger when the Indians raided, able and willing to help with farming and other heavy chores. In any peasant or subsistence econ-omy, past and present, women are considered as fit as men for hard manual labor. The chief agricultural labor force of Africa is its women, and it is generally believed that women are better suited than men for hard work. This among other lessons about the presumed biological nature of men and women was brought home to me during a research

stint in Central Africa some years ago. My African neighbors had become accustomed to the idea that my country engaged in all manner of
nonsensical practices. They were usually tactfully tolerant, but when I
said that in my country, it was the men who did the heavy work, that
women were not considered fit for it, they did not conceal disapproval.
This was a mistake, they maintained. Everybody knows that men are
not suited by nature for heavy work, that women are stronger and better workers. Men drink too much and do not eat enough to keep up
their strength; they are more tense and travel about too much to develop
the habits or the muscles needed for sustained work on the farms. And
this was all confirmed by observation of actual behavior. It should be
noted that the society in question was an old-fashioned patriarchal
feudal kingdom, in which nobody had ever heard of equality of the
sexes.

Emotional stability is another axis of variation. It is obvious, to
some, that women are by nature less stable emotionally than men, that
it is natural for women to cry easily and otherwise to show their feelings, whereas men are more easily able to control and conceal them.
But again, the belief about what is natural and whether observed behavior corresponds to belief depend on where we happen to be. Edward T. Hall, in his book, *The Silent Language* (1959), offers as his
illustration of this point the views of male-female difference in Iran.
There—in a thoroughly patriarchal society, where men are deemed the
superiors of women—it is expected that women will be practical, cool,
and calculating, whereas men are expected to show emotions, to be
sensitive and intuitive, to prefer poetry to logic. And so it is.

The last item we shall look at for a general idea of diversity in
views of male and female nature is intelligence. In a comparison of
an American Indian community—the Zuni mentioned above—with a
nearby group of Anglo-Americans, an investigating anthropologist made
this assumption: if Anglo-Americans, living in a society in which the
male is the dominant, superior sex, generally believe that men are intellectually superior to women, then the Zuni, living in a matrilineal
society where decisions are made by women, would believe that women
are intellectually superior to men. But projecting our culture-bound
views or merely reversing them is not sound procedure. The Zuni
replies to the question "Which are more intelligent, men or women?"

took this general form: "Well, some men are more intelligent than some women, and some women are more intelligent than some men. That's because some men are intelligent and some are not, and some women are intelligent and some are not." Any comment on such a judicious verdict could be only an anticlimax.

To present further cases would only be to labor the point: there is universal recognition of differences between males and females—let us be thankful for small favors—but whatever the differences, they are not so strikingly uniform that human beings everywhere must come to the same conclusions about them. We have, moreover, a hint of part of the answer to the question "What differences does a difference make?" What is believed to be true of the nature of males and females influences significantly the content of ideal models constructed for the formation of character. Within a given society, there is a statistical tendency to develop according to socially defined ideals of appropriate behavior. But viewing humanity on a world-wide scale, we find no consensus. Again, nature makes us male or female, but the beliefs and values of our society make us the kinds of men or women we become. It would nonetheless be again erring in the direction of oversimplification to assert, as some social scientists have done, that observed behavior is fully explicable by social definitions of roles. Each individual perforce has a multiplicity of biological characteristics, sexual and otherwise, which may or may not be compatible with role expectations. Actual behavior is the product of complex and usually unconscious negotiations among the demands of diverse roles and diverse individual characteristics. In the dynamics of everyday life, there is much more room for individuality than is suggested by descriptions of societal norms and ideals. Permissiveness with respect to departures from established norms varies from one place to another. However, in no society is there a demand for complete conformity. Secondary norms are regularly set up to permit scope to the multiplex character of any concrete individual.

For at least a preliminary view of the complicated relationship between a cultural ideal of woman and the behavioral realities, I am much indebted to my friends, male and female, in the African kingdom I mentioned briefly above. What follows is drawn from my paper, "The Status of Women in Burundi," in a volume on *Women of Tropical Africa* (1963). As I said, this is an old-fashioned, feudal, patriarchal society in the grand manner. Women may not call their husbands by their given names, for this would be lacking in respect. They serve their husbands from a kneeling position. Political power, judicial rights, ownership and inheritance of cattle and lands, 'and the right of independent action are traditionally for men only. A wife is paid for, so that the husband owns all the children borne by the woman during the marriage and has a right to her labor on his farms and in the home. Obedience, fertility, graciousness as a hostess, industriousness, respect for her husband are among the chief feminine virtues. All this and more is taken as serious, literal truth by men and women alike, irrespective of caste, age, or other variables. Yet, in point of fact, there are women—and not a few—who enjoy considerable authority, who own or control cattle, lands, and other forms of wealth, command large numbers of feudal inferiors, and in general realize the central values presumably intended only for their fathers and brothers. There are many charming but formidable matriarchs who rule with an iron will all those who come within their reach. Unstinted admiration is accorded to women who succeed. It seems not to have occurred to anyone that such women are unwomanly or unfeminine. What a woman cannot do as a woman she manages very well indeed to do as a person, as a member of her society.

The scope of feminine activity in Burundi is limited rather by caste than by sex, for wealth and power are distributed that way. Still, even the poorest woman can be a politician on the scale permitted by her circumstances. What is needed are the personal qualities of cleverness, ambition, energy, courage, and application—and, incidentally, men willing to do one's bidding for a share of the profits. There are always a good many of them available for projects, large and small.

A woman of Burundi who has just served her husband his dinner from the accepted kneeling position will, on leaving the house, order about her workmen or servants with the greatest authority and efficiency. This is part of her job, and there is no conflict. Each role requires different behavior, and any reasonably socialized individual goes from one to the other as naturally as breathing. While all agree that men are supposed to be more intelligent and emotionally stable than women, exceptions are readily recognized, and a stupid husband values a clever wife. Intelligence is not to be wasted. When it is applied to the advantage of husband or father or local ruler, it is duly rewarded. By the exercise of good judgment, by giving good advice, a woman earns gifts of cattle and lands. Her voice will be heard in private conclave and respected—but in public, women do not depart from the ideal of modest silence in the presence of men. There are no love songs in the otherwise rich poetic tradition of Burundi; but when a wife has proved intelligent, capable, and loyal, her husband composes a praise-poem for her, of the same form used to praise princes and generous patrons.

To be sure, there is a seamy side. Many women are not especially bright, and nobody seeks their advice and gives them gifts to reward them for judicious decisions. Some intelligent women, instead of help-ing their husbands, plot against them and destroy them. Many who find father, brother, or husband less than tractable take control of the affections of a son, in such fashion that Momism, Burundi style, makes the American version look very tame indeed. We need not go into the high cost of patriarchal systems. The point to be made is clear. Even—perhaps especially—where sex-linked role-models are rigid, individual differences are in fact permitted scope for activities which are not in accord with the ideal models but which are nevertheless socially ac-ceptable, even praiseworthy.

What conclusions can we draw, from our brief excursion into other cultures, about women, real and ideal, in our own society and about the potential of woman? An adequate descriptive account of women would have to include the variety of beliefs about the nature of women, the variety of ideal role-models assigned to women as women but also to women as persons, and the crooked course of the flow of actual behavior relative to ideal models. Even within one society, there is so high a degree of heterogeneity in the actualities that one is led to suspect that although there are millions of females in this world, there is no such thing as "woman." To study "woman," or even "women," is to study a figment of our traditional classification of humanity. For, if anything is true of "woman," it must be true of women in all times and places. To study women as female persons is another matter. Spe-cifically feminine roles and characteristics can then be viewed in their relationship with other types of roles and characteristics, and these all add up to meaningful totals.

Studies of women in Western culture encounter a peculiar problem. In most societies, ideals are kept within hailing distance of realities. They are understood as prescribing and proscribing behavior, thus as limiting development by channeling it. In the Western tradition, however, ideals tend to be so far above and beyond common reality that their realization is not likely, except perhaps in the rare instance. They are thought to elevate their object, to give it wings to raise it above the common. Denis de Rougemont, in his study of love in the western world (1939), gives us a sensitive historical account of the development of the romantic ideal and a somber sociological analysis of the damage done to both sexes by the etherealization of the female. Mere flesh and blood—or, if you will, "a rag, a bone and a hank of hair"—what can any woman do to bring to reality the fictions and fancies that have gone into the construction of "the ideal woman"? It is perhaps momentarily flattering to be raised high on a pedestal, but the higher the pedestal, the harder the bump when it crumbles beneath the weight of realities. It is probably a sign of great esteem to idealize any object. But those of us who have read some history profoundly mistrust idealizers. What has been done to human beings in the name of ideals of religion, of civilization, of progress, is painful to contemplate. Ideals of "true femininity," of "woman," of "motherhood," are emotionally pleasing, but they, too, are suspect as selfish, unconsidered wish-fulfillment for the idealizer, as delusive flattery for the idealized that can all too easily become merciless mutual exploitation.

Extravagant glorification is not the remedy for traditional degradation. Exploration of the potential of women is part of the world-wide exploration of the potential of humanity generally. Ideals too easily realized do not sufficiently spur us on to optimum growth. But we must distinguish between ideals which stimulate constructive action and the fictional products of dreams and unfulfilled needs. Impossible ideals do not bring out the best in us. They are as restrictive and deforming as the worst kind of tyranny. The construction of viable ideals for the future requires reliable factual information about humankind, male and female, not to cut down ideals to what has been achieved or can be done without much effort but rather to fit them to what can be achieved in fact, rather than in fancy, and to provide some assurance that we will be protected against the disappointments that flights from reality almost surely bring in their train. Being fully human is a high enough ideal for all; it contains the potential for woman and the potential for man, inextricably linked together. By all means, let imagination and hope soar, but untrammeled by false notions and untroubled by false problems.

References

Albert, Ethel M. The Status of Women in Burundi. In: Denise Paulme, Editor, *Women of Tropical Africa.* Berkeley, University of California Press, 1963.

Hall, Edward T. *The Silent Language.* Garden City, N.Y., Doubleday & Company, Inc., 1959.

Mead, Margaret. *Male and Female.* New York, William Morrow and Company, Inc., 1949.

Rougemont, Denis de. *L'Amour et l'occident.* Paris, Librairie Plon, 1939. (Translated into English as: *Love in the Western World.*)

Marya Mannes

THE PROBLEMS OF CREATIVE WOMEN*

Many times during the thinking and the writing of this talk—one of the hardest jobs, incidentally, that I can remember—I have asked myself: Who cares? It is not merely that creative women are a minority—that the woman who can produce intellectually and artistically as well as biologically constitute a very small proportion of the female population of this country. It is, I am reluctantly convinced, that they are neither particularly wanted nor particularly valued. Oh, you have read and I have read scores of articles these last years about the great wasted reservoir of female intelligence, about the nation's need not only for educated women but for thinking women trained and ready to apply their knowledge and skills in professions that presumably cry for them. But if the call is there, I have not heard it. And if the need is there, society—and that includes women—either ignores it or rejects it.

This rejection has been confirmed by fact as well as inferred by personal experience. Not long ago *The New York Times* published an article on the job status of women in which Martin Tolchin wrote: "The educated women of America have lost ground in their attempt to place their talent at the disposal of a nation that professes to be hungry for brainpower." And later on he says: "The decline of the professional women has been attributed to a combination of factors that include earlier marriages, misuse of education, job discrimination, and what Mary I. Bunting, president of Radcliffe College, calls 'hidden persuaders . . . the cultural forces that tell a woman it is unladylike to

* Copyright © 1963 by Marya Mannes.

use her mind.' " I would add that all these factors stem from one major cause: fear. Fear in both men and women of the next step in the continuing revolution they prefer to ignore, steps which I rashly intend to define in the course of this talk.

For what I say from now on will be subjective, the result of my own experience and observation, for I *am* a woman and I *think* I am creative. And although dozens of books and hundreds of papers and articles have been written by many wise and wiser people on this subject and although some of what they have said will be said again by me, I choose to ignore them now. What is more, I am sick—as a woman —of being talked about and written about, especially by men who cannot feel what we feel, or by women who are not what we are. And the only reason, apart from being qualified to speak for myself, that I am here adding more talk to this subject is that I feel it high time to think radically and in new terms, to clear away what I consider to be a thicket of misconceptions and timidities, and to open a window in the suffocating room of our present social patterning. Some of my ideas, therefore, are bound to be unpalatable if not repellent to the majority of our citizens who believe that prosperity and procreation—in wedlock, of course—are the only valid goals of man and woman. I happen to think that there are other goals as valid—and as valuable—both for man and woman.

How did I get that way? Well, I saw it around me when I was a small child. My mother and father were both concert musicians and both teachers, my mother of the piano, my father of the violin. There was nothing strange whatever to me in the fact that my mother, a woman, spent much of each day practicing or giving lessons, that she often went off on tour with my father, and that she couldn't boil an egg. She didn't have to. In the early part of the twentieth century even people of very modest means had cooks and nurses, and it was taken equally for granted by my brother and myself that if our mother was away, the cook, the nurse, or the great-aunt who lived with us would take care of us. There was no sense of rejection, no shocks at being "motherless" for a period of weeks. Life went on fully, we studied, ate, and slept, and when our parents did come back we were delighted to see them. It was a very loving, a very warm, family of four.

It was also quite natural to me that besides being an artist of real distinction, my mother created an extremely attractive home, took care of all my impractical father's practical needs, paid all the bills, entertained scores of fellow musicians, and was, for all her attainments, intensely feminine. What is more, her love of her children did not prevent her from being the strict disciplinarian our father was not.

Now you can say two things that I, as a child, did not then realize. One was that my mother was an exceptional woman. The other was that servants and relatives made it possible for her to maintain a professional life and a domestic life without harm to either. Both were true. I can add one more thing: that the temper of the time was different. The mass media had not enthroned the housewife as God's noblest creature and best consumer, reams of nonsense were not being written about woman's proper role, and women themselves did not regard professional or career women with that mixture of envy or disapproval, or superiority, which seems to color contemporary social attitudes. Women like my mother were then, as they are now, a minority, but an accepted and admired one.

It was therefore quite natural that I should grow up believing that all was possible for a girl or woman. Certainly, both my father and my brother made it seem so. Both spoke to me as equals of many things that girls are not supposed to be interested in. My brother passed on to me the first principles of physics, the relativity of time, and how to throw a curve with a baseball. My father discussed with me, from the age of ten years onward, such things as the nature of melancholy, how to get a vibrato on a violin, and how sickness could be caused by states of mind. I lived, therefore, for over seventeen years in the world of imagination and discovery, going steady not with the boy next door but the men out of range. I was passionately in love with Julius Caesar, Hamlet, Henry V of England, and John Barrymore of Hollywood. I did not start transferring my affections to more attainable men until I was nineteen, at which point I threw away the books along with self-restraint.

But at no time, then or since, did I throw away a sense of fierce independence as a human being and the desire to attain distinction in terms of mind and spirit and expression. Since I wanted to experience the full range of human experience, the thought that my sex should confine me exclusively to wifehood, motherhood, and domesticity was

untenable. I did not even, at that early age, want children. I wanted
that splendid but impossible thing called freedom. I still do—but I
know where it is—within—and how hard it has to be fought for.

Now I have dwelt on this background, not because it was right for
a woman or natural for a woman, but because it was right and natural
for the kind of human being which I happen to be and which a number
of women—far more than we suspect—are. It took me a good many
years to figure out what that is and why it is. It is something which
many of you would define in the precise terms of your professional
knowledge but which I can only describe very simply as this: that
each human being, male or female, is composed of both male and female components and that the proportion of one to the other varies
widely in each person. While the public generally assumes that all
normal women are or should be 100 per cent female, the truth is that
a woman can be 70 or even 60 per cent female to 30 or 40 per cent
male and still function biologically as a woman, with all the physical
attributes which this entails. Yet together with these functions and
attributes, the woman with a higher quotient of masculine qualities
must function also on other levels, whether it is in the world of ideas
or performance, or in the expression of sexual drives not necessarily
linked to procreation. Such women can love men yet not submerge
themselves in men; can love children but not dedicate themselves to
them; can enjoy domesticity but not devote themselves to it; can be
feminine but not make a fetish of it. In so being they may miss the
intense pleasures of submission, the unity of character and the security
of role which the quote normal unquote women enjoy, but they can
also gain that breadth of experience, intellectual and emotional, that
free and single identity, which their majority of sisters are often denied.
But the women who feel compelled toward creative expression, whether
in the arts or sciences, in exploration and adventure, or in the battles
of politics and government must learn to accept the losses which accompany these gains. And here we come to the basic root of the problem confronting men and women today: acceptance not of what society
thinks we should be but what we really are. Everything I have said
about creative women applies equally to noncompetitive men: the
dreamers rather than the doers, the non-go-getters, the sensitive and
gentle men who possess a higher-than-average proportion of female

components without being in any sense effeminate. Equipped neither as fighters nor—primarily—as breadwinners, lacking the desire. to impose their will on others or to dominate the women they love, they are in their own way as valuable to society as their "normal" aggressive brothers.

The trouble is, I think, that this complexity of roles within men and women—the result of a slow, long, but dramatic revolution in the sexes—has not been realized by the public as a whole. Or if it has been subconsciously recognized, it has been consciously rejected. Why? Because it challenges the whole structure of marriage, the family, society as we now know it. It challenges a good many timeworn assumptions that have been not only comfortable for men but convenient for the majority of women too.

For equality is not at issue here. Equal franchise, equal pay, the end of legal and civil discriminations against women have been, though fought for, inevitable. What is at issue is the recognition of minorities, among which creative women and nonaggressive men are the largest— far larger, I repeat, than we think. That this recognition must extend to, and include, the homosexuals at either end of the spectrum, goes without saying. Whether these manifestations of human complexity or, if you will, deviation, are desirable is not the question either. They exist, they are here, they will not go away, they may even increase. The point is to make them productive instead of destructive, to recognize what values they have, to incorporate them openly and without prejudice into our society. For it is the refusal to accept and even value their difference from the norm that causes unhappiness and ultimately harm, the problems which today I am confining to the creative woman.

What exactly are these problems? The earliest, I would think, are her parents. From infancy they give her no choice to be anything but what they think a girl should be. They smother her in pink when she might prefer blue, they give her dolls when she might prefer trains, they present her with books about girls when she might rather read about boys, and they send her to a psychiatrist if she likes books better than boys at sixteen. Now, in fact, they initiate the mating process when she is twelve in the firm conviction that the only possible future for her is early marriage, lots of children, and a suburban home. If their girl shows a desire to paint or model or write verse, the more intelligent parents, of course, encourage her. A talent is fine so long as it is kept within bounds—bounds meaning youthful expression before the real business of being a woman takes over. It is far more disturbing if the female over eighteen still wants to be a doctor or a biologist or a lawyer, although parents can comfort themselves with the hope that when she meets budding doctors, biologists, and lawyers in the course of her studies, she will choose the husband rather than the profession.

But even if her parents, like mine, are proud of her intellectual curiosity, her talent, her independence of spirit and encourage them, she can never escape the relentless, steady nudging of society: the assumption that she is in some way unfeminine, that she is jeopardizing her future happiness as a woman, that what she is doing is merely a substitute for her true—and only valid—functions. Everything she sees about her, moreover, seems to confirm this assumption. From childhood through adolescence the women she sees about her—her mother, her neighbor, her best friend's mother—are homebound and house-oriented to a degree not even experienced by *their* own mothers—and certainly not dreamed of by those valiant pioneers of sixty years ago whose militant efforts to widen women's horizons and take them *out* of the kitchen earned them ridicule along with rights. They must be turning in their graves to see most of their female descendants being not only full-time servants to their many children and to their house but serene in their sense of superiority over their career-bound sisters.

The housewife image, moreover, is exalted daily by all the mass media that find in the young, large, solvent family an inexhaustible market. In television soap operas the apron is the mark of a good woman, the career the sign of a frustrated one, the single existence the proof of a desperate one. In the fiction in the mass women's magazines the heroine·is never brilliant, original, creative, or ambitious. In all the ads in all the media, woman steps out of her four-walled role only long enough to drive the car to school, to the hairdresser, or to market.

Irresistibly, the American girl is formed in this image from childhood, and by the time she is going steady at twelve her future is so clearly indicated that only exceptional will and courage can change it. For the risk of changing it is loss of popularity, which in turn is loss of femininity, which in turn has been drummed into her as acquired characteristics of dressing, make-up, attitude, and talk that mark her as desirable. Clearly listed as undesirable in this lexicon of attraction are independence of mind, intellectual ambition, and attachment to work.

So our girl in this free country has, in truth, little choice. Security is the goal, and as soon as possible. Marry the boy right away, get the house right away, have the brood right away. No time for search of self, no time for experiments in love and life, no time for interior growth, no time for the great world outside.

Now what is wrong with that, you say? The majority of women since time began have found their greatest fulfillment in the home as wife and mother. If they hadn't, the race would have perished. Why grudge them their happiness just because it isn't yours?

I do not grudge them their happiness. I merely question whether a number of them are indeed happy: whether given a real choice by a more fluid society they might not be better doctors than mothers, better mathematicians than homemakers, better courtesans than wives. I could question equally whether a number of the young man trapped into domesticity and corporations at twenty would not be happier explorers than fathers, poets than husbands, and rakes than lawn mowers.

Ah, says society, but what about the continuance of the race, what about the structure of the family, what about the sanctity of marriage? Again, I find myself—in the light of the present—questioning whether the profound changes working on all three are either understood or accepted as reality demands that they should be.

Has not, for instance, unlimited procreation become a danger as great, or greater, than the bomb? Is not the large family now an indulgence rather than a duty—an indulgence and luxury for which the children themselves will pay with intolerable congestion, inadequate schooling, and the deprivation of those amenities and pleasures which make for civilized living? Is a proliferation of babies more important to the race now than the development of intelligence? And if all these questions suggest that man and woman may have reached a stage where love has other goals besides procreation, should they not be recognized as valid and therefore acceptable?

Whether they are or not, they exist. Nature has ways of adjusting herself to the realities. The world can sustain many different kinds of love, whether it is between man and man—a relationship, incidentally, that has often been culturally productive, between woman and woman, between man and mistress. All, in a sense, are in revolt against a society so overwhelmingly swaddled in domestic units that it cannot see beyond the next mortgage or the next car to the next holocaust. All are in revolt against concepts of the correct and normal roles for men and women which bear no relation to the sexual duality inherent in a great many people.

Of these the creative woman is, as I've said, a prime example. And her problems are not as inherent in her nature as in her relationship to a society which accepts her only on certain conditions. It is her attempt to gain this acceptance by fulfilling these conditions that make for trouble.

Let's look at some of them. Nobody objects to a woman's being a good writer or sculptor or geneticist if at the same time she manages to be a good wife, a good mother, good-looking, good-tempered, well dressed, well groomed, and unaggressive. These are the entrance charges for the approval of other men and women. They are, I maintain, exorbitant to the point of impossibility. Nobody expected George Eliot to be a beauty. Nobody worried about Jeanne d'Arc's haircut. Emily Dickinson was not scorned for being childless. Nobody urged Marie Curie to dye her hair.

To come closer to home, my own pianist mother was on the plump side, had rather limp hair, and didn't know how to use lipstick properly. She was a fine pianist and a good wife and mother, but she simply didn't have the time to fuss with herself, to reduce, to be fashionable. What's more, nobody expected her to.

I was interested to see photographs of Dr. Kelsey, who did so much to keep the drug thalidomide out of the country. It was obvious that her hair was cut without reference to current style and that her dress was—well—serviceable. It was equally clear that a woman of that degree of dedication to her work didn't have the time to have her hair teased or to cook elaborate meals for her family. Why should she be expected to? Yet we are, or think we are, because of one thing only: the fear that men will reject us. Thanks largely to the brilliant manipulation of mass media, women are obsessed with an ideal of femininity as the guarantee of happiness. Be thin, be smart, be gay, be sexy, be soft-spoken. Get new slip covers, learn new recipes, have bright children, further your man's career, help the community, drive the car, smile. And if you can write a best-seller or a Broadway hit too, that's great.

There are some women who manage to do just that, and they fill me with awe and envy. But most of us who produce in the realm of thought and ideas cannot do and be all these things and should not try. Evidence abounds that even the supposedly contented suburban house-wife with four children and no aspirations beyond her home is a victim of this multiplicity of roles. In the process of trying to be mother, wife, lover, chef, servant, and hostess, she apparently consumes alarming quantities of tranquilizers and alcohol—surely not an index of fulfill-ment. Yet those of us who aspire creatively struggle as she does to prove to the world that we too are feminine and, therefore, desirable.

This, I maintain, is a sort of craven appeasement that does no honor to a free intelligence. For the fact is, we cannot have our cake and eat it, too. We cannot enjoy our mobility, our resources, our liberties, our triumphs, our intense and heady involvements without paying for them. And these are some of the prices: The first is popularity. At school the brilliant, intense girl student with dreams in her head isn't going to get the boys unless her attractions are strong enough to de-ceive them. In this case she will probably get the wrong boys, for the right ones won't be ready for her. This is probably the right place to say that beauty is possibly the greatest hazard of a creative woman— to herself as well as to its victims. Male adoration is a powerful deter-rent to female sense, and it is extremely difficult to tear oneself from loving arms and say, "Sorry, darling, I've got to work." It is so much easier and pleasanter to drown in current delights than gird for future dreams. Also, beauty demands a degree of maintenance, and it is the strong woman who turns her back on the hairdresser to gain two extra hours of work. Certainly, creative labor has been a compensation in many women of talent for the attractions they lack, and there is no doubt that homeliness permits a dedication and continuity which beauty fragments. In this case, the advance of middle age can be a boon: as the lines increase, the distractions dwindle, and seduction can be more easily confined to the typewriter or microscope.

After school or college, the creative young woman seriously con-cerned with work will have to realize that marriage with the wrong man can be worse than no marriage. While all her sisters are marching down the aisle at nineteen and twenty for the sake of being married, she must have the nerve to resist the stampede and give herself time to learn, to experience, to grow in the direction of her free dreams. Above all, she must not be afraid of singleness or even loneliness, for I know of no woman, let alone man, who has any stature or worth without knowledge of either. It is the insecure and the immature who cannot bear the thought of their own singularity, who must hold on to another hand from puberty onward, who surround themselves with human buffers against the world.

Since vitality and curiosity are essential equipments of a creative woman, she must be willing to pay the price of trial and error—loving men who may not love her, being loved by men she cannot love. If she is worried about what others think of her, by what standards of morality she is judged, she will not stand the gaff of independence long.

If she marries, soon or late, she will be wise to find the man with sufficient female sensitivity to match her masculine liberty—for the kind of man who has to prove his masculinity through domination is not for her. She will therefore be inordinately lucky if she finds one of the relatively few men whose security lies in the full and equal partnership of a love which may—or may not—produce children.

If she has children—this creative woman of ours—she must pay for this indulgence with a long burden of guilt, for her life will be split three ways between them and her husband and her work. What she gives to one she must take from the other, and there will be no time when one or the other is not harmed. No woman with any heart can compose a paragraph when her child is in trouble or her husband ill: forever they take precedence over the companions of her mind. In this, as in many other things, the creative woman has a much tougher time than the creative man. For one thing, she has no wife, as he has, to protect her from intrusion, to maintain the machinery of living, to care for the children, to answer the doorbell. For another, no one believes her time to be sacred. A man at his desk in a room with a closed door is a man at work. A woman at a desk in any room is available.

Now most of us learn to accept this if we want both worlds of wife and work. The only alternative is to relinquish marriage in favor of men. I am quite serious about this interesting possibility: the recognition and acceptance of a special category of woman not unlike the hetaera of Periclean Athens: women who concentrate on the arts of mind and body for the delectation of brilliant men—and themselves. Brought up to date I see this as a chance for the inspired female to work alone all day and have companionship much of the night with a variety of men, similar only in that their need for stimulation is intellectual as well as physical. This would relieve them at intervals from the boredom of domesticity and rescue them gracefully from more sordid outlets. It would not be popular with wives, although it would relieve *them* in turn of their responsibility to be glamorous and amorous as well as motherly and wiferly. But perhaps I am a bit ahead of myself—and the times!

Where were we? Ah yes, the penalties of being a creative female. One of them concerns nomenclature. The gentlemen of the press carefully refrain from identifying a man as a Negro or a woman as a Negress but rarely hesitate to call a woman a poetess or a sculptress, antique phrases that suggest Victorian females painting on china. Even worse, a highly sophisticated magazine like the *New Yorker* delights in referring to "lady poets" or "lady playwrights," titles of spurious and ponderous gallantry which reveal nothing less than contempt. Have you ever read of a gentleman writer—or even a man writer? There is also a tendency in male reviewers to describe any novel written by a woman and dealing with the sensibilities of women as "a woman's book." This assumption that women are interesting only to women is as silly as the assumption that men are interesting only to men. Since neither of these assumptions exist in French literary attitudes, they appear to be largely of Anglo-Saxon origin, reflecting, I suggest, an astounding lack of communication between our men and women except on sexual levels. Why should not a man be as intensely interested in a woman's clothes, thoughts, desires, dreams, as she should be in a man's? Where does the embarrassment come in?

We now come to certain social problems which may seem equally trivial but which, over a period of time, erode the tissues of the professional female. Let us say that a woman has been a successful writer for over twenty years under the name of Jane Smith. Ten years ago she married a man called John Cooper. She is henceforth introduced at social gatherings as Mrs. Cooper. A lot of people know about Jane Smith. Nobody knows about Mrs. Cooper. Certainly not the other professionals at the party who know Jane Smith but don't know she's Mrs. Cooper. Result: no contact, desultory conversation with strangers, dull time. Why? Because the hostess has no imagination, because convention dies hard, because it takes that tiny added trouble to say— "Mr. and Mrs. Cooper—Jane Smith." As a matter of fact, along with the revival of the hetaera we might adopt the Spanish idea of hyphenating the husband's and wife's name. I have always found the obliteration of the wife's name an outmoded custom related to chattels, property, and such. Since the mark of the individual is identity, why submerge it? Has any man distinguished in his field as John Smith imagined the sensation of being introduced to colleagues or strangers by his wife's name? Another social custom I find equally antique: the segregation of women from men after dinner. I share wholeheartedly Senator Maurine Neuberger's frustration at being separated from the best male minds for the balance of an evening.

But here, of course, we get at the root of the matter. It is widely assumed, by both men and women, that men feel more comfortable without the presence of women. This is certainly true of the upper-class British and of the more socially conventional Americans. Why? Because they want to tell dirty jokes? That has long since ceased to be a male prerogative. Because women are not intellectually up to their talk? Hardly, because many women now are. Yet only intelligent men seek the company of intelligent women. The majority avoid what they think of as competition. They don't want some female deeply acquainted with foreign affairs to question their views on Berlin. They don't want any woman to tell them anything. What is asserted by a man is an opinion; what is asserted by a woman is opinionated. A woman with ideas and the ability to express them is something of a social embarrassment, like an unhousebroken pet. People like us, therefore, must learn to keep a respectful silence in the presence of men who may have a higher or lower intelligence, or speak our minds at the risk of the glassy male eye. So here we are again, supposedly intelligent and gifted women, scared of losing our femininity by the simple measure of saying what we think —and know. How much safer to play the role assigned us by the experts, to be still, to know our place, to charm—even to lie?

But since the urge to create is a search for truth, the lie does not work. We are hoist by our own honesty, by our singularity, by our identity. And yet without them none of us would be any good in the work we choose to do. That is our problem.

But why should it concern society, of which we are such a minority? Because I believe this minority to be in the vanguard of the revolution which the majority are now resisting. In fact, the American counter-revolution is a phenomenon which no one has yet explained to my satisfaction. While most other civilized countries, from Britain to Scandinavia to the Soviet Union, are incorporating more and more women of high intellectual attainments into their major professions and positions, the United States is plunged into an orgy of domesticity and childbearing. While day nurseries to take care of the children of professional women are standard community services in these countries, they are still viewed here as a communist plot against the family and motherhood. While it is a matter of course to find brilliant women statesmen, doctors, university professors, and scientists elsewhere, they are as rare as trumpeter swans over here. The exceptionally gifted and articulate woman in the United States usually finds herself the only woman in symposia and conferences, on panels and discussion groups. This could be called token integration—a delaying device which is supposed to answer certain needs and objections without actually facing the root of the problem. It is no particular satisfaction to the intelligent and articulate woman to stick out like a sore thumb, or—if you will—like a jeweled forefinger.

No—society must be trained to think differently about its men and women if the whole question of female identity as an independent human being is to be recognized as important. Certain changes, in summation, must be faced:

First, we have reached a stage in our evolution where procreation is not a duty or even a responsibility. It is both a blessing and a luxury, and a luxury to be jealously guarded for the quality rather than the quantity of our race. If men and women have any real concern for the future they will voluntarily deny themselves a large brood for the sake of their children's children in a world so overcrowded that it will prohibit the individual freedoms and privileges which we ourselves now enjoy. Self-restraint is alien to the human temperament, but humanity without restraint will dig its own grave.

Ironically, the large family is now not only considered a status symbol but has made the single or childless woman an object of derogation and pity—attitudes immensely destructive to her self-respect and happiness. Once the large family is considered an indulgence rather than a contribution, the productive values of the single woman can be recognized, and she, freed from the sense of guilt and inadequacy that now haunts her, can divert her full energies to the many crying needs of society. That the word "single woman" or "spinster" should imply inferior worth or usefulness is only one of the damaging by-products of our present consumer-based, security-mad domestic pattern.

Secondly, girls who show marked talent and a strong desire for creative expression in any field should not be made to feel that they are unfeminine if they delay marriage for the sake of work or choose to experience a variety of involvements before they settle down. Time and freedom are essential ingredients of self-knowledge, of the growth of mind and spirit. So is the man—worth waiting for—who fully recognizes these special needs.

Third, the creative woman must herself stop trying to discourage or suppress her urges for independence of spirit by trying to conform to society's image of a woman, or to "please" a man. If a man does not love her *because of* this independence, he is not for her.

Fourth, the people who deal in mass media must recognize that out of millions of women who are entirely happy and fulfilled in their classic roles as wife and mother, there are thousands who are not, and that they may represent productive values of equal use to society and the nation. The assumption that there is no possible alternative dream for a woman but domestic suburbia will have to be modified if there is to be any approximation to reality.

Finally, men will have to wake up to the fact that the identity of women as human beings is as essential to them as their identity as wife and mother. For some, this need for a separate identity is even as important as it is to man. There must be some area where they exist solely as themselves. Men should also come to learn that creativity and femininity are not only compatible but often inseparable, that a body with a brain can be more responsive than a body without, and that imagination is the sister of love. Admittedly, the recognition of these things by men is not made any easier in a society where intellectuality is suspect from adolescence and where adolescent attitudes are cherished into middle age.

In the meantime and pending these changes toward an adult, rather than an adolescent, society, the lonely few of us will just have to go on being ourselves, living our special kind of life to the fullest, accepting responsibility for what we lack as well as for what we give, and taking the sniping from those who deplore us as well as the praise of those who admire us. Above all, we are not to be either feared or pitied. We made our beds, and although they are sometimes hard, they are good for the spine—and the spirit. And although most women would not want to trade places with us, some women who question their own aspirations may now be encouraged to pursue them.

For it takes courage to know what you are—and to be what you are.

Peter Koestenbaum

THE INTERPRETATION OF ROLES

I know that I have been asked to address you primarily because of my interest in the philosophy of existentialism. The program committee must have thought that, since the purpose of the present symposium is to help woman define herself, the existentialist theory of man can contribute significantly to understanding and solving her problems. They were correct!

This morning I wish to establish the principle that the question of feminine roles can be fruitfully examined in terms of the rather remarkable existentialist contribution to contemporary philosophy and science, and to illustrate the applications of that principle by suggesting an existentialist analysis of that problem.

To implement these two purposes, we need first a definition of existentialism and an indication of its importance for the study of man; second, a brief discussion of the central themes in the existentialist theory of man; and, third, we must in each case and above all emphasize the relation of existentialism to the roles of femininity.

Existentialism is the Third Copernican Revolution. The great sixteenth-century Polish astronomer, Nikolaus Copernicus, shattered the Dantesque medieval-world picture—a drama with God at its center and salvation as its goal—by transforming the then prevailing Ptolemaic geocentrism to a heliocentric conception of the solar system. Then, in 1781, is one of history's greatest intellectual achievements, Immanuel Kant promulgated the Second Copernican Revolution by showing the astounding role of subjectivity in our conception of the external cosmos. Even space and time were assigned subjective status. It is likely that, after the turbulent dust of philosophical controversy has settled and the clear calm of historical appraisal will have prevailed, existentialism will be recognized as the Third Copernican Revolution.

Existentialism is first a method of inquiry through which we obtain the primordial, the purest, and most reliable knowledge about what it means to be human, knowledge devoid of the assumptions and presuppositions prevalent in traditional scientific methodologies. Existentialism is also a corresponding theory of man. However, the right to name existentialism to candidacy for the Third Copernican Revolution rests mostly on the scientific character of this existentialist method. Whereas the technical epistemological details cannot be worked out here, it is nonetheless essential to realize that existentialism provides a new methodological approach and a new set of categories in terms of which we can study the problems of man. In existentialism, philosophy and science—that is, philosophical ethics and the behavioral sciences—merge as never before.

In the full spectrum of electromagnetic radiation that makes up the total universe, the range of visible light is infinitesimal. Nonetheless, our common-sense conception of the world is based on that incredibly narrow band of visible radiation. Modern physics has developed instruments sensitive to all radiation, and, as a consequence, our knowledge of the physical universe has been expanded, transformed, and revolutionized. To a comparable extent, existentialism has richly expanded the data available for the construction of theories of man. This philosophy has transformed our conceptions of what it means to exist as a human being in the world, and it has revolutionized the ancient hope of finding authentic solutions to religious, ethical, psychological, and social problems.

To illuminate pithily the scientific character of existentialism, we must distinguish between precise data and fringe data. Precise data— the narrow band of visible radiation—are simple, sensory, public, measurable, and repeatable, such as the color, consistency, and weight of a precipitate in a chemical process. Fringe data, on the other hand—the rich remainder—are complex, introspective, private, nonmeasurable, and evasive, such as the wondrous titillation of first love. Traditionally, only the measurable precise data have been accepted as genuine by the sciences—including, especially, the behavioral sciences. It is the great merit of existentialism to have definitely established that what heretofore had been relegated solely to poetry and the arts is also susceptible to strict scientific treatment. The empirical data and factual observations on which a genuinely scientific understanding of man must rest—such as the inner and nonmeasurable experiences of love, anxiety, obligation, and frustration—are not simple, sensory, public, and measurably precise as are so-called ordinary scientific data, such as length, weight, time, and statistical correlations. Fringe data are different in kind from precise data, but they are data of observation just the same. It is fringe data to which William Butler Yeats refers when he says that ". . . all sounds, all colors . . . call down among us certain disembodied powers whose footsteps over our hearts we call emotions." It follows that to develop a bona fide theory of man, a theory that conforms without distortions to the actual empirical structure of human experience, we must admit fringe data into the pantheon of scientific facts. Let us look at the following two groups of expressions:

Group A: Precise Data:

1. A red, squarelike presentation.
2. The length of object x is 4 feet 3 inches.
3. Red litmus paper turned blue upon being immersed in liquid l.
4. The current in coil c measures 0.3 amperes.
5. A thermometer T reads 85.4 degrees Fahrenheit.
6. A force of 3 pounds is required to raise a weight of 16 pounds by means of a pulley system P.
7. The volume of gas G in container C doubled as the temperature rose 10 degrees centigrade.
8. A moist electrode, attached to the palm of the hand of person P at time t showed a resistance of 90,000 ohms.

Group B: Fringe Data:

Type I (Quasi-precise Data):

9. Company C has a good corporate image.
10. A sense of cohesion is established by the sense of loyalty to political and religious institutions.
11. Television provides substitute gratifications.
12. Important feelings have been repressed.

13. The capacity for sublimation leads to mental health.

14. Men search for status; happiness consists in finding one's role.

15. His problem is that in childhood he was unable to identify himself with his father.

16. A stable personality is one that has achieved a balance between cathexes and anticathexes.

17. He has reached the stage of the transference neurosis in treatment.

Type II (Fringe Data):

18. "I know I am but summer to your heart,
And not the full four seasons of the year."

(Edna St. Vincent Millay)

19. "lady through whose profound and fragile lips
the sweet small clumsy feet of April came
into the ragged meadow of my soul."

(e. e. cummings)

Expressions 1 to 8 illustrate different types of precise data, whereas expressions and terms 9 to 17 illustrate aberrant fringe data that are used in the behavioral sciences. These latter need to be made more precise, and we therefore call them quasi-precise data. Finally, expressions 18 and 19 illustrate fringe data that make no scientific pretensions at all. In point of fact, a precise introspective formulation of all fringe data, 9 to 19, is needed for an adequate theory of man, and existentialism provides these formulations. Unfortunately, the behavioral sciences (1) have ignored statements of the type illustrated in expressions 18 and 19, and (2) they have likewise tried to reduce expressions of the type in 9 to 17 to precise data, which cannot be done.

What, exactly, are the quasi-precise data of the behavioral sciences?

The social and psychological sciences, in their effort to develop a science of man, often try to reduce experiences, observations, and data that are intrinsically nonprecise to the kinds of facts we have in the natural sciences. The effort to pattern the social and psychologial sciences after the natural sciences is doomed to fail because many of the facts of the sciences of man are not precise; that is, they are not measurable, public, susceptible to mathematical operations, etc. As a consequence, many of the so-called data of the social and psychological sciences are, in effect, hybrid. The genuine nature of these facts is often that they are fringe data, whereas the expressions designating these facts imply that they are precise data. This situation places the social and psychological sciences in a no-man's land with respect to the understanding of man.

Possibly one of the best illustrations of the difference between precise and fringe data, and of the relevance the latter have to the sciences of man, is to be found in the analysis of time. "Time" is a word that denotes a cluster of ubiquitous, evasive, and protean experiences, all of them necessary to our understanding of man.

Time is a mathematically abstract dimension that serves as coordinate. Time is the period of a pendulum and the vibrations of molecules. There is also the inner sense of time. That is time as it appears to us most directly and most commonly in experience. This kind of time is clearly a fringe datum. That inner sense of time is the matrix through which human existence can be described and understood, and the scientific analysis of that inner sense is to be carried out through the theoretically justified existential analysis of fringe data. The French philosopher-biologist, Henri Bergson, has described this fundamental inner sense of time (durée) in these terms:

20. "There is, beneath these sharply cut crystals and this frozen surface [i.e., my perceptions, memories, and habits], a continuous flux which is not comparable to any flux I have ever seen. . . . This inner life may be compared to the unrolling of a coil."

There are also aesthetic descriptions of the inner sense of time, such as the famous lines in Macbeth:

21. "Tomorrow, and tomorrow, and tomorrow,
    Creeps in this petty pace from day to day,
    To the last syllable of recorded time."

(Shakespeare)

On the other hand, when we focus on the future, we can use Hamlet's description of the inexorable direction of time:

22. "There is a divinity that shapes our ends
    Rough-hew them how we will."

(Shakespeare)

It is evident that expressions 18 to 22 make reference to authentic facts of experience and to facts which are essential in the scientific understanding of man, but facts with which the traditional scientific method cannot deal without distorting them.

In the light of the above considerations, it has shown itself to be psychotherapeutically highly heuristic to interpret psychological and sociological phenomena by their effects on the inner sense of time. For example, the experienced flow of time increases with age and is a typical factor in the experience of aging. The young child experiences time as barely moving, whereas to the older person it proceeds with distressing celerity. Also, the psychological states of boredom, anxiety, depression, and sorrow can be understood when described in terms of their relation to the pathological slowness of the inner sense of time. Conversely, in states of joy, euphoria, happiness, and elation, the inner sense of time accelerates greatly, whereas if the euphoria is drug-induced, time is experienced as slow as it is during depression.[1]

Whereas in depression time flows with painful slowness, the schizophrenic illusion of immortality is the exacerbation of that time-condition: time stops altogether. When time stands still, man experiences the eternity of the present moment. It is as if we were to see, in a stream of water, a miniscule drop magnified a hundred thousand times. Conversely, the existentialist description of mania includes the highly accelerated and agitated flow of the inner sense of time.

Furthermore, existential psychiatry accounts for a number of neuroses and psychoses through distortions of the dimensions of time, such as that of the sense of the future. Since our self-image and our ideas of fulfillment lie in the dimension of the future, depression is the experience of a blocked and inaccessible future: to depressed East Berliners, the dimension of hope and of the future points to West Berlin, which is blocked off by an impenetrable wall. For manics and psychopaths, the future is empty: their erratic and irresponsible behavior is to be understood as directed toward a future that is as bereft of content as are the farthest reaches of the voids of space. If time flows toward a total vacuity, there can be no hope, no thought of consequences, no fear, nor any sense of responsibility. And that is why, in his world, the actions of a psychopath make sense.

After these preliminary methodological considerations, let us turn

[1] Cf. Rollo May, *et al.* (eds.), *Existence*, New York: Basic Books, Inc., Publishers, 1958; pp. 102ff.

our attention to existentialist conceptions of man and their responses to the problem of women's roles.

Whereas contemporary conceptions view sex as the central explanatory principle in man, existentialism substitutes for it the anticipation of my own death. We must distinguish the death of myself from the death of another. If, using the existentialist method, we examine exactly what we imagine in connection with the word "death," we will discover two altogether different constellations of meaning. The death of another means bodily death; it means a funeral, bereavement, and financial settlements. It is a minor event in the stream of history. The philosophically significant features of this image are (1) that the world continues, insouciant, after death and (2) that there is an observing ego which imagines the scene of death and envisions the continuance of the world. Both of these are denied in the death of myself. If we now try to describe what we imagine in the death of myself, we are likely to come up with a similar description, that is, the physiological symptoms, the funeral, the bereavement, and the continuance of the world, the only difference being whose body it is we are talking about. However, it is soon apparent that my ego, who supposedly died, is still imagined to be in the picture. The body may be imagined supine and interred, but there still is an ego observing this imaginary scene, and I am that ego. But I am trying to describe what I mean by the death of my ego! The death of myself is presumably the extinction of the observing ego itself. If I imagine myself in the grave then I am not really imagining myself dead, since I am still present as a disembodied observer of the death scene.

A true description of the image of the death of myself is different not in degree but in kind from the death of another. The genuine death of myself is best described as the annihilation of all being. It is the image of total nothingness—the absence of any image whatsoever—and its fully conscious anticipation is suffused with deep anxiety and uncontrollable nausea. The egoless world is the image of stepping back into a black and bottomless pit.

Our almost unconscious interpretation of the death of myself as merely a subspecies of the death of another is a rationalization that is psychologically profoundly necessary. It would be soothingly wonderful if the death of myself were no more than the death of another. But the facts of human experience, as these disclose themselves to assiduous and candid introspection, are otherwise.

Although the first impact of understanding the death of myself is like the creeping flesh at a witches' Sabbath, subsequently it rejuvenates the soul and fills it with vitality, strength, decisiveness, courage, and with hope.

For example, a woman who confronts the conflict between being a successful wife and mother and abandoning herself to a romantic love affair can solve it only in the light of her own inexorable death. Paradoxical as it may seem, death does lead to decisiveness, perspective, courage, vitality, and to truth. Let us examine each virtue in turn. First, the permanent vision of death propels her with the thrust of urgent pressures to resolve her conflict, which is, after all, that of human fulfillment. Her life is all she has and is. It will terminate she knows not when, and she must come to terms with life while it lasts. These insights give her decisiveness. Second, when she sees life as a total project, with a point of termination, she will distinguish sharply between bagatelles and the things that matter most: if necessary, what is dispensable, husband or lover, home or profession, security or excitement? She is the captain of a fast-sinking ship, who must decide between abandoning or saving her. Her values are thus in perspective. Third, no one can threaten a convict, on his march to the death chamber, with a pistol and the words, "Your money or your life!" He who has faced death can be judicious in his fears, because he has made his peace with death and can now face life. It follows that the pervasive presence of death puts the magic of courage in her life. Fourth, since she no longer thinks that death can be avoided, she has pruned her concern over roles of the entanglements of all ancillary vines. She can attack her problem directly and undisturbed. Thus, mortality leads to vitality.

Finally, fifth, the problem of roles is the problem of the meaning of life. The pressures of death demand not only that the problem be solved immediately, but also that it be solved correctly, that is, in truth. We can take no chances with the greatest of all issues. No miscalculation is permissible. If death is the end of the spectator-ego, then the universe is my present existence. I can either make sense of it or waste it. Time is running out, and we have but a single chance. If we throw

away that life, we will have lost all there is. This insight will give
woman the constant courage, decisiveness, and inner sense of power
and determination to manage the problem of the meaning of life in
its guise as her conflict of roles.

Existentialism does not decide for the individual. Existentialism
does not decide which role is best for women. A scientifically oriented
philosophy of man can only outline human nature; it cannot choose
for the individual.

Whereas the scientific view of man is deterministic—man is the
product of environmental and hereditary factors, that is, of social,
psychological, physiological, radioactive, and chemical determinants—
the existentialist theory of man, in diametric opposition, emphasizes the
central, absolute, and unqualified character of man's free will. The
existentialist methodological technique establishes convincingly that
the experience of free will is at the core of our sense of humanity.
Consequently, the analysis of all human problems, including that of the
potential of women, must take as its point of departure the miracle and
the power of free will. Because of the reality and the completeness of
man's freedom, the quality of his life is his sole and total responsibility.

For example, a key to the happiness of any woman is her free
decision that she shall face and accept full responsibility for all that
befalls her. As a mother, she must see herself as totally responsible for
the persons her children become. There are, of course, circumstances
external to her—such as the quality of the father, the schools, relatives,
friends, neighbors, income, health, and the national economic and the
international political situations—which shape her children's destiny.
But she possesses the dreadful, the powerful, and the absolute freedom
either to accept these external circumstances fatalistically and do
nothing about them but feel self-pity, or to rebel against them, shape
their own ends, and do her constant best to neutralize and counteract
illness, insanity, poverty, alcoholism, or war. Every minute of every
day she has to decide which kind of mother she is to be. In the face
of adversity—large or small, earthquakes or broken dishes, miscarriages
or runny noses—she is forced to choose freely between the two alternatives of cowardice and heroism. She must respond either with the
words "I cannot help it! I give up!" or with "I am absolutely determined
to do the very best for my children. I shall never be discouraged or give

up!" In sum, a woman is what she chooses herself to be. She may choose to allow circumstances to mold her, or she may choose to counteract these nefarious and insidious encroachments. But she cannot escape the onus of choosing.

Another aspect of man's freedom is that all his conscious acts are in reality choices. He cannot live without being forced to choose freely among fixed alternatives. He may choose to consider rationally all the alternatives that are open, or he may choose to act upon blind impulse. Each choice has indefeasible consequences which he has thereby also chosen. These consequences are like our children: we are responsible for them, even though with the years they acquire an independent life. Let us assume a woman is desperate because she can no longer stand the mother-in-law who lives with her. Her children and her marriage are on the brink of disaster. Whatever this woman does about her problem is a free choice among fixed alternatives. She can decide to feel sorry for herself; that is, she can splenetically decide to preserve the *status quo,* blame others, and thereby freely choose to invite the dismal consequences. Or she can choose to daydream with the help of *True Confessions* and *Modern Romances.* On the other hand, she may choose to exist in complete subservience to her mother-in-law. She has then chosen the consequences of being a bad example to her children, a bad wife to her husband, and an unfulfilled individual to herself. Finally, she has the option of deciding freely to examine the situation objectively and manipulate her feelings and her environment (with or without professional help) with primary regard for her children and her marriage. In general and in sum, whether she is to be a vulpine virago or a vestal virgin, a hapless harridan or a hallowed hermit, whether she is to be sanguine or saturnine in her disposition, these are matters for her own and her lonely decision.

In sum, our woman must realize the following things: First, she is not free to avoid a choice. Second, the alternatives open are fixed. Third, her choice among these alternatives is also a choice of consequences. Fourth, her choice among the alternatives is a choice of the meaning of life for her and her family; it is a matter of ultimate concern and of human fulfillment. Fifth, her choice among alternatives is totally free. She creates a decision as God created the world, that is, *ex nihilo.* Sixth, whether she succeeds or fails in life is exclusively her own responsibility, for in every case she could have chosen otherwise. As a result of these insights about the structure of her free will, she more likely than not will render an intelligent, mature, and courageous decision in her present as well as all future dilemmas.

Whereas the spirit of the implicitly prevailing scientific theory of man demands pure and uncompromising objectivity, existentialism holds that such a requirement is chimerical and consequently harmful. Science requires that man detach his inwardness from any theoretical and cognitive appraisals of the world; his investigations must be dispassionate. Consequently, the presumed correct scientific analysis of man must be altogether bereft of ego involvement and value judgments.

In response to this pervasive attitude, the existentialist position is simply that the demand for objectivity is physically and intellectually impossible; in fact, it is even logically contradictory. And since the existentialist is an unqualified realist, he does not deceive himself with hypocritical hopes. All experiences, observations, knowledge, and evaluations are first-person experiences, observations, knowledge, and evaluations. Even the putatively most objective stance is subjectively thought, subjectively constructed, and subjectively accepted. Man is the center of his universe, and man is the center of his values. Man creates the conception of his universe, and man creates his ultimate values. But lest you think of existentialism as arrant egocentric megalomania, let me explain the inevitability and the grandeur of subjectivity with an illustration.

The staggering picture of the universe drawn for us by contemporary physics and astronomy—with hundreds of millions of galaxies visible through telescopes that scan the heavens with a radius of 2 billion light years (and beyond, with radiotelescopes) and man but a momentary retardation in the reflection of the sun's radiation—certainly does not place us at the center of Being. But now consider these questions: Who created the image of the expanding universe? Who created the concepts of "billions" and of "light years"? And who accepts as true the view that man is insignificant? Man himself, of course. Moreover, that picture of the vast cosmos is based on subjective sensations (i.e., imprints on photographic plates, motions of stellar bodies, etc.), on subjective thoughts (i.e., theories, hypotheses, predictions, and mathematical operations), and it is, in the last analysis, a subjectively held mental image and a subjectively accepted view of man's place in the universe. It is I who hold within my mind the image of the vast expanse of space with man in it as an imperceptible speck. I must envision the universe *sub specie aeternitatis* (from the aspect of eternity), in order to see myself as insignificant. Man must play God so that he may see himself as dust. Whether he likes it or not, man is the cognitive center of his universe.

The same egocentric predicament obtains in the realm of values. In Kierkegaard's famous example, Abraham was told by Almighty God to slit the throat of his only son, Isaac. We think, "Poor Abraham—he has to choose between disobeying the Lord or destroying his beloved son." Such fate is bad enough. But the real facts are far worse. For one, Abraham has to decide whether the stentorian voice he heard was God or an auditory hallucination. In the second place, Abraham's decision is the predicament of us all. He could have asked the voice, "Are you God or a hallucination?" To which the voice would have obligingly replied, "I am God!" Abraham's real choice is between two dreadful risks: If he kills his son and the voice was a hallucination, he will have perpetrated an insane murder on his own child. If he saves his son and the voice was that of God, he will have blasphemed the sustainer of all Being and irreparably defiled himself and his son. This unfair decision is his, is free, is lonely, is made in a total vacuum; yet a decision must be made. It is in this burdensome and unjust manner that we create our world of values. This inescapable abyss is the structure of human subjectivity.

Our first response to "I am Who am," to this I-am experience, is deep-seated anxiety; it is despair bordering on suicide. But our second response is a profound sense of security and hope. We are the center of our universe, we possess certain genuinely creative and divine attributes, and there is a magnificence and nobility about them undreamed of and unparalleled in our ordinary and common-sense consciousness. We may have the burden of creating our universe—but what a marvelous burden it is to be able to create ourselves and our world! The individual who retains this insight about his nature is never tempted to be a traitor to himself; he will not escape into the self-deception of objectivity.

Think of a nubile girl interested in relations with a young man. Her conflict is how much initiative she is allowed without violating her feminine role and thereby making a fool of herself. She has been raised to believe that woman's role is passive, and her man refuses to take the lead. It follows that, if she is not aggressive, she will have no relationship. She now asks herself, "What is the right thing to do?"

With that question she really asks what kind of person she is to be and what meaning her life is to have. Is she to be the kind of person who takes chances and wants Bacchanalian excitement, or is she to seek security and be a jejune conservative? What kind of a future does she demand? How will she feel about the man's response, if unfavorable? In fact, how much importance is she to attach to the man's or to anyone else's response? How much heed is she to pay to her natural timidity? What does she want out of life?

The answers to these questions are not discoveries but decisions. She wants advice, but there is no one to ask. Her condition is that of Abraham: from the depth of her being and out of a total vacuum she must choose and define the person she is to be. Her most difficult question is the one question she must answer alone. Her unaided inwardness must create her ultimate values. To seek advice is to escape into a spurious objectivity. After all, she decides whom to consult—her parents, friends, counselor, minister, teacher, or God—and she decides whose advice to take. She decides if there is a God or not. There is no objective refuge. She cannot escape the lonely, anxious, and helpless burden of her subjectivity: she is the center of her world of values; she is the divine creator of her person and her life. She has no precedent, no truth, and no second chance; yet, all existence looks to her for a decision.

Once she understands and accepts the nature of her irrefragable subjectivity, she is suddenly relieved to discover a soaring, wraithlike, lissome sense of freedom. She sees that there really are no genuine obstacles whatever to her commitments. No universal law will crush her; no destiny will damn her. No one can force her. Her universe of values is precisely what she has created it to be. This is indeed the dream house for the architect of life. She now is an authentic person. As a consequence, she makes her decision intelligently, confidently, in good conscience, with no crippling sense of guilt, impotence, or regrets. The sense of subjectivity makes her a secure, solid, dignified, decisive, and happy person.

Let us now apply the existentialist analysis of man specifically to the problem of feminine roles. As our cue we take the functions of the goddesses titling the forthcoming panel. Hera is the Greek Olympian goddess of women and marriage, Ceres is the Roman goddess of the growing vegetation, and Aphrodite, the Greek goddess of love and beauty.

First, woman as Hera and Ceres functions in the noble role of homemaking, in which case her dedication is to the production of a superlative family. She thereby assumes responsibility for the physical and spiritual creation of successful children, the establishment of a happy home atmosphere, and the development of a satisfied husband. In this role, her goals are homemaking, marriage, companionship, security, husband, children, and the satisfying knowledge that she is fulfilling the traditional female role.

Second, woman can function in the role of a "creator" outside the home. She can have ambitions, seek out éclat, and dedicate herself to a profession, identify herself with a cause, or commit herself to the fulfillment of her artistic inclinations. In this role she may fear that she preempts the function of the male, and it is this role, above all others, that the twentieth century has opened up for her. Stretching the function of the goddess (who, after all, was invented at a time when this particular function was not a legitimate alternative for women), we might say this is the role of Ceres. Her creativity in this area is self-made rather than biological, physiological, or customary. She seeks worldly excitement; she searches after stature, status, recognition, independence, and aesthetic satisfactions. She is ambitious; she wants strength, influence, and money.

Her third possible cluster of roles is that of Aphrodite. She wants sexual gratification; she wants romantic first love; she wants physical beauty and the cynosure, the power, and the glory that attend it. She desires the supreme physical and spiritual experiences of which her feminine nature is capable. Again, in this area, the twentieth century has immensely increased her possibilities. Sexual mores—both real and vicarious (that is, in literature, theater, and films)—are more permissive than they were in the nineteenth-century Victorian world. Also, women's capacity for sexual enjoyment has been explored and emphasized by the medical professions in the twentieth century.

We can now state the nature of her problem in general terms. There are two clusters of problems: they are the conflicts that arise among these roles and the problem of achieving fulfillment in any chosen one.

The conflicts are obvious and notorious. Success in the role of marriage and family creation is not always compatible with genuine achievements in her role as an ambitious professional woman. Also, and importantly, the ardors and exultations of romantic love—whose paeans poets have sung and whose details novelists have exploited—are incompatible with the arduous, inexorable, and irreversible mundane, quotidian, monotonous strictures of childbearing and homemaking. As Aphrodite, woman must have a god for her man; as Hera, she recognizes that her man is human. To her, man's divinity appears in love and man's humanity in marriage.

Consequently, woman's first problem with respect to her roles is how to manage the conflicts engendered by her new freedom and by her new knowledge about her unexplored possibilities. But her second problem exists above and beyond the conflict of roles. It is the problem of reaching fulfillment in any one of these roles. Even if she finds it possible to choose a role, she still remains with the problem of how she can genuinely and successfully fulfill herself in it. In order to find meaning in life, it is not enough merely to choose a role. A woman may succeed easily in the choice of a role and yet fail catastrophically to fulfill herself in the performance of that role.

In sum, what program does existentialism offer for the resolution of these problems? Many suggestions have already been mentioned; other must still be stated.

1. Existentialism demands a new approach to research. A fuller examination and more careful description of the fringe data associated with the problem of feminine roles are required. In addition, existentialist categories—such as time, death, free will, subjectivity, and others which we have not discussed—should be used to experiment with, to explain, relate, and scientifically systematize these fringe data. These descriptions must disclose the structure of three sets of facts: (a) They must explore the exact inner experience of a particular role. What, precisely,

does a woman "feel," "experience," and "seek" when she is concerned over a role? (b) The descriptions must disclose the inner characteristics of the experience of conflict itself. Are these conflicts such that compromises are possible? Can a woman renounce truthfully and forever her aspirations for any one of these roles, such as motherhood, sexual gratification, or worldly admiration? Finally, (c) research must investigate, above all, the exact nature of the experience of authentic fulfillment. Is there such a thing as terminal fulfillment, ultimate satisfaction, and complete happiness? Does she really want such ultimate fulfillment? What is the nature of this ultimate goal of human existence?

The existentialist analysis of these states of consciousness differs fundamentally from traditional scientific approaches. Illustrations 23 to 26 are descriptions and generalizations of different facets of the experience of love. They suggest the differing approaches of the various sciences of man. Physiological descriptions consist of precise data and invoke chemical and physical laws (illustration 23), whereas psychological and sociological descriptions consist of quasi-precise data and utilize behavioristic, clinical and social facts (illustrations 24 and 25). On the other hand, existentialist descriptions and generalizations are sensitive and completely uninterpreted analyses of introspective data (illustration 26). These consist exclusively of the scientifically justified use of fringe data. The theoretical principles implicit here are among the most revolutionary philosophical developments of the twentieth century. Unfortunately, no further elaboration is possible at this time. Following are the illustrations:

23. (Precise Fact—Physiology) "Excitation and anesthesia [on the level of the cells] are to be explained on the basis of colloid chemical changes. . . . Response to stimulation appears to be due primarily to the release of calcium into the cell interior where it causes a clotting reaction to occur."[2]

24. (Quasi-precise Fact—Psychology) "The long abstinence from sexuality to which they [women] are forced and the lingering of their sensuality in phantasy have . . . another important consequence. It is often not possible for them later on to undo the connections thus formed in their minds between sensual activities and something for-

[2] L. V. Heilbrunn, *An Outline of General Physiology*, Philadelphia: W. B. Saunders Company, 1952, 3d ed..; pp. 604 and 609.

bidden, and they turn out to be psychically impotent, i.e. frigid, when at last such activities do become permissible."[3]

25. (Quasi-precise Fact—Sociology) "From the first meeting of the two prospective lovers, through gradual infatuation and the growth of associated interests and affections, we can follow a developing and increasingly richer system of emotions in which continuity and consistency are the condition of a happy and harmonious relationship. Into this complex attitude there enter, besides innate responses, social elements, such as moral rules, economic expectations and spiritual interests."[4]

Finally, the following translation from Sartre's *Being and Nothingness* illustrates an existentialist description of the inner fringe datum of love. The description must be seen in the light of several Sartrean categories. According to him, consciousness is best described as nothingness, whereas all the objects of consciousness exhaust what is called the realm of being. Furthermore, it is the general tendency of consciousness to appropriate beings (such as in the processes of knowing, of acquiring possessions and wealth, status, friends, as well as in the sexual act itself) while at the same time insisting on its separation and independence from the objects of desire. Following is the quotation:

26. (Fringe Fact—Existentialism) "This impossible synthesis of assimilation and an assimilated which maintains its integrity, has deeproot connections with basic sexual drives. The idea of 'carnal possession' offers us the irritating but seductive figure of a body perpetually possessed and perpetually new, on which possession leaves no trace. This is deeply symbolized in the quality of 'smooth' and 'polished.' What is smooth can be taken and felt but remains no less impenetrable, does not give way in the least beneath the appropriative caress—it is like water. This is the reason why erotic descriptions insist on the smooth whiteness of a woman's body. Smooth—it is what reforms itself under the caress, as water reforms itself in its passage over the stone which has pierced it. At the same time, as we have seen earlier, the lover's dream is to identify the beloved object with himself and still preserve

[3] Sigmund Freud, "The Most Prevalent Form of Degradation in Erotic Life," in *Collected Papers,* Vol. IV, London: The Hogarth Press, Ltd., and New York: Basic Books. Quoted in A. M. Krich (ed.), *The Anatomy of Love,* New York: Dell Publishing Co., Inc., 1960; p. 159.

[4] Bronislaw Malinowski, *Sex and Repression in Savage Society,* New York: Humanities Press, Inc. Quoted in *ibid.,* pp. 21–22.

for it its own individuality; let the other become me without ceasing to be the other."[5]

In this connection, it is interesting to examine, in terms of the existentialist approach, a psychological problem such as that of sexual incompatibility in marriage. Ogden Nash has said of it, "I believe a little incompatibility is the spice of life, particularly if he has income and she is pattable." The examination of this problem involves complete, sensitive, and honest descriptions of the positive and negative factors in sexual desires and sexual fears, and the further introspective analysis of their relation to our ultimate concerns. In addition, sexual incompatibility must be examined in the dimension of death, free will, and subjectivity, as well as in terms of numerous other categories not mentioned here. Of course, the details, albeit tantalizing, cannot be worked out at this time. Although it may not be apparent on the surface, the approach suggested here has all the essential characteristics of the scientific method. It follows that the problem of incompatibility is on its way to a solution if each individual fully understands—in the sense of existential understanding indicated here—his own desires, fears, and experiences, as well as those of his sexual partner.

The research outlined in point 1 above leads to the following additional and subsequent specific summary proposals regarding the conflict and the fulfillment of feminine roles.

2. Her solution to the problem of feminine roles must be primarily personal, rather than public and sociological. She must solve the issue as her own inner dilemma rather than as a matter for social criticism and social action.

3. Socrates said that virtue is knowledge. This is to say, if she understands the inner constellation of her problem as well as the nature of her humanity and her femininity, she will thereby have acquired the will to act in her own eventual best interest. Since the most any philosophical or psychological position can offer is insight, the motivation for action remains the natural corollary of right knowledge.

4. She must scrutinize all the experienced inner and outer aspects

[5] Quoted and translated by Ceasar R. Castillo, M.D., in "A Parallel between Ontological and Neurophysiological Concepts," *Journal of Existential Psychiatry,* 1 (Spring, 1960); pp. 103–104.

of her problem through the use of the existentialist method. Not only must she understand the generalized aspects of the problem of feminine roles, but she must apply those insights to her own unique frustrations and aspirations. She must be intelligent, and be prepared for pain, hard work—and hope.

5. The fact of death confronts her sharply with the immediacy and urgency of a solution. Since the problem of roles is her symbolization of the problem of the meaning of life, it is the most serious of all her problems, demanding an uncompromising, immediate, and absolutely true solution. Only death can marshal the vitality, the vigor, and the persistence she needs to manage the problem of her human fulfillment.

6. The fact of her free will shows that the solution to the problem of feminine roles is exclusively her own responsibility. To blame others for the problem is to run counter to the facts of human experience; it is to run away from the problem, having made the decision not to solve it. She freely chooses whether to solve her problem or whether to ignore it, and if she chooses to solve it, she also freely chooses the methods. She freely chooses whether her approach shall be rational or emotional, thoughtful or impulsive, liberal or conservative, temporary or continuous, effective or ineffectual. How she approaches her problem, how seriously she takes it, how much effort she expends on it, how determined she is in carrying out her decision, these choices are exclusively hers to make, and on the freely chosen quality of these choices depend the success and happiness of her life.

7. The fact of subjectivity makes clear that she can get no ultimate help from any comforting absolute objectivity, and she must therefore rely exclusively in all last issues on her own inscrutable and hieratic inwardness. As a consequence, she will not postpone decisions, neither will she fear them or feel guilty and unsure about them, but she will be proud and magnificent in the creation of her own life-world.

Let us consider the deliberately undramatic illustration of a reasonably happy woman in her early thirties, with two children, a reasonably good husband, reasonable financial security, and average good health. Suddenly, she is aware that a pallor of meaninglessness covers her life like a sheet. Although she is reasonably happy in her role of homemaker, she occasionally discovers deep longings for an exciting romantic adventure, while at other times she feels cheated, heinously betrayed, because she is unable to express her bohemian and artistic urges. These longings become clearest whenever she realizes that she lives only once.

Her alternatives are either to deal with her problem or to repress it. If she chooses the former, she must once more decide how profoundly or superficially she is to handle her problem. Above all, it is she and no one else who is in charge of the problem. As long as she lives she deals with it, whether she wants to or not. It is a law of her nature that by living she chooses the quality of her life, just as it is a law of nature that her heart is beating. Furthermore, she has numerous significant alternatives. She must decide whether or not she is to keep these alternatives honestly before her mind, or whether she is to consider some and repress others. The alternatives among which she is forced to choose are many. She may choose a single role from among those available to the female sex, and make her Carthaginian peace with the excluded roles. On the other hand, she may choose one of an enormous supply of compromises. Each choice in this concatenation creates her personality and defines her humanity, just as God created the universe and defined its values. Once she understands with the fullness of her feminine being that she is condemned to be free, she will not and cannot hesitate to know and to make the right decisions.

She cannot abrogate the necessity for choice; she cannot escape from freedom. Since it is a law of woman's nature that she inevitably and constantly chooses one role freely and also chooses freely the degree of her participation in that role, she is thereby granted the divine capacity to solve her problems. That capacity is found in the vitality of death, in the power of free will, and in the security of subjectivity.

But I am a man, not a woman. On the existentialist principles of scientific introspection enunciated here, only a woman has the right to talk about women. Man's ultimate knowledge of woman was well expressed by the poet, when he wrote,

> A Woman is a foreign land,
> Of which, though there he settle young,
> A man will ne'er quite understand
> The customs, politics, and tongue.
>
> (Coventry Patmore)

HERA, CERES, AND APHRODITE:
THE MULTIPLICITY OF ROLES

> *This is an actual transcription of the formal but spontaneous panel discussion of the papers immediately preceding. Only minor editing has been done where continuity and clarity required it. The editors feel that the spontaneity of the actual discussion gives a particular value to the panel in this form, since it amplifies questions arising from the formal presentations of the participants as well as answering questions from the audience.*

Moderator: Klaus W. Berblinger
Panel Members: Ethel M. Albert, Peter Koestenbaum, Marya Mannes

Dr. Berblinger The papers of this session have given rise to an enormous number of written questions which I have in front of me. Since there will be further opportunities to discuss among ourselves, I am going to act rather as the mouthpiece of these questions than as a moderator of a panel discussion. First to Dr. Koestenbaum, who in his paper spoke about the subjectivity of the existentialist approach and how this correlates with empathy: "How can a man on this basis understand or fear for, with, or perhaps against a woman?"

Dr. Koestenbaum Using the illustration of the narrow band of visible radiation as compared to the total amount of radiation that exists, the data on which we ordinarily base our concept of man and the world are only a few selected data which lend themselves to particular kinds of manipulation, such as mathematical formulation. There is nothing wrong with these data but there are many more. There are the fringe data which poets have elucidated and pointed to which cannot be expressed in clear, concise, mathematical language, and the behavioral sciences have tended to ignore these. These fringe data are not substitutes for precise data, but it is my contention that in the behavioral sciences a tremendous revolution could be effected if the fringe data, the vague experiences of anxiety, frustration, and of love that are so important in the liberal arts would be expanded and used as a scientific basis for a theory of man.

This does not have much to do with empathy; this would be in mostly introspective exploration. But it applies to the problems that women face uniquely and which have to be investigated from the inside, as was very well illustrated by Miss Mannes.

Dr. Berblinger   Miss Mannes has been asked, "Why didn't you go to college? Would you now if you were eighteen?"

Miss Mannes   I didn't go to college, I think, for two reasons: one was that I had been cooped up in school with girls for ten years and could not contemplate another four with women; the other was that I had spent most of those ten years with books, reading like a maniac and studying very hard, and I thought it was time I started to live with a capital L. Also I had been left a very small sum of money, enough to send me abroad for a year alone, and I thought that was what I wanted to do.

I think I would go to college if I were eighteen now. I feel great gaps in my knowledge, and with things as they are today, where you are not even let into the door without a degree, that I would need one—I would go.

Dr. Berblinger   Dr. Albert is asked, "In which societies in Africa does the matriarchal society still exist?"

Dr. Albert   Technically, societies are not matriarchal but rather matrilineal, that is, those in which women own property and in which the children belong to the women. In much of West Africa, there is still predominantly the matrilineal society, in which families are based on the mother and children inherit from her. There are many other parts of the world in which this phenomenon is still to be found, including a good many American Indian reservations.

Dr. Berblinger   Another question reads, "In view of Dr. Koestenbaum's theory of free choice and Dr. Albert's women who succeed to domination in a patriarchal society, how do you explain the fact that there are extremely few creative women? Could it be just they do not have the necessary equipment?"

Dr. Koestenbaum The views that I tried to present are no attempt to explain any sociological fact. Nothing in what I have said would tend to explain why women have achieved less in a man's world, if that is true. It is simply a fact that man is free.

Dr. Berblinger Dr. Albert has a question: "Please comment on the either-or phenomenon in the usual discussion of male and female differences. Is it not true that we men and women have some things in common just because we are human and that we have individual differences which are simultaneous, not either-or?"

Dr. Albert One of the ways we can approach that kind of question is indeed through anthropology, and it is peculiar to several cultures, our own primarily, to think precisely in either-or terms and to seek the essential characteristics; ignoring the rest. If we have anything to learn from comparative studies it will be above all, that we deprive ourselves of the truth if we look only at bits and pieces. The either-or approach is characteristic not only for distinguishing males from females but is seen in virtually every relation of problems. We see things in black and white, good or bad; if things don't come out in pairs, we don't know what to do with them. In Africa, things don't always come in pairs; they can be very mismated, like men and women.

The problem is largely one of long-established habit of thought which has to be broadened and made more sophisticated, so that instead of thinking in either-or, we think in terms of this and that. In other words, we must acquire a pluralistic way of thinking.

Dr. Berblinger Miss Mannes has a whole stack of questions, two of which say very much the same thing: "Can a creative woman be happy in a compromise situation with a family and its ties?" And: "You point out what a creative woman gives to one area of endeavor, she must take away from another. This requires decision making and acceptance of consequences for one's choice. Please comment on the aspect of accepting the responsibility for one's decision."

Miss Mannes I firmly believe whatever decision one makes, one pays for. Therefore there is such a thing as complete acceptance of choice but no such thing as finite and complete fulfillment. We make a mistake in thinking, "Will I be happy if I do this or that?" We cannot be entirely happy all the time, and conflict, in a creative woman, often makes for pain and difficulty along with its joys. We must accept a degree of unhappiness, which I think is the natural condition of man.

Dr. Berblinger "Granted a certain equality of the sexes, where equal opportunity and status are present, is it a false assumption that the majority of outstanding prodigies (especially in childhood) have been male?" And as examples are given Mozart, Leonardo da Vinci, Schubert. "Come the revolution, may we anticipate this rare phenomenon in women?"

Mozart had a sister.

Miss Mannes I wouldn't be surprised if, in time, there will be more first-rate creative people among women. There has been a very long conditioning. This kind of woman is a minority and has suffered, as the Negroes have, for centuries from a kind of second-class situation. If this ultimate partnership of male and female with the woman being a complete human being is allowed to exist over a period of time, we will find more women of great talent and productivity.

Dr. Berblinger This question is addressed to Dr. Koestenbaum, and it is about free choices, which I felt was going to give us food for thought.

"If a woman has a free will and a free choice, why doesn't she always choose the right way?"

It reminds one subtly of how major responsibilities in a household might be resolved: Husband and wife finally decided on an ideal way, so that they never had any conflicts. She said, "All the minor decisions I will take over, such as where the children go to college, etc. Now the real major decisions are left to you, such as whether we recognize Red China."

Here is a question of free choice: for that matter, does she know the right way, and if not, what determines her choice?

Dr. Koestenbaum There are no right and wrong choices, there are just plain choices. She has decided, she has freely chosen. There are wrong choices and right choices, and she has freely chosen to make the wrong choice. But this brings up the whole question of determinants operating on free will.

People say, "You know, there is no such thing as free will." This merely proves the existentialists are right in their sense of contemporary society, which has chosen to escape behind the unconscious, behind the deterministic conception of man. It is a free choice of having decided not to assume responsibility; it works for a while, but it is not a permanent nostrum. The first thing to recognize in the existentialist position is that it is a call to arms to assume responsibility for our destiny. This is the general flavor of the existentialist position: go ahead and take charge of your own life. But the existentialists point out that you are doing it anyway; if you don't take charge of your life, you are the kind of person who has decided not to do so, which makes you into a particular kind of person which you might or might not want to be.

There is such a thing as the experience of free will, the experience of making a spontaneous decision. Many of you probably watched President Kennedy when he gave his address on the Cuban situation in which he said there would be a quarantine around Cuba. Now I should think that he may have had some butterflies in his stomach while he made the speech, because it was a momentous major decision. Up to the very end he could have said, "Well, I changed my mind, and I am not going to read this particular speech." It was in the actual process of reading it that he must have had the attitude of saying, "Well, the die is cast, I am forgetting all the reasoning that went behind it. I am just taking a leap; I am taking a chance."

This experience which is, of course, magnified when the decision is momentous is nonetheless present in all decisions, even which shoe you put on first in the morning. Now this decision, this experience of spontaneity, of self-determination, of having to make a choice, is a fundamental fact of human experience. All theories and conceptions of man, to the contrary notwithstanding, must begin with that. Then we read, develop, dream about truths on several theories of man, including such things as unconsciously repressed determinants and similar things. These are our own theories about ourselves; there have been different theories which may or may not be correct.

I am not at all saying every man can do anything he wants. In a repressed state there are many strictures, but there are always some alternatives. To put it in the crassest possible way, there is always the alternative of either committing suicide or continuing living; it is an alternative, however narrow, and a free choice is always made.

Even if man is not able to do anything he wants to under any circumstance, he has this little core of free will on which he can build and expand.

Dr. Berblinger   I feel somewhat encouraged by Dr. Koestenbaum's definition of the so-called free choice, or the choice. It reminds me a little bit of our field, where, in the psychogenesis of schizophrenia, it is often said that if the mother is rather cold and seemingly rejecting, then she withholds friendly feelings from the child. But if she is overly warm, then she is actually making up for feelings of rejection, so she can't do right either way.

Miss Mannes is asked, "I have the impression that many professional women feel insecure and perhaps therefore have a need to constantly and obtrusively demonstrate what are thought of as masculine attributes. Is this true; if so, why is it so?"

Miss Mannes   I think this is true, but less true now than in a slightly older generation where resistance and hostility to the so-called career woman caused them to feel they had to battle hard in order to get a hearing and be recognized. Therefore, they put on a kind of a casing and an armor of aggressiveness which never did any good. As this hostility and criticism is reduced, more women will be more themselves.

This brings up the problem of how parents recognize a creative girl when the forces of her colleagues about her tend to subdue her creativity in the cover of conformity. You recognize real creativity in a girl when she shows a marked and consistent desire to pursue a special work. Many girls are talented and think they want to act, write poetry, or paint. This is a sort of spiritual adolescence which is very healthy but does not mean that they should become actors, writers, or painters. The wise parent can recognize something worth fostering when it lasts over a period of time and when the girl herself sacrifices a certain amount of her dating or popularity in order to pursue her chosen ambition.

Dr. Berblinger   So many questions tend to converge into "Why don't women do better, and why do men not allow women to do what they could do so much better than men?" For instance, we have here one about the admission to medical schools, and we find out that there is really no *numerus clausus* but that medical schools apparently don't advertise sufficiently that women can be admitted, too. Another refers to a prominent female physiologist, and so on, but here is one which is perhaps of the most general nature for the panel: "Nothing has been mentioned of great women, of Mary the Mother of Christ, of Florence Nightingale. Perhaps men were too proud to mention the works of others."

Dr. Koestenbaum The premise and implication in so many of the questions you have read is that there is something particularly desirable about notoriety and fame, but we must go back further and decide just what is the purpose of human existence. We cannot assume that it is good to be famous, remembered, and read about by people in schools. We have to make a fundamental decision as to what it is that is worth living for before any such questions can be brought forth.

Dr. Berblinger The problem of what is greatness and creativity would have to come up, and whether this is sex specific. I was encouraged in the previous panel to learn that genetics is no longer an immutable science and that even our genetic environment before birth can be influenced; and I was somewhat frightened by this.

Miss Mannes Florence Nightingale obviously was a creative woman; in my sense of the word, creativity need not be confined to the cultural field. Anybody that gives to humanity in a major way, who has an impact on the thinking or feeling of other people in a constructive way, is creative. This includes a great many people and a number of women, but still very much fewer than men. There is no question about this fact. I do not know the answer.

Dr. Berblinger Some of the questions can be summarized. They seem to ask for some practical advice, as well as about the timing, in regard to how either the counterrevolution is to be stalled or furthered. On the other side of the fence, I have been cheered throughout your speeches not to have men being discriminated against as the detractor for creativity for women. This is a social and sociological function, but I would be interested to know how you explain what you consider the counterrevolution.

Miss Mannes The counterrevolution is making women really stay home and consume. This is the great thing you see in the mass media where the woman is always in the domestic role. This goes for television, for fiction in mass magazines, and for popular novels where there has been a shrinking away from, rather than a going toward, the singularity and independence of the female.

Dr. Berblinger Could it have to do also with our overemphasis on youth? You will rarely see a middle-aged woman in any advertisement. You see a little girl with a Coca Cola bottle and, later on, a grandmother describing "How we retired to Florida on $100 a month," but in between there is no woman. A man may at least appear as a "Man of Distinction" on an advertising poster. Perhaps our general emphasis on youth and on physical health and vigor might have something to do with interrupting the process of creativity.

Dr. Albert I think that the problem may cut a little bit deeper. Many of the people I know who started out as ambitious as I to achieve some kind of professional status fell by the wayside when they got married and had children. In any case I continued to speak to them, and it becomes very much a practical problem when the subject is approached with good will, one which has been called attention to in the past in other contexts. A woman who has a home and children to look after must, if she wishes also to have a career, split her time up. On a simple time and energy basis, there is no way to feed a two-year-old and get hubby's dinner and do whatever else she wants to get done. The female Ph.D.s I know who combine careers at home and at the university are just single individuals and don't have the energy or time to be in two places at once. Nobody has worked out a fully satisfactory solution. The best I know of is the increasing number of part-time jobs for women who have professional training, which is better than nothing. Also there is a remarkable trend of going back to school after the children are old enough to take care of themselves. Now this isn't bad. At the same time, there are women of real distinction and ability who are not able to achieve what their potential will allow them, because they have, in effect, made a sacrifice for building a population that is already oversized.

Dr. Koestenbaum I have a question here which seems to broach a new topic: "With regard to terminal fulfillment, should we not accept what is often called divine discontent? A feeling of fulfillment or content may indicate stagnation."

What are we after? Is it notoriety or not? We are after happiness, and a happy person is not necessarily a person who is or is not in the limelight.

In my paper I spoke only about the strictures in a sense, and some of the possibilities that exist in man, and the question of death and the problem of man's finality. I said nothing about some of the positive contents for material suggestions that can be made, and since the notion of divine discontent has been brought up, I think religion is one of the central problems. I do not wish to rule out the religious solutions; I think some of them are among the most profound solutions of the human equation. But man first has to make the decision as to whether that is the direction he wants to go in and if that is the chance he is going to take.

Dr. Berblinger   It is important at this moment to stress that none of you imply that any role which you assume as a woman, be it creative, as a scientist, a housewife, or a mother, would exclude or not influence any and all partners, that it is not a unilateral role.

Miss Mannes   Everything that anybody does affects not only another person but very often a number of other people and sometimes may have a great general influence. You are not isolated; but there is a great difference between isolation and independence of self, an inner core that remains more or less inviolate while at the same time necessary adjustments to your environment, your partners, and your children take place. We are all referring to this inviolate core of the self, but such a thing as being totally free and totally separate is not possible.

Dr. Berblinger   You made a remark in your paper about the adolescent aspects of the middle years. Will you tell us more of what you referred to in particular?

Miss Mannes   This is all about us. Men go to conventions wearing little hats with fringes falling over them, drinking more than they really want, telling funny stories, talking about their college life, and watching girls come out of pies. The other side with women is an absolutely insane chase after youth. Here is the baby-faced matron who wears all sorts of little hats, clips, and make-ups, and has baby-blond hair at the age of sixty-five or seventy, when really she would look much better again being herself. These are what I call adolescent hangovers.

Dr. Berblinger   One of the first questions asked was: "Are we not to explore in the whole new continent of the mind which was discovered by Freud, whose chances are a composite full of loose screws?"

One contribution which psychoanalytic theory and early Freudian theory certainly did not make was to change the role of woman. In fact, it has been acknowledged that Freud's rather great orthodoxy took the role of woman itself into its concepts of developmental psychology, which concepts were strictly in accord with his morality and sociology, if not in his religion.

Dr. Koestenbaum   I have been asked to comment on Erich Fromm's idea that the source of all human anxieties lies in the separateness and that there are three ways to deal with it: injustice, conformity, and creativity.

I think apropos the phrase that "man's project is God." Considering human activity in general, the purpose and the satisfying experience of human existence seem to be to achieve some kind of identity with as much of the totality as possible. The scholar is a good example. As Nietzsche said, "The scholar conquers the Universe." That is even better than conquering the ancient world as Alexander the Great did, and it is an attempt to identify one's self with an ever-increasing totality which can ultimately be symbolized by the notion of God. This desire of man to go beyond himself, to identify himself with another being, a woman, a society, an art form, or anything else is frustrated in a fundamental sense. It is frustrated by man's finitude: the most dramatic expression of this is the inexorable fact of his death. It becomes a central problem that the questions of the meaning of life and how to achieve fulfillment are in a covert sense the problem of human death. What is to be done about this extraordinary paradox? On the one hand, we want to be like God. We have perhaps created the image of God as the symbol of fulfillment for man, or if there really is a God, we have not really created it, since it is a fulfillment of man. Opposed to this is the crushing realization that we can never achieve it, that we are going to die, and the argument that we are finite. It is in this area that we have to solve issues of guilt and anxiety, and ultimately what is satisfying to human existence.

Dr. Berblinger   I have reserved for Miss Mannes the crowning blow: "Can we possibly overcome the pressures of mass media?"

Miss Mannes   We can only do it if we exercise the muscles of discrimination daily, doing setting-up exercises of rejection or acceptance according to whatever standard of values we have.

We can also support those institutions that are free from commercial pressures, such as the educational television that we are on which broadcasts this program, and all sorts of pure enterprises in which the soul and spirit of man are reasonably free.

PART FOUR

THE CONSEQUENCES
OF EQUALITY

Chairman: Katherine A. Towle

A discussion of the reality of rivalry and its implications in modern American culture opened the
session. The fundamental effects of education in
emphasizing rivalry and its relation to the concept
of careers for women were then considered. The
final paper of this session presented both a historical
and a current view of American culture and a cri-
tique of the real meaning of equality. In the panel
concluding this session the speakers achieved considerable unanimity as to the meaning of equality
and the dangers today of stereotyped equality of an
unreal nature.

Barbara Bates Gunderson

THE IMPLICATION OF RIVALRY

Should any of you have an ordeal of sitting up all night alone in a cheerless small airport in the never-never time after 2 A.M., while the torn newspapers and the peanut shells drift between the hard benches—you will be very, very grateful *if* you have a book along. If you do not (as I did not recently), may I suggest a fascinating way to pass the sleepless and unending stretch of time? Simply start listing and cataloging all the examples of rivalry you can think of in the evolution of woman.

The list—like the debris in the airport waiting room—is endless, the implication of it so fraught with twists, turns, unexpectedness of character, irrational and logical by turns, that you will become amused, angered, startled, hopeful, and depressed, then hopeful again. You will forget your aching back and your fierce temper at certain unreliable common carriers. You will be launched on a wide-screen history of human life and the oft-reiterated promise of "Action! Passion! Conflict! Drama! Love and Hate!" will for once actually be realized.

We fade in on 93,000 B.C. or a few years after. The first rivalry was one that a baby girl could not even know about, though she was certainly involved. She was born, discovered to be a girl, and left quickly in the bush without a backward glance. The chieftains had decreed that the ratio of girls to boys was too high. Had she been permitted to survive, her next bout of rivalry would have been with boy babies who promised more in the life of the tribe and so got better food and much more attention.

Eventually, of course, her big rivalry was to be with the man who mated with her. Her rivals here were the basic necessities of hunting, killing preying beasts, and fighting enemy tribesmen. To do these things required freedom, and primitive man resisted any enslavement by demanding, tiresome woman. He considered it silly of her to bind herself to a dependent infant, and he had no inclination to help her in the tedious life she lived. He liked her well enough on occasion. She was warm, comforting, and able to minister to many of his needs, but it was disappointing to discover all too soon that she had carelessly exposed herself to the full moon on the tenth day after a thunderstorm and now had grown clumsy and dependent with a baby sure to be born before too long.

He knew it angered her to have him withdraw his protection and assistance with provisions just when she was weak from childbearing and forced to carry the infant always at her breast, but that was the way of the world. He had arrows to polish and a charm to make and she had no claim on him. Why did women always get the notion that a man should fix her a cave and find meat enough for two more? In his experience, if you weakened—and some did—there were more and more mouths to feed and less and less time for important matters.

How painful and lopsided such a rivalry must have been for early woman. Think of the fortitude, cunning, and psychology she must have acquired to win, through passing centuries, a custom which gradually froze into law for her own and the child's protection. The linking of her weakness with his strength and the dependence of the child with a continuing cooperation between herself and a man must stand as the most remarkable proof that women, even some ninety thousand years before Christ, were not to be underestimated.

Passing over the rivalry that probably flourished with our primitive heroine Op and the mother of her primitive mate Ug—a rivalry that helped found a matriarchal form of life in many tribes and exists today in mother-in-law jokes, we find our early couple in their split-level cave enacting another aspect of rivalry. They have quarreled. Ug has been unable to provide meat for the family, and Op has been accused of indifferent housekeeping. Besides that, she hasn't chewed the leather for his winter shift as she promised. Their tempers flare, and Ug wins an advantage which rankles deeply. Muttering, "A cooker's place is in the cave," he walks down to the big skin common tent at the end of the clearing from which all women and children are permanently excluded. Op feels the injustice of this ploy of his keenly. The Men Only Tent has always been a source of annoyance to the women of the tribe. "Why can't we be allowed in on rare occasions?" they have asked wheedlingly many times.

The answer is always the same: "Because it is just for men."

"But what do you do in the Men Only Tent?"

"Nothing special. Talk mostly. Fool around and work on our knives and our arrows."

"Well, that's what you do anyway, in the cave or down in the clearing. Why have a special exclusive place for more of the same?"

"We like it."

"But wouldn't you like it if some of the women came down once in a while and fixed fishtails or sang for you?"

"Not in the Men Only Tent."

"What do you require of a candidate for membership?"

"That he be a man."

"Yes, but not all the men belong. Poo and Zun and others don't belong."

"They don't hunt well enough to be in the Men Only Tent."

"But some of the women of the tribe hunt better than many members."

"I don't want to hear another word about it. You cannot come into the Men Only Tent—do you understand?"

And even in that primitive time woman did understand—only too well. It was part of the reason that she became club-minded herself. Keenly feeling this rejection by her man, she set out to rival him by starting the Weaving and Beading Group. It consisted of the same women who met every day anyway to wash utensils and polish weapons. But there was a subtle difference. They put on their best shells to go to Club. They devised rituals which pleased them and which they suspected paralleled those of the Men Only Tent. Eventually some brilliant president of the Beading and Weaving Club conceived a guest night for mates. The men came and found themselves, without intending to, issuing a return invitation to the Men Only Tent. Rivalry had written another chapter in its endless history. The men put on a nice party, but once the women had seen the inside of the tent with the pitiful relics and the garish appointments, some magic had gone out of the whole idea. The men were hurt at this reaction and were more than ever contemptuous of the Beading and Weaving group. There was no second invitation to the Men Only Tent. The division between the two groups grew from that time on. The women believed now that the Men Only Tent was just a smoky, ill-lighted place for men to hide in. The men had deeper feelings of resentment. They hadn't asked to go to the Beading and Weaving meeting. They'd been invited. It had been stiff, unnatural, and full of talk, and it had ended up with the women prying their way in where they weren't wanted and then refusing to see anything remarkable in the tradition and sentiment of the Men Only Tent. "Women don't understand," they told themselves.

Was this rivalry notable only in ancient days? Ladies who would be astronauts think not. Ladies who are bid by a man to come to his club for a luncheon date and cool their heels in the tiny waiting room off the Ladies' Entrance think not. The masculine delight in the late Helen Hokinson's cartoons would seem to indicate that men are still finding vast amusement in clubwomen and women's clubs. And what of the extra flourish of metropolitan hotel opulence—the Men's Bar? It would seem that the plenty of People's Bars would suffice, but the maintenance of exclusive male bars must be profitable. Women's bars, on the other hand, are a most unlikely thing. However much men would favor equality in this aspect of modern living, the idea would have faint appeal to women. It is notable, however, that London's oldest ladies' club, the Alexandria, denied entrance to any male. It is a proud footnote to history in the Alexandria Club annals that the Prince of Wales, afterward King Edward, was once refused entrance on accompanying the Princess who was a member there, and Lord Roberts used to be seen waiting outside for Lady Roberts, presumably with amused impatience.

The Women's Clubs–versus–Men's Clubs rivalry underwent many mutations in our mythical village, just as it does today. Not even the most dedicated member of the Beaders and Weavers was anything but admiring and respectful of all the Men Only Tent meant when her son was being initiated into its solemn rites. "It's a wonderful thing," she would tell proudly. "Ug's father before him was a Tenter—and now our little Icky is going in." And the most disdainful of the Men Only Tenters grew tolerant and frankly admiring when it was his own woman who became Head Fan Weaver of the ladies' club. "I'm very proud," he would tell her. "You women do a lot of good around the village." He might have added that a man whose woman had top post in the Beaders and Weavers was apt to learn village gossip faster and wield more influence in other places than the average. And this, he would affirm, was as it should be.

Today some amusing aspects of this strain of club rivalry, but tacit approval, include the disdain women feel for anything but a male speaker at their club meetings and the shortage of exclusively male golf courses. It is also interesting to note that while men choose to avoid "Ye Tea Shoppe" motifs when dining out, women are captivated by decor, thick with paneling and portraits of impressive males in uniform, deep chairs, and thick carpets in the "Men's Club Manner."

In our primitive community one day comes the inevitable challenge from without. War with a formidable enemy. The men take the first line of defense—protecting the village. Women begin rituals of appeasement to the gods, weapon refurbishing, and extreme measures of domestic self-discipline and economy. But the marauding enemy wins skirmish after skirmish. Soon the old men of the village are taken from their supply posts and put into the fight; then the young boys are sent in. Grudgingly, under the desperate war conditions, the strongest women are allowed to join the men as fighters. They are both a headache to the seasoned officers and a pleasant surprise. They can fight with great ferocity. But they also waste time attempting to help the wounded and are prone to bicker among themselves. A few men, impressed by conspicuous gallantry on the part of some of the women, praise them wholeheartedly. More of the men refuse the whole concept of women as the equal of men in war. When the war is finally over, the women give the big credit for their victory to the men, and the men agree with them. But a few continue to acknowledge to themselves that one or two of the women were prodigious warriors. Here, may have been coined for the first time the lofty accolade which men insist on tendering outstanding women. "She thinks like a man."

At a later date Dean Virginia Gildersleeve in speaking of the WAVES, said, "If the Navy could possibly have used dogs, ducks, or monkeys . . . certain of the elder Admirals would probably have greatly preferred them to women."

For the purposes of unwrapping the fascinating human condition called rivalry and seeing clearly a few of its implications, let us go once again to the tribe of Ug and Op. Let us suppose that a fifteen-year-old woman, Yula, astonished everyone with her bravery, cool-headedness, and physical stamina during the late war. Let us further suppose that her twin brother, Yole, did a conspicuously bad job of fighting. As a soldier he was a dud. His father was at him time and time again to get into the fight. Instead Yole seemed only to cower and to seek safety. Yula, on the other hand, was thrilled when she was finally permitted to get into the fight, and she distinguished herself from the onset. In the exhilaration and danger of battle, Yula knew the deep joy of being one with all the other fighters and tasting their ap-proval. Even after the victory she was the one woman singled out to say a few words about the fight before the big Ceremonial Victory Fire. While Yula blossomed under the approval of her father, his fellows of the council, and the men with whom she had borne arms, Yole grew quieter and more subdued. Unlike the others, he had not liked a bit of the dreadful war, but Yole went to the Men Only Tent where war and gallantry and heroes who had fallen were the sole topic of con-cern, while poor Yula had to wash clothes, gather yams and gourds, braid and weave and bead in the dreary company of her mother and the other women. It was almost as it had always been—but much, much duller. And there was a new quality which hurt and confused her. When, as she sat working with the other women on some communal task, she brought up the subject of her war experience, there was a polite indifference from the others. Her own mother would frequently very firmly introduce an entirely different subject or bid Yula to hush. In the eyes of the other women she saw expressions of contemptuous amusement. They did not see her as a brave warrior or as a gallant heroine. They saw, Yula discovered with grieved astonishment, a kind of pitiable freak—one who was not quite a woman, nor yet half a man. A number of pieces fell into place then. She recalled her mother's penetrating look of challenge when, after the Victory Bon Fire, the young men fighters each chose a girl from the village to walk home with—but she was allowed to depart with her family and no overture of protection from any of the warriors with whom she had shared the battle. She remembered how she had half-teased Yole for his weakness in the war, and her father had not laughed. Instead he had silenced her and pretended to recall some incident in Yole's defense. Indeed, as she thought hard about it, her mother and father had spent most of the time since the end of the war minimizing her glory and her conquests in battle and pretending that Yole had been fearless and heroic.

Stung by the unfairness of everyone in the village, Yula sought her mother out in private. "At the Bon Fire I was as much of a hero as any man in the village," she said, "and now you pay me no more honor. Where is the justice in this?"

The mother looked at her without pity or apology. "What you did was fine while the enemy threatened us all. But now it is peacetime again and you must forget your part in the war."

"But I won't. I can't. Why should I?"

"Hush!" her mother said evenly. "War may come again or it may not. But I will tell you one thing that will surely come—a time when you will either have a man want you for his woman or a time when no man will have you and you will join the outcasts."

"But I won't be an outcast!" Yula said proudly. "Our family is one of the best in all the village. I will surely be chosen. Many of the young men praised me in the battle and commended my strength."

"Yula." Her mother shook her head sadly. "Stop and make yourself think. Tell me this: why do young men of the tribe choose one woman to be their own?"

"So that they will have a warm, clean place and a woman to show off the hides and shells which they get. So that they can have children and tasty food to eat."

"Without choosing one woman, they can have all that. There was a time when no man chose one woman. I have heard the tales of those times, Yula. The men and women could hunt together and fight together until the woman must take care of herself for bearing the child.

Then she was an outcast. Then her life was hard, much harder than your days in the war. You think you were so brave and magnificent during the fighting. But I can tell you that it took much more strength and courage from women before men were led to choose one woman for their own. Daughter, do not give any man the impression that you are as brave as he is—for the time must come when you will be the weaker, and you must look to him for your protection. Do not prove yourself in battle any longer. Start a new conquest. Give your father and me the pleasure of seeing one of Yole's friends seek you out after the next village ceremony."

Rivalry wears a new look now. It is a rivalry with a hundred different sides, and it flourishes today—the rivalry with all the other interests that a man responds to, a rivalry to surpass them all and get him to the altar. After that challenge comes the rivalry of woman against woman for his attention and eventual love. This consuming struggle is followed by the rivalry of wife against wife to have the most successful, or the most contented, or the most generous husband. Chugging along behind this car is one marked rival of mother against mother for the healthiest, smartest, most popular and devoted children. Later cars on the train include the rivalry of at-home woman with go-to-business woman for the prize of being considered most feminine and most worthy of respect; the rivalry with his absorption in business; the rivalry of woman against woman and man, too, to be most youthful-appearing, considered most fun, or most dynamic, or most remarkable grandparent or most mentally alive.

Implicit in all this is that man roams the world of his natural inclinations and woman hunts on a smaller preserve with as much concentration and effort as he brings to his full-size life. If man, in modern society, reserves to himself the glory which comes of uninterrupted years of mounting competence in a job or profession, woman takes to herself the reflection of his glory, and its light is surpassingly important to her. In a society which theoretically stands for equality of the sexes her battle is rarely hinted at, but she is nonetheless engaged in a shadowy struggle all her own. He gets the big account—she manages a sit-down dinner for twenty. He moves ahead in the company—she gets Janey through algebra. He is asked into the better shooting club—

she acquires a chin strap and a rare and expensive, imported facial ointment. "It is," one can almost hear her saying in pride and envy of his accomplishments, "the least I can do." In today's sophisticated arena where raw, red rivalry has been toned down to subtle, soft, marrow-warping rivalry, women feel the necessity to take the hurdles presented in their world each time their husbands take another high one. To have a lovely home, set a fine table, possess well-bred children, look beautiful—these are proper goals for worthy women. They are time-consuming, painful, and oftentimes boring, but there are no taboos on this kind of rivaling.

Why does a wife's waistline tend to go down as a husband's income goes up? It is her way of matching his success—of helping him. Companies study wives carefully. A svelte wife will not only catch the light better, but she will also demonstrate conspicuous consumption of his growing income to more artistic advantage if she is slender.

What our cave-age mama was telling little Yula is still being told today's Yulas on mother's knee, at school, in the periodicals, on TV—it is prevalent in the atmosphere of 1963. "Make sure to get your man early." And today mother may well add, "And after you get him, don't let down for one minute."

Contrast the freedom of our young men, who may choose to wait until they are over thirty to marry, with an American young woman, who, no matter what her abilities or aspirations, fails as a woman if she does not marry early.

We can imagine our cave mother when she is alone with Yole rather encouraging his gentleness, exclaiming over his love of bird feathers and pretty shells. "Your arrow tips are much the most handsome of our tribe," she might tell him approvingly. But we cannot imagine her giving the same comfort and encouragement to the uniquely special quality possessed by his twin sister, Yula.

"It is a fine thing to have a daring nature, Yula. Your resourcefulness and executive skill may have saved this entire tribe. But now that peace has come, you must put aside these special qualities of yours. Our tribe has need of finding new land. We must organize trading parties and see if we can trade our yams for the needed sewing quills which another tribe may have in abundance. We must get the Tribal Chiefs to consider proper use of you." Such a conversation between our ancient mother and daughter? Impossible. And, sad to say, highly unlikely even today.

Does this puzzling quiescence between the older and younger woman of the same sex who are bound together by ties of love and habit have any aspects of rivalry? I believe it does. Yula's mother and her mother and the mother before her and a long line of grandmothers have all been subjected to the male's most lethal and effective secret weapon. Economic sanctions? No. Physician coercion? Certainly not. False doctrine? Not exactly. The weapon that has kept the Yulas of the world from freely seeking and holding their true place in the field of their competence and the weapon that seals the lips of mothers and woman teachers who could help so much is one that men do not even appreciate as a significant weapon. They use it, get results, and don't even fully comprehend that it is the ace of trumps in this lifelong game of rivalry. It is quite simply the weapon of ridicule.

Try to stop women with sticks and stones, and you will have to reassess the "weaker sex" delineation. Women have been uncomplaining prisoners of war in starvation compounds where the bones of the unburied, the sobs of the fever-wracked, and the brutality of guards could break the strongest spirit. Women have slugged it out in the Dakota winter blizzards of the eighties and the summer blizzards of grasshoppers that blackened the skies and stripped every vestige of vegetation from the parched earth. Women were cool and game and reliable in the London bombings, and the tales of army and navy nurses in the last war are a match for Roger Young's gallantry. Use force, and women will not buckle. Use ridicule, and a strange thing happens. It doesn't stop a Pankhurst, a Sanger, a Nation, or a Barton, but it stops her followers. "But darling," said with just the right amount of sophisticated disbelief to the fledgling suffragette, "you aren't going to become one of those drabs in flat heels and horrible bonnet who go about wreaking vengeance on society at large because no man ever took notice of them? You're much too fine, much too attractive for that sort of thing."

The portrait of the American woman as a militant matriarch who exploits the male, strips him of his masculinity, and forces him into the image of Hubert Housebroke is a far cry from reality.

True or not, the ridicule gimmick has been working at this level very well for a long time. Terrified at giving any substance in her own conduct to the charge that the modern American matron is a man-eater, Mrs. America avoids taking even the tiniest nibble (however much it is justified) from the supersensitive male ego which she has been taught since infancy to revere.

A familiar picture of the wife with an insatiable demand for more and more money to spend in a marathon with the lavish Joneses next door grows fuzzy and distorted when we learn that research by a leading advertising firm shows that it's Caspar Milquetoast, not Battleaxe Milquetoast, who decides what kind of car to buy and, moreover, consistently chooses a higher-priced one than that favored by her.[1]

Whether the reasons lie with entrenched tradition or overburdened and unimaginative gag writers, it is a fact of life that women bear a heavy burden of ridicule and disapproval today. Let Pop be a weakling who wends his way home to cold beer and a hot TV tube each night, avoiding involvement with the problems of teaching and disciplining the children, and let his wife wear the pants of the family *because she must*—no one is going to hand her a bouquet for trying to be both parents in the family. Indeed not. She will be excoriated as that dreadful American Mom while the uncommunicative, listless man watching fights on TV will never be categorized as a do-nothing father and a humbug husband. Instead, he will be the pathetic, endearing, pleasant little hag-ridden guy that American vulpine women make of their husbands.

"I am troubled," write the brief visitors from other lands (who always find time to write despite their trouble), "to account for the apparent unhappiness of the privileged, pampered, well-educated American wives"—and we're off again, to be called Gunpowder Women, Victims of Infantilism, Victims of Ennui, Victims of Leisure, Victims of Drink, Unfulfilled, Empty, Dull, Tension-ridden, Bored, Frustrated.

Are all these horrible charges aspects of rivalry? I believe that they all partake of the struggle between man and woman to strive to equal, to emulate, or to excel each other.

When the Yulas of society learn where they may not walk and

[1] William J. Callihan, vice-president, Young and Rubicam Inc. advertising agency, in an address to wives of national Wholesale Druggists' Association.

what they must not expect, when they are told what they should want and how they may best achieve it—life becomes smaller and more immediate. Success for a man means using his powers to lead, to buy, to sell, to compose, to teach, to invest, to preach, to coach, to fly, to farm—in the field of his choice. In addition to this he may, if he choose, marry and enjoy home and children. Success for a woman means using her powers to achieve a marriage proposal from a man she loves—to make him a comfortable home and bear him children. If she also is by nature deeply motivated to be a leader, a buyer, a dancer, a painter, a banker, a scientist, an inventor, she is subject to deep conflicts and feelings of guilt which express themselves in devious ways. What is she to do? She throws herself into charity work and is frequently appalled at its superficiality or incensed that the really responsible posts are filled by manipulative careerists—frequently charming men who "dear lady" her to death. Or, she may go back to her old love of music or begin art lessons. These are admirable pursuits and, if she has some genuine talent and a persevering nature, may supply valid enrichment to her life. She will discover, however, her art lessons lack the status in her household that her husband's golf dates have. For one of the painful realities of her life in the modern scheme is that pursuits which yield no profit must follow money-making endeavor. Frequent and lavish family vacations come after her husband's intense effort and money making. He, after hours at work, has "earned" his golf time. A bored, unemployed woman does not add to her stature with hobbies which have no commercial value. She will also discover that the work of which she is most proud is rated "below average amateur" by her instructor and a source of loving raillery at home. A feeling that the late forties is *too* late to start this sort of thing—despite Grandma Moses—comes over her. If she persists nonetheless, more power to her! If she puts aside the art material, there are still many fascinating possibilities.

Isn't someone always beseeching women to get into the political party of their choice and work? Yula does. It is campaign time, and she is soon whirling through exciting, punishing rounds of meetings, telephonings, letter writing, all interspersed with crises of rumor, conflicts of scheduling, promised speakers who do not appear, cunning and corrupt opponents, and cauldrons of coffee. Her work is lauded from the platform by every candidate and party bigwig (all male). She stuffs envelopes, works blocks, plans meetings, decorates halls, runs up phone bills, and is given the impossible grade school age volunteers to corral.

Leaving her family to shift for themselves most of the time, Yula works feverishly. She is certain that she has made a tremendous contribution to the party's cause. Indeed, she has seen enough of the listless headquarters' staff and the blandly comfortable men to know that the election couldn't be managed without her. Try as she does, she cannot help feeling in her bones that this is just the beginning. She even dreams of running for party office. When the election is over, some of her candidates have won. She congratulates them ecstatically and waits for congratulations for herself. Eventually two letters arrive. One is from the top candidate. It is mimeographed with her name handwritten and misspelled. The other is a personal note from the party's county chairman. Neither writer appears aware of just what sort of contribution she has made. But both use the same phrase: "I will never forget your splendid contribution to our cause."

Later she reads of a Victory Dinner, but she has received no invitation or notification. She wasn't an "old pro."

In the modern world's hottest bed of male-female rivalry—*politics*—Yula has been drained dry and thrown away. The campaign manager who rang her phone off the hook during the tense election doesn't even intend to be unjust. He will ask for her help again in two years, but he will choose another socially acceptable, inexperienced, willing woman for the big job that Yula handled this time. "Women?" he'll say candidly. "They're fine. You gotta know how to use 'em, and you gotta know how to handle 'em."

Sit, as I have done, at state inner-sanctum central committee meetings to pick out a slate of delegates to a presidential convention. Propose able, hard-working Mrs. Brown or respected, party-serving Mrs. Jones to the men around the table. They will praise Mrs. Jones. They will laud Mrs. Brown, but they will refuse to consider them as convention delegates. The explanation is either intensely clever or brutally unjust. I have never been able to decide. "It wouldn't work to have a woman on the slate," they say; then they add the knockout blow: "The other women would be jealous."

Women are not excluded from politics. They are always begged to work, and they work and are worked relentlessly. But men call the shots, and not one woman in sixty thousand gains any party advantage, no matter how skillfully and loyally she performs. Women don't know how to handle men politicians who "know how to handle women"!

Last year in Washington, men labor leaders organized a conference on the problem of working women.[2] For three days running, the women they invited to come and talk said their greatest problem was sex discrimination. They said further that the labor movement itself was guilty of more discrimination than any other segment of society. The sharpest attack came from Mrs. Sidney Hillman, widow of one of the labor movement's heroes and herself a union official. Mrs. Hillman's cool eyes snapped behind her bifocals as she described the union leaders as "the greatest offenders so far as discrimination against women is concerned." Bessie Hillman, peppery grandmother of sixty-five, took the microphone unexpectedly as the men were talking their well-intentioned generalities. "I am," she said, "very annoyed with these men who come to us and say that women have got to do this and that." Women, she said, had advanced to higher positions of leadership in every other walk of life than they had achieved in the trade-union movement. She pointed out that there was not one woman on the thirty-one-member executive council which governed AFL–CIO and that not one woman had ever been sent abroad to represent the big labor federation at international conferences. She said that the best proof of her contention was that men deliberately ignored women; that the 150 women from twenty-five international unions had heard speaker after speaker address the assemblage in fawning tones as "leaders." "Yet not one of you is on the executive or policy-making level of your union," she declared. "Very few of you are even presidents of locals. They let you be shop stewards, business agents, education directors." While she herself is a union executive, this was due to unusual circumstances, Mrs. Hillman declared. An early organizer in the garment industry before her marriage, she was named a vice-president of Amalgamated in 1945 after the death of Mr. Hillman, long-time president and one of the founders of the union.

Mrs. Hillman is a delightful exception to a sorry prevailing rule in the saga of rivalry. Too often the picture of a woman invited to the

[2] Labor Conference of AFL–CIO held in Washington, D.C. Reported by Isabelle Shelton, *Washington Star*, 1962.

councils of men "for exceptional circumstances" and because men have been getting considerable pressure to recognize the woman of the organization offers a contrasting performance. For one thing men are inclined to choose the woman who will be easiest on the eyes at long conferences and, before that, the one who seems to threaten them with the least trouble. If only we could say to men in authority, "When you do decide to recognize women, for heaven's sake choose someone whose history of experience and achievement satisfies the women. Don't look around for old Bill's pretty little wife, Dotty, who always seems so pleasant at dinner parties. That kind of appointment only infuriates the hard-working, able women, and then they have the millstone of Dotty's performance record to contend with later on."

The pressures of rivalry between women for the approval of men; the desire for the coveted tribute "truly feminine"; the years of effort to achieve a reputation for being cooperative and acceptable to men in the work situation stifle effectiveness in overcoming the handicaps the female sex labors under in the union, business, political, and governmental world.

Note the time-honored method of appointive segregation. In many public, private, and charitable organizations, a committee of men makes the policy and then a committee of women is named for window dressing.

Do these things happen because our male rivals fear us or because we are on a lofty pedestal and they are loath to bring us down to their level? I am sometimes reminded of the primitive religious custom in this not very reverent age. For physiological reasons, the primitive hedged woman around with sanctity and specialness, all the time doing all in his power to inspire awe of his powers in her by keeping religion largely in his own hand. The result of all this so far as woman is concerned was to make her something apart. Hence she tended as a sex to lose as much in freedom as she gained in respect.

Leaving aside the natural happy-to-be-staying-at-home woman, the unmarried woman who is genuinely fulfilled in teaching, nursing, or business, and the woman whose skill embraces a big job, a smoothly running home, and happy children—all completely approved by her husband (and let us fervently thank God for such women!), think about another modern woman.

She loves home, husband, and children, but her skill can bring badly needed money to the family. She likes working, because she has had a good education and she is putting it to work on the job. Happy and sufficient as she may be in the work, indispensable as her check is for the children's education and the house they had to buy, she is nonetheless forced to pay a steady daily debt of guilt. Business is oriented to the value system expounded by Yula's mother. Our working wife-mother is doing a man's job, and she is leaving a houseful of woman's jobs to do it. In America today, her story is commonplace, but the pretense goes on that she is a malefactor and a traitor. From the pulpit, the soap opera, the woman's magazine, the screen and stage rises up a mist of negation. The attitude gets through to her insidiously.

"It's true Fred doesn't mind," she tells herself, "but American men are apt to die first. Is my job denying him the special attentions, the serene atmosphere; the interest in his job at a time when his life may be snuffed out any minute?"

She reads of nice children from comfortable homes involved in delinquency. A shudder goes through her. "Does Anna really know where Danny goes after he checks in from school?"

Buffeted by these chilling thoughts, she reminds herself that many working women are excellent mothers and successful wives. It is good that she has them to think about, for rivalry within the office is masked but caustic. Unmarried women tell her flatly, "Believe me, when I get married I'll be perfectly delighted to stay home." The speaker doesn't have to add, "You unnatural woman, you!" It is implicit in tone and expression. The men say the same thing in an abundance of different ways. When the promotion which she has been counting on goes to Charlie, who has always let her do most of the work, she demands an explanation from their superior. The boss admits freely that she is much better qualified for the advancement. "But," he says closing the discussion with a firm, moral tone, "Charlie has four mouths to feed."

As a Civil Service Commissioner, I sat in on agency promotion discussion and listened with fascination to just this sort of argument *for* Willie and *against* Wilma. When, as was frequently the case, Wilma also had mouths to feed and was the sole support of those mouths, she still didn't always make the grade. She was said to be reluctant to take responsibility, or she was weak "at the operating level," or (apparently no man under consideration had anything but a Perry Como disposition) "has difficulties in her dealings with people." The numbing thing here was that the men didn't dream they were being unfair rivals. They just couldn't see these particular women in the higher job.

Look at the fruits of this male-female competition when it relates to unmarried and overage women who have never risen beyond a modest clerical job. When you laugh at the eternal struggle to stay young-looking which occupies the modern woman, think of that lonely, pathetic older woman who has had years in the same office at a low-level job. She can tell you (as one did in my office at the Commission) that the first rule of men-run government offices is that the staff of women should be young and pretty. Most particularly the women in the front office should be. The time has long passed since many working women were either. They have been trespassed against through the years and, in too many cases, responded to the hurt by becoming crabbed, difficult, and just a little bit queer. In their meager lodgings, they keep food overlong in the icebox and a gray cat. They knit things for a brother's children out in California and are sometimes thanked for it. They feel that their supervisor "has it in for them" and that other women don't have to take the desks next to the air-conditioning unit. They suspect from continual criticism and harassment that the agency is trying to get them mad and make them quit. Often this is exactly what is happening. A vague claim that the woman (still some years from the time she will legally retire) is not quite right mentally is offered by the agency to induce a medical discharge. It is understandable. Years of unsuccessful rivalry—with men for status and promotions in the office, with younger women for courtesy and attention—have made the woman eccentric and pathetic.

Of course, there will always be such women in the world. But isn't it possible that the double standard in American business has helped make many of these pitiable creatures?

Top educators are concerned for girls with youth and promising mental endowment who come to college only for fun and romance. At a time when America needs the best brains for both men and women, some of the best female brains have already discovered that the smart girl wastes no time on learning she'll never get to use. The smart girl, the happy woman, the feminine success gets a man, a college man with a future. When that mighty mission is accomplished and the children are receding in their demands on her, what does she do with the restlessness and the time? She rips up her kitchen, installing radar ovens and antique coffee mills, she takes rhumba lessons, or heads for Main Chance and the Arden cure. All of it with the approval of her husband.

This "play work" suffices briefly; then she feels wasted and lost again. "What," she wonders, "am I really seeking? What am I *really* like?"

Women are not the gentler sex. They are not naturally the glamorous sex (though she has emphasized the path of glamour and committed atrocities of idiocy in its pursuit as the counterpart of your own consuming pursuit of success in business and industry). Women are not rulers of the world. It is kind of you to talk about the hand at the cradle and make those fulsome implications, but they are as thin as the banquet speeches which Mrs. Hillman protested so forthrightly. Women know that children need a cradle builder and a cradle rocker, and some of them have spent enough time and money at the psychiatrist's to know that the time you invest in knowing and helping your children is the best insurance policy you can ever give her.

Women are not natural business geniuses, no matter how many generalities are made about the control of wealth in this country. (Women may have the first place as inheritors of wealth, but the wealth they inherit is largely managed, invested, and manipulated by men.) Women can become business executives—shrewd and calculating and imposing. They would like you to recognize this as readily as you agree that they can become nurses and cooks.

Women are not naturally lawyers. But some of the finest legal minds belong to women despite the incalculable difficulties they must labor under even in the year 1963. Think of the progress they have made with honored positions on the bench and high posts in some of the world's best firms. In the 1872 case of Bradwell *vs.* Illinois, the Supreme Court of the United States upheld an Illinois decision that refused to grant a woman a license to practice law on the ground that: [3]

[3] *Case and Comment.* Issue of July–August, 1962.

The natural and proper timidity and delicacy which belongs to the female sex evidently unfits it for many of the occupations of civil life. The constitution of the family organization, which is founded in the divine ordinance, as well as the nature of things, indicates the domestic sphere as that which properly belongs to the domain and functions of womanhood. The harmony, not to say identity of interest and views which belong, or should belong, to the family institution is repugnant to the idea of a woman adopting a distinct and independent career from that of her husband . . . the paramount destiny and mission of women are to fulfill the noble and benign offices of wife and mother. This is the law of the Creator.

Women are not natural doctors, statisticians, industrial designers. They have no sex-given preeminence in the field of teaching, meal planning, or choreography, but some women possess astounding abilities in these fields.

Why shut them out of any field in which they have ability? Does an *Esquire Magazine* writer come close to the mark when he suggests that men fear and dislike women in top business jobs for two reasons? (1) that they deeply fear the extraordinary sexual attraction of women and the business ascendancy it may lead to for them and (2) that the men don't want women to find out how easy business really is?

Whatever the reasons for this rivalry, it is wasteful of woman's natural gifts, conducive to neurosis and estrangement. It is an injustice to man and to the blessed democratic concept of each individual's gifts and sacred rights.

Beyond all that, it is *so* unnecessary. Women have themselves in a strange dilemma today. They have won extraordinary freedom. They may vote, seek elective office, own property, sit on juries, practice birth control, sue for divorce, gain custody of the children, receive alimony or child-support money, marry again. They may enjoy social acceptability while smoking and drinking in public. They may dye their hair, wear bikinis, attend prize fights. The standards of Winsome Womanhood which the Supreme Court upheld in its decision on the woman lawyer from Illinois have undergone astounding changes. Some years back, a *New Yorker* cartoon showed the familiar interior of a neighborhood bar. Each stool around the bar was occupied by a woman. Some were elegantly dressed and engaged in sociable conversation. Some were moodily studying their watches. One, in some disarray on the center stool, was demanding the attention of the house. "I can," she said loudly and with understandable satisfaction, "lick any women in this place!"

Why with so much equality, so much freedom should there continue to be a painful side to rivalry?

Why, with the great wide world of knowledge and human need, should so many of the most promising young American girls prefer beauty-contest laurels to national scholarship honors? Why have we witnessed rising nationwide "Miss Teenager" contests taking their place with the dreadful "Mrs. America" spectacle? Does the glowingly healthy, well-reared, long-stemmed American college girl leave the campus and knock at schools of law, medicine? Seek a job in the fields of social work, teaching, foreign service? She may, and for this: four cheers. But she is just as apt to shoot for becoming a photographer's model or a mannequin. Here, if she is good, she will run no risk of alienating the admiration and attention of marriageable men.

The modern girl lives in two worlds: the wide world of men which claims to believe in and uphold equality of the sexes and the secret "other world" with its strictures and insistent goals. The great law in this "other world" of women deals with the true "success" of a female. It says, "Thou shalt be loved by a man. Become a wife. Have a family. Do it early. Do it now." The second law is like unto the first! "Dissemble under a facade of charm and glamour your inherent strength, ambition, and intellectual power. All these abilities will serve you best within the framework of the first law's achievement and are most successful when they stay invisible."

What are the implications of the rivalry between the world and the "other world"?

Degrading waste and degrading dishonesty are two of the commonly seen results. The cost of these sanctioned acts of fraud is appalling. Woman has not lost her ability to love—indeed she has never pinned so much hope, need, desperation on love. But she has become less lovable. Her failure to achieve reality for herself has cost terrible wages for society and led to corrosion and distortion in the man-woman relationship. When she fights the system, she is apt to become a kind of She-Man freak or a witch-on-wheels, or a much-married glamour-girl mercenary to appear on TV panel shows and catch verbal custard pies. The failure of this and other methods of "fighting City Hall" has twisted children's lives out of shape, increased in the population the number of effeminate men, raised the score of alcoholism and drug addiction. If we look only at the appalling divorce and desertion figures, we can see that it's time to consider how far off the track the natural rivalry between the sexes has gone.

In the days of our primitive cave couple, Op and Ug, there was a good reason for tough rivalry: we could see that the visceral turbulence between the sexes was the very stuff of survival. Men and women were born to be rivals, not only of each other, but of most members of their own sex. Struggle, competitive effort, even a splendid belligerence was required for all that was to follow in man's development. The need for rivalry will never depart. Eleanor Roosevelt, Helen Keller, Marian Anderson, Dr. Kelsey, Althea Gibson, Margaret Mead, Jacqueline Cochran, Jacqueline Kennedy—all have known it. Yet all such women and thousands more whom you and I know personally and give thanks for have refused to be less than their unique and special selves even under the intense pressures of their personal challenge.

There is no one way to be a woman. She is both weak and strong. She may be saint or shrew. She can be a seducer or an ennobling teacher. She is often a healer, a helper, a comforter. She is often a discoverer, experimenter, destroyer. She can be courtesan and troublemaker; peacemaker and catalyst. Her history has given all these sides to her make-up, and no one has yet given her wise direction in how to use them. Perhaps she has come such a long way in the first sixty-three years of this century that she deserves thirty-seven more years of grace, a period of patience from her rivals, men, and her rivals, other women, in an atmosphere of respect and confidence, so that she may pull all the skeins of her complex and awesome self together.

To do it, she will need immense generosity of spirit from men— men who are confident enough of themselves to know they can enjoy a deeper, more meaningful rivalry with a stronger, more natural woman. To assist women in their "days of grace," men will need to lay aside much automatic and superficial praise of "the better half" and be impersonally critical and constructively stern with women. Too often women hear pearls of praise for their qualities and no reminder of the things they had better set right.

Just as often the chirpings "How right you are, darling" and "Oh,

you incredible strong man, you!" cover with "other world" veneer facts
that men ought to know about themselves. "What demon possessed me
that I behaved so well?" [4] could apply to the whole area of rivalry today.
Neither side has been honest.

Our message—woman's for man and man's for woman—hasn't been
getting through. We have let ourselves forget that men and women are
one in a great and good essential which is common humanity.

It could be that a rival tribe is coming toward our clearing in the
jungle, again. Every human will be needed *at his best,* if we are to hold
our own.

It is time we abandoned a blind and destructive rivalry founded
upon myth, moonshine, and stubborn unwillingness to understand each
other. We must be ourselves—our very best selves—for the engagement
and for the sake of what is to follow. Our rivalry, man and woman's,
needs scouring and burnishing.

It needs the great word, compounded of hope, need, and trust,
placed in front of it like a banner. It must become *loving* rivalry.

Let us rediscover ourselves by rediscovering each other, our special
gifts and our mutual dependence, promise, challenge, achievement, and
zest.

We need each other. We are capable of learning. The implication
of rivalry is that we must start to shake off the old hobbles and become
loving rivals determined to match in heart and spirit the best the other
has to offer.

[4] Henry David Thoreau.

References

Books

Encyclopaedia Britannica, 1951, V1-pp. 780; V5-pp. 860c; V7-pp. 650; V6-pp.
    696; V1-pp. 433–434; V15-pp. 689; V19-pp. 106.
The American Woman, E. J. Dingwall, New York, Signet Books, 1956.
The American Woman as Lover, Mate and Rival, Morton M. Hunt, New York,
    Harper & Row, 1962.
Susan B. Anthony: Rebel, Crusader, Humanitarian, A. Lutz, Boston, Beacon Press.
I Learned about Women from Them, I. Taves, New York, McKay, 1962.
Male and Female, M. Mead, New York, Mentor Books, 1955.

Articles

Entire issue on "The American Woman," *Life,* 1-7-57.

"Party of One," C. Fadiman, *Holiday,* 6-61.

"Are Women Losing Their Femininity," poll report, *Parade,* 5-15-60.

"Your Job and Your Emotions," J. Skardon, *American Weekly,* 11-15-59.

Special "Looks at Woman" issue, *Realities,* 11-61.

"Such Interesting People," M. Pines, *Reporter,* 6-7-62.

"All about Women," B. Crowther, *The New York Times,* 3-18-62.

"My ABC's," M. Dietrich, *Look,* 10-24-61.

"The Organization Bimbo," *Newsweek,* 7-2-62.

Issue on "The American Woman," *Esquire,* 7-62.

"Fifty Years of American Women," W. Sargeant, *Life,* 1-2-50.

Supplement on "The American Female," *Harper's,* 10-62.

"The Girl with the Harvard Degree," M. J. Arlen, *The New York Times Magazine,* 6-10-62.

"The Quiet Revolution," E. Harrison, *Civil Service Journal,* 10-12-62.

"The Ascent of Woman," E. M. Borghese, *Glamour,* 7-62.

"Hows and Howevers of the Woman Voter," P. K. Hastings, *The New York Times Magazine,* 6-12-62.

"The Language Barrier," R. Gehman, *Cosmopolitan,* 1-58.

"Change and Choice for the College Woman," entire issue, *AAUW Journal,* 5-62.

Esther Peterson

THE IMPACT OF EDUCATION

I appreciate the opportunity to reflect with you about the impact of education on women's past, present, and potential status in our society. The very title of my presentation, without any elaboration, recognizes that the impact of education is profound. President Kennedy in a message to Congress on the educational needs of our country made this point in these words:

. . . education is both the foundation and the unifying force of our democratic way of life—it is the mainspring of our economic and social progress— it is the highest expression of achievement in our society, ennobling and enriching human life. In short, it is at the same time the most profitable investment society can make and the richest reward it can confer.[1]

The title "The Impact of Education" has the additional advantage of being so comprehensive that I feel free to concentrate on the "impact" of my choice. That is the impact of education on women's economic status in our democracy.

I most certainly appreciate the many noneconomic aspects of education in a woman's whole life. It increases her contributions to family life by expanding and deepening her understanding, interests, values, and family goals. A sharpened intellect and a wider perception of the world bring the possibility for a rich and satisfying life. A good educa-

[1] President John F. Kennedy, message on education to the Congress of the United States, 1962.

tion should make a woman more aware of her responsibilities toward her fellow men and of the need for her talents in public service.

Whether or not a woman ever goes into the labor force, her education—the best education she can obtain—is of as much importance to our nation and to humanity as it is to her own satisfaction and sense of achievement. Since I am concentrating on education and vocation here, I want to emphasize my full commitment to good education per se—without regard to economic implications. Whether the education is for the pure joy of learning or for a definite vocational objective and whether for men or for women, it is a national asset of vastly greater use and durability in the stockpile of total national assets than any material thing we could acquire and treasure.

We do recognize, though, that education, once acquired, *eventually* is put to financial use by most of our educated women. Therefore, the United States Department of Labor, while enthusiastically applauding the idea of educating women for all the many reasons which make education so important, does not lose sight of the fact that an educated American woman is an invaluable addition to our labor resources.

From kindergarten through high school we provide virtually the same academic education for boys and girls. In most instances, the 22 million boys and 21 million girls in our "regular school system" today study under similar conditions. The boy who wants to be an astronaut or chemist will learn about Shakespeare and the sonnets of Milton, just as the girl who hopes for a stage career or whose ambition is early marriage and a large family must nevertheless master the theorems of plane geometry and the life cycle of the earthworm.

After graduation from high school, however, the situation changes. Although higher education is generally available to both sexes, fewer women than men go to college. A recent Bureau of Labor Statistics survey showed that 41 per cent of the girls and 56 per cent of the boys who graduated from high school in June, 1961, were college students the following fall.[2] We know, of course, that the proportions of all young people seeking a college education have been rising in recent years. Although the same type of statistical measure is not available for

[2] *Employment of High School Graduates and Dropouts in 1961,* Bureau of Labor Statistics, Special Labor Force Report No. 21, May, 1962.

an earlier decade, it is significant that the percentage of 18- and 19-year-old girls in school jumped from 18 to 29 per cent in the years 1920 to 1961. I am optimistically confident that this trend will continue. Education is so valuable an asset that we must not only make it available to all on an equal basis, but we must also motivate women and girls to take full advantage of their opportunities.

The rise in women's educational attainment has paralleled their participation in paid employment. Although a two-way influence certainly exists, there is no doubt that women's education has had a strong impact on women's interest in, and qualifications for, more and better jobs. So many women have paid jobs today that our economy would be brought to a halt if all women decided to stop working outside the home.

Each decade of the twentieth century contains a larger percentage of better-educated women than the one before, as well as a higher proportion of the woman population in the labor force. In 1920, the formal education of the typical woman stopped after grammar school, and there were less than ⅓ million women college students. Women workers numbered a mere 8¼ million. Today's typical woman is a high school graduate; there are about 1½ million women students in college; and almost 25 million women work outside the home.

Who are the working women? They represent about one-third of the women in our population. Of those between 18 and 24 years of age, 45 per cent are employed—nearly one out of every two. These are traditionally the premarital years or the years of newlywed status, when the girl is trying out her job skills, acquiring a work record, and perhaps helping a young husband financially while he completes his education and strives for a foothold in his chosen field. Between the ages of 25 and 34 the percentage of working women drops by 10 points, to 35 per cent—still one out of three. Many of those not in the labor market stay home to care for their family but then come back into the work force again after age 35, remaining until retirement age and even beyond. Thus, 43 per cent of all women between the ages of 35 and 44 were working at the time of the 1960 census. At that time, 42 per cent of those between the ages of 45 and 64 were working. And even in the group 65 and over, the percentage of women still working was a surprisingly high 10 per cent.[3] So we have this picture of peaks and valleys on the chart of working women at different age levels—going into the labor market in large numbers after completing their education, dropping out because of marriage and family responsibilities, and then returning for another period of employment.

What is the impact of education on this situation? In terms of statistics, the impact is clear. Over one-half of all women college graduates in the United States had paid employment in 1959. By comparison, only two-fifths of the high school graduates were working, and only one-third of those whose education ended after elementary school. Of course, the better-educated women have the better-paying jobs—three-fourths of the women college graduates who are working are found in professional employment. As we raise the level of a woman's education, we open to her a greater number and a greater variety of vocational choices.

There is some tendency to moralize on the role of the working wife or working mother, but I don't think we have a right to do so. Whether a woman works or stays home should be her own and her family's decision, based on their judgment of what is best for her and best for the family. Whether we think it should be or not, more than three million of our women workers are the mothers of young children. Many women who are married—33 per cent of them—*are* working. This is a fact of our times. I am not sure of the relative influence of all the reasons for this situation, but there is no doubt that economic necessity and the availability of job opportunities have a great deal to do with the decision of a married woman to work.

Other factors also have considerable influence on the college woman. At some period in her life, she is likely to realize the economic value of her education—whether she consciously anticipates a lifetime working career or considers it an investment she may need or choose to expend some day. We tend to minimize how important it is to a husband to know that his wife can contribute to the family income if need should arise. Dr. Farber has found in clinical practice that this knowledge takes considerable pressure off a husband. His wife's potential

---

[3] *Women Workers in 1960: Geographical Differences,* Women's Bureau Bulletin 284, 1962.

earning ability is especially appreciated if a husband wants to change his career, if he has to retire early, or if his financial resources cannot cover the cost of a college education for his children.

The woman who has an education and is not using it in a way she considers productive tends to feel dissatisfied with the waste of her talents. This feeling was acknowledged by many of the women interviewed in a survey of college alumnae fifteen years after graduation.[4] Exactly one-third of these women were employed and most of them on a full-time basis. Among the two-thirds not working, 5 out of 6 were either seeking positions or considering going to work at some later date. Only 1 out of 6 expressed no interest whatsoever in future employment. But there was a feeling among many that they would need additional training or education to obtain the kind of position they would like to have.

Not surprisingly, a significant number of the "fifteen-year alumnae" wanted to take courses leading toward teacher certification. During their college days, most of the women in this group had been attracted to other fields. But their recent experiences with their own children and with parent-teacher activities and other community projects had brought them into close contact with local educational problems. They had become aware of the urgent need for more and better-trained teachers and the many personal rewards of teaching. Of course, for a woman with children of school age, there is the further consideration that a teaching position will enable her to be at home with her children after school and during vacations. So it is quite natural that when their children reach school age, many college-trained women give serious consideration to the idea of resuming their education in order to qualify for schoolteaching.

But as increasing numbers of intelligent and well-educated mature women are discovering, there is an endless variety of employment possibilities available to them if they are willing to acquire the necessary training. There are new fields which did not exist when many of them were in college. The electronic computer, for instance, is spawning careers in everything from space sciences to banking.

I find it very interesting to consider the experiences of one group

[4] *Fifteen Years after College: A Study of Alumnae of the Class of 1945,* Women's Bureau Bulletin 283, 1962.

of mothers who became acquainted through a cooperative nursery school. Most were college women who had worked after graduation and for a number of years after marriage. When they came together in the nursery school, however, most of these women were full-time home-makers. Gradually, over the following years, one after another went back to work, either to her previous profession or into a new one. The new careers were often ones which they had never considered seriously while in college. For instance, several became so interested in preschool education as a result of the nursery school experience that they went back to school to train professionally for this work. One took a gradu-ate course in library science and became a professional librarian in the highly specialized field of scientific research. Another took a master's degree in social work and is now conducting an experimental and ex-tremely significant project dealing with the problems of disadvantaged children. One became an audiologist at a local hospital. Another went back to writing. Still another moved from part-time volunteer work to directing the public relations activities of a community agency on a full-time professional basis. Several went into local politics, and two of them —a former teacher and an economist—were elected to their school board and served with distinction.

Thus, even this one small group, whose experiences we have fol-lowed over a period of time, contains example after example of the pat-tern of the college-trained woman returning to work.

It seems to me that the secret, if there is a secret, in the success of mature women's going back into professional employment after a hiatus of from five to fifteen years lies in the broad gauge of their education and experiences. Shouldn't we strive for the kind of basic education for our women which provides them later with the greatest degree of flexi-bility in building new careers after marriage? I ask this question here because I think this is a good forum for considering it.

Since men and women have different life patterns, shouldn't we consider different educational approaches for them? A young man going to college either has or seeks quickly to find a career objective—one that he can prepare for as thoroughly as possible to equip him for a lifetime of work of progressively increasing importance. Many young women also determine during their college days what they want to do profes-sionally. And, of course, they should be given every encouragement to concentrate and specialize. We need experts—we need them desperately. But we have a resource in our women which is not generally appreciated, except in periods of great national emergency. Our educated women constitute what I call a skill bank—a reserve of women who have the potential to undertake specialized training and move into areas of acute need.

When we have a fuller appreciation of this latent national resource, I think we shall be more energetic about finding easier ways for mature women to continue their education or training. More colleges will consider relaxing strict regulations, thereby encouraging mature women to enroll in selected courses, possibly at unusual hours. More employers will look favorably on hiring mature women and providing in-company training to refresh their rusty skills.

During recent wartime periods, many women rose to the challenge and proved that they could learn virtually any skill, both well and quickly, when sufficiently motivated. "Rosie the Riveter" and her colleagues became wartime heroines. Shouldn't we continue to have faith in them and their daughters' ability to make an important contribution to our economic life?

Virtually every girl in today's world can expect to have a paying job during some years of her adult life. But at what? With little education, she will be in and out of the labor force more by chance than by choice—a marginal worker who, unfortunately, may desperately need the paycheck she will find so elusive. There are, of course, many things she *could* be trained for—fields in which the return would be commensurate with the training required. As mentioned previously, her best bet—her best course of action—is a good, broad, general education on which she can build at any time the specialized skills she may need for employment in a new field, perhaps one of the glamour jobs in space technology, or any field which appeals to her in her middle years.

Our girls must look to the future and plan an educational program which features flexibility and adjustment to change. We know that practically all occupations are undergoing revolutionary changes. Automation is eliminating not only jobs but fields of skill and knowledge; it is also creating new jobs and many specializations within old jobs. Therefore, we must be able to change and adjust as individuals.

Education should provide us with this ability—this flexibility. The charge is often made that most girls go to college with only one great objective—matrimony. It is said that they consider the college environment excellent for meeting many eligible young men with good prospects, but if a suitable husband is not found while they are in school, then skills acquired in college will qualify them for jobs where there are other promising young men. Of course, this is an oversimplification, an easy generality, which is nevertheless often confirmed. What's wrong with having a better opportunity to meet a likely mate? Nothing at all. But if it is true, as it undoubtedly is, that most college women plan to marry, then it seems to me there must be more support among students, faculty members, and parents for educational policies geared to the future needs of our women students. And this is not necessarily education identical to, or equal to, that needed by young men.

I am delighted at the magnitude of interest in this problem among educators, and among those interested in the status of women. Dr. Mary Bunting, the president of Radcliffe, not only has been pioneering in this field of continuing education for women at her own institution but, as chairman of the committee on education of the President's Commission on the Status of Women, is directing a study on the timing and tailoring of education for the special needs of women in our complex society. I am sure you will all be interested to know that the chairman of our symposium here, Dr. Seymour M. Farber, who is also nationally known for his work in the field of continuing education, is a valuable member of Dr. Bunting's committee.

In this consideration of the impact of education, I think we should give some attention to the financial impact of education on the parents of our boys and girls. A college education is assuming comparable importance in family life today to the high school education of a generation ago. Then, a boy or girl who stayed in high school until graduation deprived his family of very little other than the money he might have earned, assuming he could find a job. Today, the results are quite different. By going on to college for another four years, the young person may possibly deprive the family of some financial contribution to family expenses. But more importantly, he or she generally imposes a heavy financial burden on the parents. For many families, the burden is impossible to bear. And if the parents decide that they are able to send some of their children to college but not others, the chances are that preference will be given to the boys. This seems to me to be a very unfortunate situation, as it hurts women in a very strategic manner—by restricting their opportunities for improvement and achievement.

The answer for me is to try to make it financially possible for all who want to go to college to be able to do so. A very important recommendation in President Kennedy's education program has been for Federal loans to needy and talented high school seniors who would otherwise not be able to continue their education. He has also supported proposals for funds for the building and expanding of community colleges. Such colleges help bring higher education within the reach of the millions who can attend school only if they can commute.

If what we seek is equality of opportunity for women, then this is the place to start—this is the doorway to a world where girls really have as much opportunity as their brothers to go to college. None of the recommendations for aid to higher education represent a newfangled "spending scheme" or anything very different from what we are doing and have been doing for a long time for a variety of specific purposes. We were willing for the Federal government to help millions get a college education under the GI Bill of Rights. That program stemmed, of course, from a national emergency, but it became an investment in education. Where would we be today if so many of our veterans had not been able to obtain training in engineering, science, and the other professions?

The Federal government is currently financing the education of nursing supervisors and practical nurses, agronomists and astronauts, linguists, researchers, teachers—the list is very long. In every instance, however, it has been specified that the training must be in conformity with specific occupational objectives in areas of national defense need or industrial or agricultural skills. The purpose in most cases is to guide qualified people into shortage occupations. The President's Advisory Committee on Vocational Education recently called for a tremendous expansion in the whole vocational education program. And in all the health professions, there is general agreement on the urgent need for the expansion of teaching facilities, loan programs, scholarships, and fellowships for more doctors, dentists, public health officers, and other health personnel. We are now training teachers for specialized work with mentally retarded children and those with speech and hearing defects. It is also agreed that this program must be expanded for all categories of exceptional children, including the gifted.

Aren't we thwarting our country's advancement when we fail to extend opportunities for higher education to all our qualified young men and women? This means making available broad, basic education in the humanities, as well as in the sciences. What better foundation for a better society, for better family living, even for national defense? With millions more men and women who are well educated, we would have a reservoir of talent for new and challenging occupational needs.

We have observed that education has a most profound impact on the economic status of women. Basically, it means improving their work skills and thereby broadening their employment opportunities. But lack of it or an insufficient amount often means rejection and poverty rather than a productive and satisfying work life. The unemployment rates of those who "have" obtained an education with those who "have not" are strategic indicators of the unfavorable position of the uneducated and the unskilled. In November, 1962, the highest rate of unemployment (12.1 per cent) was reported among laborers and one of the lowest rates (1.5 per cent) among professional workers.

In summary, then, continually larger numbers and proportions of women are seeking employment after their children are in school or college. The better educated they are, the more satisfactory are the jobs they get—both psychologically and financially. These facts must guide us toward the development of educational and training policies which will prepare women for the kinds of lives they are going to live. Counselors must make their recommendations in terms of the multiple roles of a woman's life. Young girls must realize while still in school that marriage will probably be combined with employment outside the home. If they follow the typical pattern of today's married women, their life will include initial education and possibly some employment, a period of interruption concentrating on home and family, and then later return to school and/or the labor market.

The increasing number of women with incomplete college programs who wish to continue their education suggests that we must alter our sense of timing about women's formal education and make it easier for them by giving more flexibility to admission requirements, time schedules, and the variety of courses offered. The flexibility we want should include a willingness to set up special short-term courses to train people so that they can qualify for special job needs. The fact that many of the women who are seeking retraining or resuming their education are mature women means we need to rethink the content and methodology of some college courses to make them more suitable and meaningful for adults. More and better facilities for counseling these women are also indicated, as well as willingness on the part of employers to give greater consideration to hiring qualified mature women for professional positions and developing mutually satisfactory working arrangements, such as part-time assignments when feasible.

In the work force projected for 1970, there will be 56 million men and 29 million women. It is estimated that over 10 million of these will be professional workers.[5] This is approximately 40 per cent more than the 7½ million professional workers employed in 1960. If women are to share in the new jobs of the future and obtain full partnership with men in our economic life, they must be encouraged and enabled to obtain appropriate education. It is important, therefore, that special attention be given to their educational needs and interests.

[5] U.S. Department of Labor, Bureau of Labor Statistics.

Adrienne Koch

TWO CHEERS FOR EQUALITY

Rarely does one have the luck to speak to a group in the guise of a natural, bona fide authority. Today this is possible for me despite the fact that my subject is not within the usual area of my professional interests. By the mere fact that I am female, I am become an expert—for this conference is symbolically and institutionally prepared to recognize (for three days) that women are people, and that they have ambitions, abilities, and something called "potential." On the curious belief that a member of a class is the best person to analyze the properties of his class (a Christian to give you the truth about Christianity, a Communist about communism, or on the same logic Moby Dick about white whales, and perchance a bigot about bigotry?) I have been summoned from the ivory tower nestling under the shadows of great laboratories in Berkeley to give you the low-down on whether women are equal to men.

   This is not quite a fair description. The men who planned this conference, in a masterly and accommodating spirit, agreed that I might define the question as I saw fit, presumably so that I could be free to substitute the scars of experience for the scantiness of what we normally settle for as knowledge. I am therefore disposed to consider with you not whether women are equal to men, or superior to them, or inherently unequal but involved, or equal but separate—but whether they are persons in the moral and philosophical sense of the term and whether they are so recognized in the institutions of higher learning in America. I am thus proposing one very wide and fundamental question—the ethics of equality for women—and one rather narrow question of what the prevailing conditions are for women who are "professors" in a democratic culture that "emancipated" its women, politically and to some extent legally, more than forty years ago. It is possible that my second question, concerning the academic woman, is somewhat broader than it appears to be on the surface—since it may suggest the situation of other professional women in America and since the educator, by the nature of her work, is placed in a chain of ever-fresh and impressionable younger Americans.

Are women persons? Not if "anatomy is her destiny," surely. Not if she is "the second sex"—for to be a second anything—second-class citizen, second choice, secondhand, always a bridesmaid never a bride—is intolerable to a person of spirit as an *eternal and absolute foreordination*. *Primus inter pares* has its charms; *secundus inter pares,* mortifications. Surprisingly enough, women do not normally consider themselves to be a "second" and inferior sex—although they often mime and mug the role for what it is worth. *"Vive la différence"* is a sentiment common to both sexes; and it is a different sex, not a second sex, that listened to the serpent in the Garden of Eden and "being deceived" conspired with Adam (who was not deceived!) to eat the forbidden fruit! Since God was angry with them both and ordered them to leave, certain theologians have maintained that all mankind inherited *Adam's sin.* Thus there is some logic in the position that both sexes are sinful or at least immoral, fallible, and in subtly different ways "fallen." Nonetheless, the male of the species became, in due time, "enlightened." He demanded and won first a measure of liberty and then, in the lush but rough wilderness of America, equality—in principle at least. Even fraternity, in sporadic and somewhat external ways, came to sweeten his pilgrimage in the new American world.

It is no secret that the document from which this nation dates its independence proclaimed, for the first time in a public paper, the fundamental proposition that "all men are created equal" and joined to this basic value the inherent rights of life, liberty, and the pursuit of happiness. But what of women? Were they intended to be included in the generic term "men," or were the author of the Declaration and his learned and emancipated associates confining the term to its reference to one sex alone? On this matter one is free to speculate. For while it is clear that no one then thought of making women equal in political, legal, social, and educational rights with men immediately, there was a consciousness of a new spirit, a dynamic moral principle that was expected to lead to unexpected consequences of further growth. For it was an era when confidence in human capacities and pride in human reasonableness had its passionate advocates. Jefferson was one; his good friend Benjamin Rush another; and Benjamin Franklin at that time and in the tolerance of his age and wisdom was a likely third—not to mention a veritable army of less illustrious but farseeing men.

That this daring thought was being voiced explicitly, and by women, is also fact—for we have many proofs, among them a remarkable letter which Abigail Adams wrote to her not so liberal husband in the Continental Congress on the eve of independence. Pleading for her dependent sex, Abigail Adams wrote:

In the new code of laws which I suppose it will be necessary for you to make, I desire you would remember the ladies and be more generous and favorable to them than your ancestors! Do not put such unlimited power into the hands of the husbands. Remember all men would be tyrants if they could. If particular care and attention is not paid to the ladies, we are determined to foment a rebellion, and will not hold ourselves bound by any laws in which we have no voice or representation.

She concluded this appeal by recommending the substitution of the title of "friend" for the harsh title of "master," and ended with the question

Why not put it out of the power of the vicious and lawless to use us with cruelty . . . ?

To this fetching appeal, John Adams wrote a heavily bantering reply.

As to your extraordinary code of laws, I cannot but laugh! We have been told that our struggle has loosened the bonds of government everywhere—children and apprentices . . . schools and colleges . . . Indians, Negroes grow insolent. But your letter was the first intimation that another tribe, more numerous and powerful than all the rest, were grown discontented. . . . Depend upon it, we know better than to repeal our masculine systems. Although they are in full force, you know they are little more than theory. We dare not exert our power in its full latitude. We are obliged to go fair and softly, and in practice you know we are the subjects.

To this affectionate evasion his loving "friend" responded in kind:

I cannot say that I think you are very generous to the ladies, for whilst you are . . . emancipating all nations, you insist upon retaining an absolute power over your wives.

Then gracefully accepting the implied role, she quoted the couplet:

"Charm by accepting, by submitting sway,
Yet have our humor most when we obey."

This good-humored dialog could take place only in a pervasively dominant "man's world." When issues of human rights more insistent and tragic than Mrs. Adams contemplated were before the nation, the full moral and intellectual argument was formulated in terms so compelling that they live still.

This second case for women's rights was formulated early in the 1830s by two remarkable women abolitionists, the sisters Angelina and Sarah Grimké of Charleston, South Carolina, who had been drawn North to work for the emancipation of the slaves. These young women had personally witnessed the tragic facts of slave life on neighboring and on their own prosperous plantation; and in behalf of human rights they became the first American women leaders to speak from a public lecture platform before mixed (male-female) audiences. The jibes, insults, and mob scenes which interfered with their lectures did not deter them one whit from the crusade they were serving but made it painfully clear that women could not work as reformers unless they were recognized fully as persons and as citizens—entitled to and granted every right— social, political, educational, and economic—accorded to free males. Mercifully, the Grimké sisters were endowed with beauty and with angelic voices. John Greenleaf Whittier suggested their effect on the other sex when he called them "Carolina's high-souled daughters." The Grimkés and the thousands of conscious feminists who joined the cause as it developed were all schooled in public organization and political campaigning through their work for abolitionism—even though they often felt, as the century progressed, the ruthlessness of the abolitionists' decisions to abandon the cause of women's rights whenever necessary or expedient in the antislavery struggle.

Both the Grimké sisters were brilliant polemicists and writers. But it is to Sarah Grimké that America owes its first effective moral justification of women's human rights and their place in society. Her pamphlet, *The Equality of the Sexes and the Condition of Women* (1838) antedates by six years Margaret Fuller's *Woman in the Nineteenth Century,* and had been well studied in England in the 1840s when abolitionist leaders visited there. The argument leaves no aspect of the condition of women in America unexplored—social relations between the sexes, equal pay for equal work, the mistreatment of slave women by white men and the psychological and moral effects of this upon white women, the legal disabilities of all women, their Christian right to enter the ministry (and indeed their natural right to any occupation for which they could qualify by training and merit). There is a brief but telling section on the history of other civilizations and the slavery, serfdom, or degradation of women and a brilliant discussion, in an early application of "Higher Criticism" to the Scriptures, denying that they are divine in origin, just as she had denied any Biblical justification for the inferiority of women.

The Biblical phase of the argument was of great importance, since it was a reply to the "Pastoral Letter" issued against the Grimkés and other women reformers by the Council of Congregational Ministers of Massachusetts. The "Pastoral Letter," it is evident, breathed anything but pastoral understanding, pronouncing the work of public reform by women as "unnatural" to their character, observing that the ". . . power of woman is her dependence, flowing from the consciousness of the weakness which God has given her for her protection." Pompous metaphor was introduced to censure these courageous women: "If the vine," the Pastoral Letter announced, "whose strength and beauty is to lean on the trellis-work, and half conceal its cluster, thinks to assume the independence and the over-shadowing nature of the elm, it will not only cease to bear fruit, but fall in shame and dishonor into the dust."

None of the masked threats in this letter were lost on Sarah Grimké, as we may infer from the unerring sense of human dignity which suffuses her argument. Cannot all at last see, she wrote, ". . . the simple truth, that God has made no distinction between men and

women as *moral* beings. . . . To me it is perfectly clear that whatsoever it is morally right for a man to do, it is morally right for a woman
to do." Leaning neither on trelliswork nor yearning to become the
overshadowing elm, she developed her position with analytic depth,
marshaling proofs of the intelligence, skill, courage, endurance, and
deep moral concern of women, all cultivated despite the discourage-
ments of a social world that refused them full education, brainwashed
their will and sense of purpose, and bribed them by trinkets, favors,
and approbation. As Sarah Grimké put it in "Southerny" terms, women
were created to believe that they should first be "butterflies" and "dolls"
and then docile churchgoing homebodies. At the time of writing, it
should be pointed out, Sarah Grimké was a Quaker who still wore
Quaker garb. She was later to break with the Quakers over matters of
discrimination against Negro members. Her argument for independence of spirit and self-direction must therefore not be assimilated to any
flamboyant pattern of licentious liberty. In any event, before Sarah
Grimké closed her powerful essay, she had established a case against
double standards and divided worlds for male and female. We will state
in her own words what she tried to prove:

"*That intellect is not sexed;* that strength of mind is not sexed;
and that our views about the duties of man . . . and the duties of
women, the spheres of man and the spheres of woman are merely arbitrary opinions, differing in different ages and countries, and dependent
solely on the will and judgment of erring mortals."

This was the fundamental truth: that intellect is not sexed! But as
she looked around her at the restraints and disabilities thrust upon
women, Sarah Grimké judged the situation to be appalling. The laws
had left women ". . . very little more liberty or power, in some respects,
than the slave." Not that free women could be compared in suffering
or in degradation to the slaves. "Still I believe the laws which deprive
married women of their rights and privileges, have a tendency to lessen
them in their own estimation as moral and responsible beings, and that
their being made by civil law inferior to their husbands, has a debasing
. . . effect upon them, teaching them practically the fatal lesson to
look unto man for protection and indulgence." She found that the laws
had crushed woman's individuality and quoted Blackstone effectively to
show that the legal existence of the woman is incorporated and con-

solidated into that of the husband under whose wing, protection, and cover she performs everything. These legal disabilities were furthered by a deliberate policy of keeping women ignorant, just as slaves in her own state were forbidden to be taught to read—to keep them "better slaves." It is to this issue that she talked when she spurned the male dictum that "She that knoweth how to compound a pudding is more desirable than she who skilfully compounds a poem," pointing proudly to women of intellect in past ages, as in the present age, who could compound something more than a pudding! Hypatia, Vittoria Colonna, Lady Jane Gray, and Miss Grimké's contemporary Harriet Martineau—these were some of the women whose learning and gifted intellects probed for truth without quarter. As for the standard comparison with men, Miss Grimké asked: what of Elizabeth of England, Maria Theresa of Germany, Catherine of Russia, and Isabella of Spain? Had not these women shown the world they were at least as well qualified to govern and sway the scepter of royalty as men? And had not these illustrious rulers purchased their celebrity by individual strength of character? Yet as she cited their example, she knew well that they were exceptional and that essentially men had so effectively monopolized the opportunities for knowledge and action that to expect women to assume the burden of proof of equal achievement was already an injustice, an unwarranted demand. How can one prove what women are capable of, when it is women deprived of educational opportunity and denied practical experience, deprived of expression, and of those subtle but essential inducements of admiration and incentive, who must be measured against quite differently privileged men?

In effect, then, Sarah Grimké perceived that the real issue concerned social and educational equality as much as it did the narrower sphere of equal legal and political rights. She herself was much indebted to her fond brother, Thomas S. Grimké, whose liberal views on female education she cited with approval. Give me, he said,

. . . a host of educated mothers and sisters and I will do more to revolutionize a country, in moral and religious taste, in manners and in social virtues and intellectual cultivation than I can possibly do in double or treble the time with a similar host of educated men. I cannot but think that the miserable condition of the great body of the people in all ancient communities is to be ascribed in a very great degree to the degradation of women.

Sarah Grimké saw the point, and in her final argument, the justification for full moral equality for women lay in its consequences for men and for the indivisible human society in which men, women, and children ceaselessly interact. If only men could see beyond the cake of custom and conventional pride, they would be able to share their heavy responsibilities of lifelong work. Sharing too in self-respect, men would benefit by the increased understanding and sympathy of women who had become their equals. They would see in truth that "woman, as their equal, was unspeakably more valuable than woman as their inferior."

Sarah Grimké's tract on equality, written a century and a quarter ago, provided the rationale for a movement that did not come to full political culmination until the ratification of the Nineteenth Amendment in 1920. In some ways, the story of this ultimate trial and costly struggle that consumed a century of human effort has never been fully told, nor has it been properly estimated in American history. Sad to say it is a story which is peculiarly muted and callously misunderstood, especially in our own times. The skill, the fortitude, the imagination and the moral tenacity of these feminists tend to be taken for granted or quite overlooked, while the caricatures, the vulgar jokes and jibes, and the bloomers are vividly relished and remembered.

No, the "suffragist" has not had a good press, and her image is barnacled: we see her as a strident and sexless female, her hatchet face rising above a mannish collar, sour, dour, shoving her angular frame into places and corners where healthy bully-boy males retreat for convivial moments. She is known to us as more shrew than sibyl, the zealot whose envy and hatred of male power is a pre-Freudian rampage, unchecked by visits to the therapeutic couch. As always, some of the image, part of the caricature, is related to actuality. The movement for woman's rights was a most complex and long-lived affair, and it certainly had its full share of bigots, its fanatics, its absurdities, and its mistakes. Reformers are troublemakers by any definition and by anyone's lights. To reform is to take trouble and to make trouble—even if the larger purpose is to make things better after the trouble subsides. To reform is to decide to resist drift; it is to unsettle fixities and challenge "normal" (some mistakenly think "natural") habits and ways. But the stunning irreducible fact about the feminist movement in America is the proved intelligence and good sense, the conscience and courage which the best of the women leaders effectively maintained. Much like the American colonial woman or her later sister on the moving frontier, these women reformers possessed the resourcefulness and inventiveness to put salt in their stew.

Think of women who could become, overnight in some cases, editors of newspapers—like Susan Anthony and Elizabeth Cady Stanton when the wealthy eccentric, George Francis Train, suddenly decided to establish *The Revolution* for them to edit—and handed them, with his check, a motto which they kept while the newspaper ran: "Men, their rights and nothing more; women, their rights and nothing less!" Or think of women like Margaret Fuller, who could count as friends and supporters the circle of writers and philosophers to which Emerson, Thoreau, Channing, and Alcott belonged; women who became educators of underprivileged white children and freed Negroes, in the North and eventually in the South; women who survived the isolation-cell welcome of medical school until they passed their exams and then knocked on hospital doors begging the chance to practice medicine; women who literally drove themselves to early graves via exhausting speaking tours, in bitter weather, over wretched roads, to cold and barnlike halls and bedbug-infested beds for rest—in the innumerable state campaigns for the suffrage. And reflect for a moment on the feelings of all the women workers in this cause, who had to walk a daily line between hostile men and spiteful women, "sisters" whose imaginations rested content with trelliswork and overshadowing elm, and whose generosity could not encompass a single migrant from their painted garden. Rousseau's *aperçu* is fitting here: "Slaves lose everything in their chains, even the desire of escaping from them; they love their servitude, as the comrades of Ulysses loved their brutish condition."

But having reviewed these moments of America's past, we must ask to what purpose? Biographically, I am tempted to say that part of my purpose has been to confess, "Peccavi." For like so many so-called "emancipated" modern women I had accepted the view that the abstract issue of "equal rights" for women was old hat—the battle had been won, long ago and far away, by crusaders who were too single-minded to be interesting, too righteous to be admired, and too graceless to be accepted into my private family of ideal types. My academic journey began in the crude and innocent belief that the life of the mind and the republic of humanistic scholarship was wide open to work and worth, regardless of race, creed, color, or previous condition of sexual servitude. I am now an older and, if not wiser, at least a less ebullient believer in equality, as she is practiced in this advanced and democratic world. It has occurred to me, with respect to the Grimkés and other courageous women who served this cause, that possibly most Americans, as well as myself, might say with T. S. Eliot, "We had the experience but missed the meaning."

Why so? As we look about us in the 1960s, only mop-up operations remain to complete the victory of full legal rights for women, to match the suffrage for which so much was expended, and from which so much was hoped for. This era of the sixties is distinctively the post-World War II complex; for in that war women served in the Armed Forces and on every industrial production line, and they now continue to participate in the labor force in increasing numbers. In 1960, the United States Census reported that 35 per cent of all women over fourteen were in the nation's labor force and that a marked increase in participation rates for married women and middle-aged women was an established trend. In higher education, it is now the case that universities and colleges are by and large open to women on an equal basis with men (except of course in traditionally noncoeducational institutions), and it was true by 1958 that women made up 35 per cent of the total opening enrollment of degree-credit students in all institutions. Meanwhile even graduate education reflects the growing participation of women. In 1957–1958, 11 plus per cent of all Ph.D. degrees in the country were awarded to women—despite the warning statement in the *National Manpower Council Report on Womanpower* that only 1 woman out of every 300 capable of earning a doctoral degree does so. To be sure, in scholarships and fellowships women do not have as many opportunities as, or equal opportunities with, men; and in salary rewards there remains, in most cases, a gap.

No one in his right mind (or even in her right mind) can question this very real progress in the past twenty years in the position of women, both in the labor force in general and in the educational world as students and faculty. And yet there is an ineradicable sense of unhealthy confusion which echoes the past: Are women inferior, should they retire once again to the sanctity of their predestined roles as wives, mothers, homemakers? Should they withdraw from the "competition" with men and express their unused energies in a variety of voluntary organization tasks—typically in PTA work, League of Women Voters' work, culture clubs, hospital committees, Red Cross activities? Or—if they must do more than "compound a pudding"—let them write a poem (novel, short story, children's story)? Perhaps, in this industrial age, encourage them to weave cloth, make crude silver jewelry, paint between times, or bake small ceramic objects in kilns? While it may be clear that I do not find this kind of program acceptable, it is important to do it justice and to state it in its best terms.

The revived "second sex" approach often flows from moral values that are themselves undeniably good. For example, Lynn White, Jr., in a stimulating book called *Educating Our Daughters*, some years ago entered a plea that women's education should recognize an "equality of differences as well as equality of identities." He felt that a better preparation would be provided by colleges for "our daughters" if the so-called minor arts were emphasized in a special college curriculum for them. On this kind of proposal, I myself find a recent Barnard College report on the liberal arts curriculum an effective rejoinder. It says: "Men and women differ, but the liberal arts college addresses itself to them as human beings. . . . A curriculum intelligently devised to develop the intelligence, artistic and social potentialities of the students would, in general, serve men and women equally well."

Harder to meet is a position which maintains that the feminist movement, with its emphasis upon competition with men for place and power, was a "false-lead" and overlooked and minimized the woman's role as the guardian of life, morality, and human compassion.

This position is wrong insofar as it is prescriptive and universal. No moral value and no human right is absolute. It is right in maintaining that the demand for equal rights can become a negative value if it fails to meet the test of intelligent scrutiny in terms of its consequences and costs. But if we examine the argument more closely, we see that it will not do. For who can limit the horizon or chart the loyalty that all women must serve? After World War II, a Rockefeller Foundation report pointed out that in the war an American soldier fighting in the

Far East had been saved from tetanus by the discoveries of a Japanese scientist; a Russian had been given blood transfusion developed by an Austrian; and a German soldier was protected from typhoid by the labors of a Russian. It commented: "From birth to death we are surrounded by an invisible host of the spirit of men who never thought in terms of flags or boundaries and who never served a lesser loyalty than the welfare of mankind." Was it not the meaning of Sarah Grimké's angle of vision that there would always be women who would settle for no lesser loyalty than the welfare of mankind, and that the self-respect, self-confidence, and limitless aspiration of every human being should not be crippled by a system of invidious restraints? Would any sane person refuse to benefit by a new drug because it had been discovered, perchance, by a woman rather than a man? Is sex to limit freedom of inquiry, freedom of search, freedom to invent and to serve the highest intellectual and moral goals?

In a sense, the position that woman's role is that of moral arbiter is female chauvinism. It is the reverse of the "inferiority" argument, although paradoxically itself an outgrowth from the doctrine of two quite separate spheres of male and female moral and intellectual traits. Women are people, some say, but people who cannot think like men, cannot administer, solve practical public problems, or master the same type of subject matter that comes more naturally to the masculine intelligence and to male character. Women are supposedly gifted in intuitive, artistic matters. Their talent and role is presumably that of great feeling and heart—they are the peacemakers, the civilizers par excellence.

Not so—however subtly flattering or subtly degrading one considers the description. Women, alas, are people: some good, some bad (relatively), some intelligent, some not so; as often as men, quarrelsome (who sits for the portrait of the termagant and shrew?) and often the bane of moralists in their compliance with every type of vice. The only thing we can be sure of in terms of intellectual and moral traits is that there should be no prior restraint on seeing what, with proper training, women actually make themselves competent of. In this century, the philosophical and logical powers of analysis of Susan Stebbing in England were never questioned on the grounds of sex, nor, for that matter, has anyone found Simone de Beauvoir (whatever one thinks of existentialism as a philosophy) an intelligence inferior to her male associates. Incidentally, it is Miss de Beauvoir's use of Thomas Jefferson's strategy of piecemeal moral advance that accurately disposes of the argument of ineradicably different intellectual and moral roles for women. She paraphrases the Jeffersonian strategy as "Let us come into existence before being asked to justify our existence." In short, let us be, before you define what we are. The female adoption of the position I have called "female chauvinism" is rife with ironies, making one think of the statement in Ecclesiastes: "A man who wishes you ill is better than a woman who wishes you well."

In appraising the situation of women today who seek professional standing and a policy of unhampered scope for work and for the realities of economic and prestige reward for merit, I must say that the ideal of equal rights is heavily compromised. If there is any courage left in the class of professional American women who seem to fear the stereotype of the female reformer more than they love justice, their work is cut out for them. For in truth, with all our scrupulous efforts to set the house of democracy in order in a world in which we anxiously work on the "image of America," sending a peace corps abroad and informational and cultural programs in quantity to fortify the technological and financial assistance our policy wisely sustains, professional talent and creativity in this nation, regardless of sex, cannot afford to be discouraged. This is a practical argument, in the first instance, but essentially a moral and social argument in the long run. It implies that in the context of the academy, as in every learned profession, the basic American ideal of equality of opportunity must not be permitted to become a jest.

What women face, for example, as they try to carry out their professional tasks is what R. H. Tawney once described as ". . . the impertinent courtesy of an invitation offered to unwelcome guests, in the certainty that circumstances will prevent them from accepting it." That is why I have called my paper "Two Cheers for Equality." I am reserving three cheers not for the jest but for the cheerful acceptance of full human rights in some indistinct future. For the peculiar half-world of limited tolerance in which professional women work is democratic in pose only. "Treat another as inferior," remarked the philosopher Ralph Barton Perry, "and you place him in a dilemma. He must either suffer humiliation or show resentment. You either break his will or antagonize it." Employers who will not train women for executive tasks;

department chairmen who will not consider hiring a woman for professional openings; administrators who will not concern themselves with equal (perhaps even greater) opportunities for graduate fellowship and scholarship programs for women students and promotion up the ladder for faculty members of proved merit—these are only the most visible tokens of the discrimination which in fact exists against women today. A thousand subterranean attitudes and devices in effect make up a systematic pattern of discrimination, which even to identify and name is to invite the charge of female "aggression" and troublemaking. Sensitive women have consequently learned to see, to be silent, and to convert a measure of hope to either cynicism or despair. Another way to describe this attitude in terms of its latent irony is to recommend a policy of Leibnitzian optimism, which holds that this is the best of all possible worlds and that everything in it is a necessary evil!

The most corrosive effect of the discrimination against women is the psychological effect it has of reducing a sense of personal competence, of encouraging women to disqualify themselves before the male managerial world has a chance to rebuff them. The *Radcliffe Report on Graduate Education for Women* discusses the varieties of discrimination which women are subject to in staying out of fields which are traditionally thought to be "men's," in having to compete for jobs on a curious ratio which one Radcliffe-trained faculty woman reported as being that ". . . a woman has to be twice as good and work twice as hard as a man." The bargaining power of women is invariably less than that of men, and the so-called "nepotism" rule in effect on many campuses further reduces the chance for academic employment when women move to a campus where their husbands are employed. Administrative positions, chairmanships of faculty committees, real power, in short, in the academic decision-making process is, as one might expect, even more scarce for women than the professional-employment ratio suggests.

In line with this pattern of covert discrimination is the fact discussed in the Civil Service Commission survey a few years ago that 94 per cent of the requests they received from government agencies for top management jobs specified men. The assurance that the new policy of the Civil Service Commission would be to compel agencies to specify reasons for requesting men (in short, the principle of introducing the difference of sex only where it is relevant to the performance of the job) was encouraging. It was limited, however, by what limits all compulsory and legal advances—namely, that with sufficient motivation and ingenious reason to aid and abet them, respectable reasons can be devised for circumventing almost any law. Again, the Radcliffe Ph.D. comes to mind who reported of her professional progress: "I think I am more acceptable in my present work if I do not attempt to press forward as strenuously as a man would, but such matters are subtle, and it is hard to separate trying to keep my head in general from trying not to be a strident female." Part of the program of reformation which lies ahead must, alas, reduce such hypersensitivity to the "strident female" tag. How to do this without becoming reduced in human and civilized terms is indeed a request for the wisdom of the serpent.

Surprisingly enough, the Radcliffe report which I cited came to an unexpected decision in its advice on how to solve the discrimination against professional women. It proposed that women should do work of such high quality that no question of "competition" should arise. It says:

It would take a very prejudiced anti-feminist to refuse to employ, on the ground of sex, a woman who has demonstrated ability and achievement clearly superior to that of the men available. To take an example outside the academic field, the only woman member of a famous symphony orchestra was engaged as a flutist because she far excelled the male applicants for the post. Her superiority demanded acceptance, and without question.

I hereby propose that this solution be known in American history as the "magic flute" position on female underprivilege. For if women must become magic flutists, playing tunes no male in the country can perform, out of a background which has already discouraged women from believing they can or should play at all, then "equality" for women has come to mean achieved mastery, unquestionable superiority, or genius— even before the hiring begins!

My solution is different. It takes the guise of the advice given by my old friend Thomas Jefferson to Madame de Staël, when he wrote: "Where wrongs are pressed, because it is believed they will be borne, resistance becomes morality." The indispensable and uncompromising meaning of equality is the principle of the intrinsic dignity of the human person—a postulate which is the presupposition of civilization and moral behavior. Equality is not mathematical equivalence, but as a mathematical logician suggested, a "mathematical metaphysics of the incommensurable," in which each person speaks for himself and demands consideration on his own behalf. No person in a democratic society should be forced by social inequality to live his life on different moral terms than others, for this is the meaning of a caste distinction. It degrades the person and forces him to lower the moral level of his life.

I should like to conclude with three specific implications, for the decade ahead, of the two cardinal policies I have advocated: that women should be treated as persons and that "intellect is not sexed."

First, the policy of certain superior colleges in refusing admittance to girls who have proved ability and motivation is antiquated. This suggestion may create the customary amusement inspired by every claim for equal rights. But I submit that any serious concern for equality of persons and for the requirements of economic growth in this critical decade of the 1960s necessitates the education and advancement of all our youths in skills and intelligence. I would even suspect that the increasing share of the vote by women should make everyone alive to the need for having an informed and intelligent comprehensive citizenry.

Second, there will be growing demands for professionally qualified teachers to meet the accelerated enrollment in colleges. Here clearly there should be no discrimination against properly qualified academic women. But there is one problem that must be dealt with forthrightly. Women, even academic women, want and have "the potential" to give birth to children. This potential is usually recognized, but it normally reenforces prejudice and discrimination against giving real positions to women in the academy. I propose that we meet this double problem of the increased demand for qualified teachers and the stated potential of woman by providing leaves of absence with the assurance that positions are held open.

Third, the sixties may provide conditions for increased discrimination against women in the labor force, including professional women. The labor force is growing at the rate of almost two million every year. At the same time increased productivity and automation are displacing workers in many major industries, such as transportation, construction, and even in the clerical occupations which are traditionally considered women's work sphere. If the demand for labor does not grow with the increasing labor supply, high rates of unemployment may persist. If so, women will find that men feel they are unduly competing for their jobs, and therefore increasingly expendable. This possible discrimination must be guarded against if we are concerned with equality and economic growth. Other means must be found than discrimination against women to meet the issues of full employment so as to provide for the fuller employment of all human resources.

The conclusion is out of concern for the multifarious riches and the diverse varieties of self-development inherent in the equality and liberty at the core of American ideals. Above all, it is not in any sense a fight with men. Of all the absurdities to be imagined in this turmoiled world, the quarrel of one-half of the human race with the other is not even material for science fiction. On the contrary, I feel like poor Thoreau on his deathbed, who was asked by a bumbling friend whether he had made his peace with God. He replied: "I did not know that we had ever quarreled."

Finally, returning to my point of origin in this talk, I wish to acknowledge that the title "Two Cheers for Equality" is borrowed from a book by E. M. Forster called *Two Cheers for Democracy*. In it he explains: "Two Cheers for Democracy: one because it admits variety and two because it permits criticism. Two cheers are quite enough: there is no occasion to give three. Only Love the Beloved Republic deserves that." I, too, after my fashion have been keeping in mind love the beloved republic and asking only that the gates of the city be not inscribed: "For men only."

PSEUDO OR REAL EQUALITY

This is an actual transcription of the formal but spontaneous panel discussion of the papers immediately preceding. Only minor editing has been done where continuity and clarity required it. The editors feel that the spontaneity of the actual discussion gives a particular value to the panel in this form, since it amplifies questions arising from the formal presentations of the participants as well as answering questions from the audience.

Moderator: J. Fenton McKenna
Panel Members: Barbara Bates Gunderson, Adrienne Koch, Esther Peterson

Dr. McKenna   Our purpose is to discuss equality, real or pseudo. It seems to me that we are faced with a question very similar to some raised by one of our early comedians: How high is up? How long is a piece of string? How equal is equal? And to what is she or he equal? One of our bromides is that everyone is equal but some are more equal than others. Personally, I have been trying to determine in my own mind what in the world there is in a man or in man's outlook that any balanced woman would want to be equal to? That, however, may not be as scientific as it should be and may be a reflection on self-discovery. I would like first to refer to a challenge that was presented by Mrs. Peterson. This concerned our educational process and its inflexibility in terms of the development of potential leadership in women. I would ask the others on the panel if it does not appear that we are moving backward rather than forward in these terms, that our admissions policies in general throughout colleges and universities are moving much more positively toward the traditional aspect of the educational process. Even in the arts, as well as in the area of taking individual differences into account, we have the problem of everyone's being faced with the same pattern and process in education, particularly at the secondary level, where there is such intense pressure. This seems to me to present a deleterious effect. It certainly touches on those young men, for example, who have some sensitivity to the more delicate aspects of life, who exhibit in their responses more femininity than others, and who are deeply interested in the nonanalytical.

Dr. Koch I think the increasing traditionalism which has reasserted a hold particularly over secondary education but is being felt also in the colleges is somehow the effect of that whole post-Sputnik cycle from which we have not quite recovered. Sputnik generated a feeling of the intense need to compete and to cut out all kinds of experimental things that might have proved to be worthwhile. I doubt it is a lasting thing and think our attitude is already changing. It was more true three to five years ago than it is today, although that does not mean that there are not very vigorous attacks and attempts still supposedly to cleanse the secondary or primary school systems of any trace of a child-oriented program. On the whole, if those who really believe in innovation and experimentation would be a little more vocal and effective in making their opposition to a peak emphasis upon discipline without rebuttal, we would probably be able to stop some of these trends.

I have heard so many people launch wide attacks on Dewey's progressivism. They often know very little about this but agree blindly: "Oh, yes, that was a terrible thing." But it was not a terrible thing; it was a great advance. Historically it was a great innovation in the sense of the freshness of learning and relating it to life. But some of the fringe movements and later developments were exceedingly shallow. Consequently people settled for the stereotypes and became unwilling to consider the theory and philosophy behind progressivism, and evaluate how much of it was good and how much a series of mistakes.

Dr. McKenna Wouldn't you feel that this is an area in which women's leadership could become a very pronounced factor and be very valuable, since they do have stronger affiliations with the educational system, especially in organizations peripheral to the system itself?

Mrs. Gunderson I have been asked to elaborate on my statement that women do not carry through in the long haul.

I remember the wonderful fantasy of James Thurber, "Is Sex Necessary?" To paraphrase one of his ideas: women leave the country (for instance South Dakota) and go to New York to seek adventure, mad passion, and a wonderful new life. But they find a little rented room which they have to fix up, and they get lost in lamp shades.

It seems to me that a man and woman contemplating a life of marriage together say, "Darling, we will have these long talks by the fireside. I intend to continue with my violin, and you simply must write that book you're always talking about." They mean it and dearly love the idea, but like the unfortunate Kennecott, the cigar band is eventually found on the Stradivarius on the piano. As Miss Mannes put it, a woman is available in any room in the house; she simply does not say, "I am now busy working at my desk." Her inability to carry through in the long haul has to be faced.

Dr. Koch It depends on the kind of long haul it is. I think of somebody like Mary Somerville, the first English woman scientist for whom I have rather a feeling. Imagine this woman who educated herself and was able to compete with men in science, physics, chemistry and mathematics. Her daughter told that when Dr. Somerville was ninety years old she reported with delight that she was so pleased that her mind had lost none of its sharpness; she continued to enjoy her mathematical equations and reading. This was a haul of seventy years.

Dr. McKenna I would like to reverse this thought and ask Mrs. Peterson: Is it possible that many women who could find meaningful work are really not interested? Is it really their own apathy accounting for much of the slight degree of significant movement forward? Is there perhaps a tendency even to be concerned and anxious about the damage to their femininity, which was suggested several times during this symposium? Is it possible that we here are talking in terms of a very brilliant, able minority or a very positively interesting minority and that the great majority are quite definitely interested in other directions?

Mrs. Peterson I think it is tragic that there are many women who don't see it. I blame our mass media, magazines, television, and the nature of our community for their failure to stimulate and really to awaken women to these needs. But this is part of the whole problem discussed throughout this program.

Dr. McKenna This is true, but I was thinking, rather, in terms of directions and movements. I take it that you would indicate that the educational processes at the time and the home pattern we project have profound influence in this aspect.

Mrs. Gunderson I would like to tell a story from my experience in Washington. I became interested in a letter from a woman who wanted an opportunity to be a tower supervisor in air traffic control. She explained that she was a pilot, was fascinated by this, and felt she had a real vocation here, but was being restricted because only women who had such tower experience during the war were being employed. Looking into it, I found there was no reason why such a criterion had to continue, made a call on the Administrator of the FAA, and was eventually able to tell her that there was a job waiting for her; since she was breaking into a field which had been very predominantly masculine, I hoped she would let me know how it worked out. I even said to her, "I know this is going to be tough; you have to convince people that you can do this job." Three months passed and she wrote me a letter which broke my heart; she said that the men had not been very nice to her and that she had quit.

Dr. Koch That question is in line with one I have been asked: "All our speakers of this session are obviously gifted and superior, competent to prescribe for women who are not all gifted or superior. Are not the problems of inequality, in fact, only their problem? Is not their status superior to that of the mass of men?"

While this question is full of that sort of ambiguity of emotional dart and peck, there is something to say about it. What is essential to realize is that a woman is a person exactly in the sense in which a man is a person. Some men are dull and unimaginative, and some men read nothing but the comics; some women are like that, too, so there is no sense in prescription. Moreover, a man who is dull and interested in nothing except the area around his life space is not normally invited to participate in a conference. There has been some selection, to be sure, and it would be false to pretend otherwise.

Nobody is prescribing any policy. What we are saying is that those who have inner desires and ambitions that are objectively concentrated on some kind of conquest of knowledge or work, or who can play some sort of role other than the traditional, should be given the chance to escape. We are not saying that women must be interested in careers or that to be a housewife is a deplorable thing. But I think most women in America, which is a highly advanced and comfortable civilization, want more than simply the housewife role. They themselves, for reasons good, bad, and derivative, often apologize for being housewives. I sometimes think longingly of these women who can retreat, do not have to get up early in the morning to make classes and meet strict criteria all the time while keeping the home show going. Sometimes I wish there would be more frequent sabbaticals. But I have heard from innumerable women who stopped after a certain amount of graduate work or the beginning of a career that they are deplorably bored, and I feel sorry for them.

Mrs. Peterson   In this connection, I am asked: "Aren't you encouraging women to leave home and neglect their children?"

Certainly we are not, because we just hope that the home can become the place that we would all like it to be: the place where there is the security, economic strength, and the possibility of developing people to their fullest, which is not just a place to sleep and raise your head. That is what we want. But we must say that in many cases the home is happier if the woman is out working and making a contribution. Just bearing a child does not necessarily make a person a good mother.

Dr. Koch   I think the home is a mess, but it is not due to the fact that there are a few women, or increasingly many women, who have jobs. It is a mess for all kinds of complex reasons, having to do with the past history of America, the present crisis in which we live, the missile race, and automation and change-overs; men are just as messy as women.

Dr. McKenna   Here is an interesting question: "Does it not take an unusual male to allow this equality or independence of woman without trauma for his own ego?"

Dr. Koch   I think the three of us on this panel want to get up and applaud the males, the husbands who have always been willing to tolerate us. There is no question that any career of a married woman with children could possibly go on unless the husband were more than willing to help and take a lot of deprivations. It is the unsung story.

Dr. McKenna Would Mrs. Peterson comment on the specific areas of opportunity open to women?

Mrs. Peterson There is a whole list of shortage occupations: the health services, technology, mathematics, the new computer industry, and program planning. Teaching is one of the great ones as are nursing and the social services, all of which are expanding. There is a tremendous shortage in these areas, but these are all jobs that require skills and education; and here is a special problem. Everything is so flexible and fluid that we don't know exactly what we are educating for. A person may be prepared and trained now, but will require something completely different when the time comes for employment.

A question that comes up here is: "What do women particularly need to know to perform their home and childbearing tasks?" There are certain skills and tasks one should know something about such as child psychology, housing, design, and other homemaking areas. I think increasingly of how to buy, how to shop, and similar real needs. Whether this is taught by the family, by schools and colleges, or through community activities, these remain skills that are needed. Nowadays you often see a woman in a store buying with a slide rule because it is the only way to compute which package to buy; everything is sold as "giant economy," "super deluxe," and other sizes. The way to figure it out is to use this little mathematical device, so maybe a good advanced course in mathematics is something we would recommend. Also there is a question of organizing one's time. All of us who have worked and managed our homes know that if the housework can be done in a short time, then we do other things. Women have the intelligence to be able to manage their time, but this kind of education needs to become more general. Another facet is the services for women who are homebound. I think in our society we must look to day-care centers, not just as places to put a child to reject it, but to aid the child to develop. Many of these services could be made possible, so that women during those years would be free to have more opportunities and get out into the community to a larger extent.

Dr. McKenna A traditional question which has some reference in terms of the desirability of more opportunities for women to move up into higher administrative posts is: "Why do so many women say they would rather work for a man than a woman?"

Dr. Koch   That is easy to answer. First of all, you know that women like men.

Secondly, we are the kind of creature we are because we have been subjected to all these pressures and brainwashing that I referred to, and we tend to distrust a woman simply because we feel in some way she has bested us by being in a position in which she is over us. Some women are intolerable people, and others superb to work for. I have loathed and loved women bosses, but the same is true for men. I think it depends on the woman.

Dr. McKenna   Returning to the area of the person who has not had the background for some creative activity: "What is the role of the truly domestic woman to be when her children are grown and her husband is less demanding?" It seems the least creative women, the majority, should be considered in the study of woman.

Mrs. Gunderson   Let us say some women have a gift such as painting. But we all face the fact that domesticity is essential; it is a proper place for women's ambitions. I believe some women have gifts that parallel Wanda Landowska or Emily Dickinson in that they can do something with two bits and a bit of chintz that is awesome. I do my own housework, and I keep a very neat shop. I work on it; it is just ordinary, but it meets my stringent requirements. This is a natural, proper place for women who desire it, and I respect them as we all should. I can't believe that their fate after the domestic role is over is any more terrible than that of a woman with a gift for tightrope walking who finds she is sixty. In fact we are crying for the domestic arts as we survey these awful, hopeless air terminals with no comfort or convenience, and the sterile cubicle of a hotel room. How can we become real life partners if the schools do not supplement the home training? Each one of our ideas might be interesting. For one thing, I would like to see an end to the idea of the Little League just for boys and the Camp Fire for girls. Why cannot boys and girls get together and paint, listen to music, and have a tug of war? Perhaps we need less coeducational school and more coeducational play.

Dr. Koch   I agree with that and also think that there is a good deal of excitement that we often forget in simply talking about books and ideas that are fun. Back in the antediluvian age when I was a college student there used to be things like book clubs, where books were reviewed, and debating societies; these seem to have disappeared from the world. Maybe they are there, but I never hear much about them. I am sure lots more interesting things can be done which include both girls and boys.

Mrs. Peterson I have been asked about the equal pay issue: "What is the present situation, and are the equal pay laws merely a safety valve?"

I have just gone through the last session of Congress, a sort of fiery furnace, where a bill for the first time passed through the House, the Senate, only to get caught in the last throes of Congress, as usually happens. So far as the laws go, I would say that there is a very good chance of a Federal equal-pay law's being passed this year. But I don't think that it will answer all the questions, because the subtleties are far too deep. It cannot deal with many of the traditional differentials between men's and women's wages. However, in situations where there is a different rate for a man and a woman for the same job, as there is in many situations, such a law is applicable, and it should give an impetus to breaking down the more subtle barriers.

I receive many letters in which a woman will write, for example, "I am employed as a bank clerk, and I get $15 a week less than a man who is doing exactly the same thing. This man, who is working right next to me, has a wife who is employed and no children. I am a widow with three children, but because I am a woman, although I am doing exactly the same thing, I am getting $15 a week less." Now we have many cases like that, and often employers write to the employment service, "I am looking for an accountant; I will pay $1.95 for a man or $1.75 for a woman." We can by legislation get at some of these remaining existing inequalities, just as we did in the Attorney General's reversal of the old ruling, which are real substantive barriers, but we will not solve the whole thing. I think that over the period of years, the differential has decreased between men and women, but a recent article in the *Wall Street Journal* told of college girls who said that they expected a considerably lower entrance rate for jobs than men in the same positions. Now, of course, there are many myths as to why this is so, and I cannot go into that now. I do think we should encourage moving away these artificial barriers as rapidly as we can. If legislation does it, then we should support the legislation; as barriers fall, soon it will not be needed.

Dr. McKenna Can you speak of social and political equality of human rights without laying the economic base for it?

Mrs. Peterson They must be related. A classic letter from a girl might read: "They try to put us on a pedestal; they value us highly but they price us low," and there is some justice in her complaint. I examine a job where the rate for a woman is lower than the rate for a man and ask, "Why is this rate lower?" I will be told, "Her work is not worth as much." How do you measure worth in these areas? It opens a lot of questions, but usually you find that they are myths.

Mrs. Gunderson Isn't it also true that quite serious and sober-minded men will represent to you, Mrs. Peterson, that their experience is that a woman won't take responsibility? I have heard discussion in one of the agencies of the Federal government about promoting a woman to a job for which she shows qualities. I am always so amused; they say, "No, I don't see her in this job, she has difficulty in dealing with people," as though every man who gets a promotion is Perry Como himself. But I have discovered, particularly among married women, that they like to leave exactly at five o'clock, because there may be a young-ster waiting for them or a meal to fix. Employers can make a fairly strong case that a man has a little bit more general utility.

Mrs. Peterson But when you come right down to the fact, it isn't so, because the quitting time is a certain time.

Dr. Koch Some of the most efficient people I ever knew in gov-ernment are the ones who went home on time rather than working around the clock and proving their virtue.

Mrs. Peterson That is so true. These are individual differences, and it doesn't matter much which body they happen to be in actually.

Dr. McKenna Here is a question which seems to me to imply that the discriminatory attitude begins in early years, and the reactions from the first school years on. The question is, "What do you do if a ten-year old boy pulls the hair of a girl in the play group? She has slapped his face, he slaps her back; he gets punished, she doesn't. Why are girls in school discriminated against or for, whichever it is?"

Dr. Koch They are discriminated *for* in school so they can be discriminated *against* later. We should dispose of the old argument that women want to argue for equal rights but they also want people to give them seats when they are standing in the bus. The matter of wanting a seat if you are tired has to be treated as a subspecies of civilized behavior of a discriminating sort. There is such a thing as discrimination between and discrimination against. There is nothing wrong with discrimination between a pregnant woman who sits down, or a very fat man who has varicose veins for whom you would do well to get up. I have seen young women get up for both elderly and disabled men; it is discrimination between what is appropriate and what is mannerly or what is generous and what is courteous.

Mrs. Gunderson We must admit when we are taking all the blinders off that there is a provocative nature in women, and the teacher may know that this poor boy pulled her hair because of something that the girl did repeatedly. My older brother and I would wrestle, and I held my own in every fight until I heard my father's steps on the porch, then I fell on the carpet and held my breath, and my father would say, "What have you done to Barbara?"

Mrs. Peterson It reminds me of a little boy that came home and said, "There is a bully bothering me in school no end," and the father said, "You just go ahead and take care of that person," and the boy came home next day, and the father said, "How about the bully?" and the boy said, "Boy, did I beat her up."

Dr. McKenna This new question from the audience is, "What about the present and potential roles of Negro women? Little has been said here of this and how you see this."

Mrs. Peterson I feel strongly on this question. What I tried to point out was interesting, that in Negro families it is the women who are given the chance of education, probably because through history they have had to hold the family together in so many cases. Also some opportunities may be open for them where they are not for men. Certainly we find that the skills and abilities are there, and to deny this large group of our population both education and opportunity is to deny ourselves a great deal. I shall never forget a case where a Negro woman testified before one of our committees. She was asked, "Do you feel any discrimination?" She said, "I have a double discrimination, I am a Negro and a woman."

Also I think that women do not feel that we are doing enough to help women realize that they have a responsibility to contribute, when you consider how much is being done to improve our civilization. Femininity or leisure is a kind of a sweet coating for a bitter pill if it implies uselessness. What we need is usefulness and a feeling on the part of people that they ought to contribute.

Dr. McKenna   We have a question here which deals again with the possibility of working with the educational process in terms of the problems in some countries—Cuba is indicated here—where there is a greater than equal opportunity for Negroes to get education through governmental scholarships which were established to compensate for previous discrimination.

Do you think a similar policy for women would be highly desirable, and is there a potential in this direction bringing them into the colleges and universities?

Mrs. Peterson   It raises a question of how far we want to go in special legislation and special areas. I think it will take us a long time before we can give the Negro population the kind of education that should be available. If teachers are not well qualified, this in turn makes a chain that means there has not been the opportunity. I know myself in government, where we seek and want qualified talent, it is difficult sometimes to find a qualified Negro who is trained and can take a job. On the other hand, we start with extra points for veterans, for women, for the young and the handicapped. Sometime perhaps we will come to the type of society where we will group what I would like to call nonmerit factors together. Then perhaps we can evolve to a stage where nonmerit factors are not part of the requirements for jobs. We are not there yet, and we may arrive by picking at these various ways and trying to catch up, we have a long way to go in this.

Dr. Koch   I am sure you mean, Mrs. Peterson, essentially there is no compromising with excellence, and whenever you suggest some sort of resort to national legislation, it is to right an imbalance which does not permit excellence to be the criterion that you want. I hate this kind of token thinking, and I think any person of color would join me on the sex issue when people use it as a token saying, "We have a woman in the department of——and you see we have demonstrated our moral purity." I remember a shocking suggestion made when somebody once, in a history department, proposed acquiring an African historian and said, "Wouldn't it be a good thing to have a Negro for this position?" It is dreadful that this was said before looking for prospects and finding that there was a good Negro applicant. He should be considered along with everybody else, and if he is better qualified, you should hire him. Similarly with the woman; you don't want more than that, and you don't want to continue to serve as a token for your whole sex. Just as you dislike the "professional" Jew, the "professional" Negro, you must also dislike the "professional" woman, and I hate to be treated as a token for that with all one's silliness imputed to everybody else.

Dr. McKenna   Equality of opportunity.

Dr. Koch   For the person.

Mrs. Peterson   And the best-qualified person.

Dr. Koch   A metaphysical mathematics of the incommensurable—that is what I am recommending—not transposable into somebody else or something else. That is what is meant by the infinite worth of the human person.

PART FIVE

THE MALE REVOLT

Chairman: Helen E. Nahm

This opened with the study of a woman, Marilyn Monroe, and the events leading to her tragic suicide considered as a result of the Western view of values in women. An investment banker then discussed the important position that women hold in the economic world today and the reality of their participation. The final paper considered the direction in the future that we may expect from feminine evolution as we consider previous and current Western societies. The panel concerned itself particularly with male valuations of women and how they might relate to the values that had previously been presented.

PART TWO

THE MALE REVOLT

Mark Harris

ONE AMERICAN WOMAN:
A SPECULATION UPON DISBELIEF

Norma Jean Mortenson, known also as Norma Jean Baker, was born June 1, 1926, in or near Los Angeles under circumstances whose mysteries, after discommoding her childhood, would aggravate her mature anxieties. Of her father it was sometimes said that he died by automobile, sometimes that he died by motorcycle. Perhaps he was a baker. In any case, from the beginning he was effectively gone. The little girl dreamed of a father who looked like Clark Gable.

Of her mother more is known, but it is not encouraging. A film cutter at RKO, she was reputed beautiful, but no claim was made for her peace of mind: betrayed and abandoned, penultimately widowed, and finally insane, she in turn abandoned Norma Jean to a sequence of orphanages and foster homes. Norma Jean, who lost count, later estimated that she had lived with twelve families, each receiving, in those Depression days, $20 a month in public money for her care. Her first home, she recalled, was a "semi-rural semi-slum." She could turn a phrase.

Photographs show a lovely child, but the childhood wasn't. At the age of two she was almost smothered to death by an hysterical neighbor and at six almost raped by "a friend of the family." One family taught her to recite.

> I promise, God helping me, not to buy, drink, sell, or give
> Alcoholic liquor while I live.

From all tobaccos I'll abstain
And never take God's name in vain

but at the hearth of another her playthings were whiskey bottles.

At nine, in the Los Angeles Orphans' Home, her first big money was a nickel a month for pantry labor, of which a penny a Sunday went into the church basket. With the surplus penny she bought a hair ribbon. So runs the legend. She stuttered, she heard noises in her head, and she contemplated suicide.

At sixteen, working in a wartime aricraft plant, she was photographed by an Army publicity man who thought that the distribution of her picture among the fighting forces would serve an inspirational end. Indeed, one unit soon named her Miss Flamethrower, soldiers in the Aleutians voted her the girl most likely to thaw Alaska, and the Seventh Division Medical Corps elected her the girl they would most like to examine.

Then she married, perhaps to avoid being returned to an orphanage. She called him Daddy, and he called her Baby. For a while they lived with his parents, later in "a little fold-up-bed place." It was a marriage which brought her, she afterward said, neither happiness nor pain, just an aimless silence. He entered military service. She modeled.

By the time of their divorce, in October, 1946, her face and figure had appeared upon several magazine covers and been seen by, among others, 20th Century-Fox, who signed her to a one-year contract at $125 a week and changed her name to Marilyn Monroe. A cameraman said, "Her natural beauty plus her inferiority complex give her a look of mystery."

She was twenty years old, and she must have believed, in her youth and relative innocence, that she was headed somewhere, like Up, like Success. She knew by her mirror that she was radiant, and she knew by her history that she had a nimble, preserving intelligence: had she not thus far survived neglect, poverty, and a mistaken marriage? She thought, too, putting radiance and intelligence together, that she had a talent for acting. She studied acting at The Actors' Lab in Hollywood and literature at U.C.L.A. downtown, and she lived frugally. She would afterward play in a moving picture called *How to Marry a*

Millionaire, but in the life that was her own she was unmoved by millionaires. "I was never kept, to be blunt about it. I always kept myself. I have always had a pride in the fact that I was on my own." She owned 200 books (Schweitzer, Tolstoy, Emerson, Whitman, Rilke, Milton, Lincoln Steffens, and Arthur Miller) and records of Beethoven and Jelly Roll Morton.

It is not difficult to see, especially in retrospect, that she was uncommon, though to 20th Century-Fox, which paid a great many young ladies $125 a week, she was only one blonde girl in a world of blonde girls where even here or there an uncommon blonde was common enough. After a year, for lack of a clear motivation to renew, the studio allowed her contract to lapse.

Still she modeled. Once, for $50, she modeled anonymously nude on red velvet for a photographer named Tom Kelley, who was afterward proud of the fact that no matter how you turned the photograph its composition was impeccably symmetrical. The photograph, turned calendar, brought him $900 from a printer who sold it in quantity for ¾ million dollars to barber shops, gasoline stations, ships' galleys and soldiers' barracks, wherever men mark time across the world. Several years later, when her proprietors feared that the revelation of the calendar would damage her career, she refused to disclaim it. "Sure I posed. I was hungry." As a child she had had persistent dreams of walking naked in church over the prostrate forms of her friends, neighbors, and foster parents, "being careful not to step on anyone."

In 1950, in a pair of lounging pajamas, she played a small part in a motion picture called *The Asphalt Jungle.* She had auditioned for the director, John Huston. "I remember she was nervous," Huston remembered. "But she knew what she wanted. She insisted on reading for the role sprawled on the floor. She wasn't satisfied. She asked if she could do it again. But she had the part the first time. . . ." Joseph Mankiewicz, watching her in *The Asphalt Jungle,* wanted her for a picture called *All About Eve,* and Zanuck, watching her in *All About Eve,* reclaimed her for 20th Century-Fox, this time with a seven-year contract beginning at $500 a week.

So much money resounds with authority. But it was less than star money, and Hollywood above all is stars—names and faces capable of magically drawing the public into movie houses in spite of the force of such competing attractions as television, bowling, motoring, and bed rest. Miss Monroe was not yet a star.

Of course, she was soon to become one, and she must have believed, at twenty-five years and $500 a week, that the choices and decisions of her life had thus far been more right than wrong. Almost everything her culture had ever taught her and all that she had ever known or seen or heard must have impressed upon her mind the American fact that More is Up: Success. Or even if she doubted this, alone of an evening with Schweitzer or Tolstoy (she took little pleasure in night life, felt no necessity to be seen), who in Hollywood could possibly have corroborated or encouraged her skepticism, or explored its implications with her, or really seriously persuaded her or anyone that the shape of death might early appear even in the indisputably happy form of a moving picture invitingly entitled *Don't Bother to Knock,* which grossed $26,000 in its first week in New York in spite of bad movie-going weather and bad newspaper reviews?

The pictures *Niagara* and *Gentlemen Prefer Blondes* quickly followed. In the first she showered in silhouette, in the latter she danced à la burlesque, bumps and grinds pruriently denatured to satisfy a code which, forbidding nakedness, provides the basic material from which interested persons may labor independently upon their own fantasies. ("American culture," Isaac Rosenfeld has written, "is contradictory with respect to sex, urging its members on in a riot of stimulation, while it upholds conventional and moral restraints and taboos.")

For Marilyn Monroe a formula had been found. Henceforth she would be compelled to perform according to the formula so long as the profit flowed. The very titles of the moving pictures with which she was associated during the early 1950s suggest the restrictions of that formula—*Ladies of the Chorus, Love Happy, Let's Make It Legal, Love Nest, Pink Tights.*

By 1954 she was a star. In that year she made *The Seven-year Itch* and after the shooting attended a supper in her honor, arriving an hour late in a red chiffon gown borrowed from the studio. She had never owned an evening gown. Now for the first time she met Clark Gable, once the fantasy father of the fatherless child. She was twenty-eight years old, and she danced in his arms.

How is 20th Century-Fox like a little girl in a borrowed blue sweater?

In West Los Angeles, when Norma Jean was twelve years old, she went to school one day in a borrowed blue sweater. The boys of her class "suddenly began screaming and groaning and throwing themselves on the floor." After school they went to her house. "For the first time in my life I had friends. I prayed that they wouldn't go away." But there was a way of keeping them even more effective than prayer, and so she wore the blue sweater again. This she learned.

Marilyn Monroe and 20th Century-Fox produced happiness by formula. In a decade of crisis in Hollywood she was one answer to the single question the industry asked: what sells? It no longer even pretended to be serious. (In 1820 an Englishman asked, "In the four quarters of the globe, who reads an American book?" Now one might ask, "Who sees an American movie?") Its principal function had become its exclusive function—to respect the ultimate consumer's sacred whimsy. What's good for Hollywood is good for the U.S.A. Profit and democracy are sisters under the skin.

Having learned to produce happiness by formula, what would happen to Marilyn Monroe if what she became should disgust her and poison her with self-contempt? The course of her career had received its first impetus from the odd penchant of large numbers of men for photographs—pin-ups—to be hung upon walls for the purpose of study. If claim may pass as fact, Miss Monroe, by the end of 1951, hung upon more walls than any other American woman; 20th Century-Fox was soon receiving, says one report, "thousands of letters a month" requesting her photograph.

Why Marilyn Monroe? Few of her admirers had ever seen her act in a movie, and to most of them her name was unknown. Why not any of a hundred or a thousand young ladies who had contrived to appear upon the cover of a magazine?

My first inclination is to search for publicity machinery behind a phenomenon so irrational. But no, whatever it was, Miss Monroe had it. It was hers. It came through. It was felt. It defied imitation, like the syrup of Coca-Cola.

And her very namelessness may have been chief among her charms.

Was this not the simplest and purest and least menacing relationship most of her admirers had known? Perfectly sexual, she was also absolutely silent. So long as she was only a picture on the wall she could never outwit or outsmart her partner, while, like the paper doll of the song, she was always waiting, she could never be stolen. A relationship with her was therefore effortless, without mess or obligation, totally uncomplicated. Above all, she provided that highest of all selfish pleasure, for she demanded no equality of pleasure, no exchange, no collaboration, no mutuality.

In the film *The Seven-year Itch* the pin-up turned to flesh. Marilyn Monroe played The Girl upstairs whom Tom Ewell downstairs more or less hopes to seduce while his wife's away. But he doesn't really dare, or can't, or won't. Like the red-blooded Americans peeping at pin-ups in gas stations and ships' galleys, he can't relate with sufficient grace to a live and superior beauty. Such a relationship would force him to grant all her humanity, as if he believed not only in her tape-measure dimensions (finally paper-thin for safety's sake) but in the dimensions of her mind and spirit.

As the success of her formula increasingly bored her, Marilyn Monroe more and more expressed her desire to become an actress, thus to employ the larger range of her womanhood. This desire was generally viewed as amusing but impractical. *Life* magazine called this ambition "irrational," and *Time* said that "her acting talents, if any, run a needless second" to her truest virtues—"her moist 'come-on' look . . . moist, half-closed eyes and moist, half-opened mouth." The journalists, incapable of believing in motivations not their own—believing in fame and gross receipts and the easiest popular expectations of women—could never imagine what more Miss Monroe might have wished to be. Didn't she, after all, fulfill *their* idea of a woman? "You know, journalists," said Arthur Miller—the playwright, her third husband—"usually come around with an angle. They *have* to. They simply never get the time or the opportunity to hang around long enough to decide anything. Over the years that angle becomes the easiest thing to do."

Above all, the danger lies in the thinking that makes it so. Sufficiently propagandized, the innocent believes in his guilt, as Marilyn Monroe learned to believe in her limitations, and as women in general perhaps do. Of course we freely say, "I don't care what anybody thinks," but of course we care. At the time of her marriage to Joe DiMaggio in 1954 she must herself have capitulated to a public image of herself which had overwhelmed her private conviction. His life was his body, his power was his power. It must have seemed to her a proper wedding because a proper definition of herself. Within a year it ended. Mrs. Joe DiMaggio she wasn't. That she knew. Nor The Girl upstairs. Nor a pin-up. At this time of her life, said a friend, she was engaged in "an absolute desperate attempt to find out what she was and what she wanted."

One thing she didn't want was 20th Century-Fox's film, *How to Be Very Very Popular.* She walked out, announcing the formation of an independent company to be known as Marilyn Monroe Productions, Inc. More money? Perhaps so. But she had been "drowning in Hollywood" (Eli Wallach's phrase), and she was determined, he said, not to spend the rest of her life "just wiggling [her] behind."

"I want to expand," said Miss Monroe, "to get into other fields, to broaden my scope. . . . People have scope, you know, they *really* do." She declared herself, at this time, with a remark which was to plague her. She said, "I want to play strong dramatic parts, like Grushenka," an assertion which was to be hurled mockingly back at her, quite as if her experiences as waif and queen among peasants and lechers rich and poor in Southern California necessarily deprived her of a Dostoevskian outlook.

Hollywood minimized her by laughing at her. Director Billy Wilder, cynically reducing her new hope to the old focus, cheerfully said he would be pleased to direct her not only in *The Brothers Karamazov* but in a series of *Karamazov* sequels, such as *The Brothers Karamazov Meet Abbott and Costello,* etc. Disputing her claim that she needed training in acting, Wilder expressed in a breath the ruling conviction of both commercial Hollywood and an America gaping at pin-ups: "God gave her everything. The first day a photographer took a picture of her she was a genius." Her employer summed it up more formally. "20th Century-Fox," said 20th Century-Fox, "is very satisfied with both the artistic and financial results from the pictures in which Miss Monroe has appeared."

For a year, in New York, she led a private life. She studied acting with Lee and Paula Strasberg at The Actors Studio. I say *studied,* implying teachers, though I suspect that the Strasbergs served mainly as counselors, cheerleaders, psychologists whose task was perhaps less instruction than a demonstration of faith. All teachers of adults have had the experience of the woman touching thirty who has come to realize that she has for some time known what exists to be known but who needs an outer voice to confirm the inner. "For the first time I felt accepted, not as a freak, but as myself." Praised for her acting, her health improved. Here her circle of friends also included Arthur Miller.

Miller's interior, like hers, baffled the press. The marriage of Miller and Miss Monroe was described by one reporter as "the most unlikely . . . since the Owl and the Pussycat"—the familiar insistence, in the language of American disbelief, upon the imagined incongruity between brains and beauty, love and intellect, flesh and sensibility. Owning no matching veil for her beige wedding dress, she dyed one in coffee. The groom, though he was wealthy enough, owned only two suits—"the one he was married in," the bride said, "and the other one." Miller posed for photographers awkwardly, perhaps because grudgingly, resisting the insolence of the expectation that a man married to Marilyn Monroe must necessarily embrace her during every waking moment. Nor did Miller ever answer the question most often asked by obsessed reporters, "What does Marilyn wear to bed?" On the back of a wedding picture the bride wrote, "Hope, Hope, Hope."

He spoke of her always as actress, person; as mind, never as freak. Of her acting he said, "I took her as a serious actress before I ever met her. I think she's an adroit comedienne, but I also think that she might turn into the greatest tragic actress that can be imagined." His own arduous habits of labor enabled him to share her distress at moments when others viewed her as merely petulant. "In a whole picture," he said, "there may be only two scenes of which she is really proud. She has great respect for the idea of acting, so great that some part of her is always put to shame by the distance between what she achieves and the goal she has set for herself."

It was a noble strategy and a clearheaded loyalty, too late. Nor is it irrelevant that at the time of their marriage Miller's dispute with the Congressional Un-American Activities Committee centered about the question of loyalty—his refusal to implicate associates of his political past. "The only real territory left," he said in another connection, "is relationship to other people. There really never was any other territory. . . ."

Miller said once, "Marilyn identifies powerfully with all living things, but her extraordinary embrace of life is intermingled with great sadness." This conception of her he carried into a short story, *Please Don't Kill Anything*, in which a girl with a "startling shape" laments fish dying upon a beach. She wants to throw them back. Her less anquished escort—her husband—points out that there are twenty-five miles of beach alive with dying fish. "He did not bend to pick them up because she seemed prepared to sacrifice them and he went back to her, feeling, somehow, that if he let those two die on the beach she might come to terms with this kind of waste." Once, during her first marriage, she had tried to bring a cow indoors out of the rain; as Rosalyn, in Miller's screenplay *The Misfits*, she would oppose the killing of horses.

In the autumn of 1956 the Millers went to England, where she made *The Prince and the Showgirl* with Sir Laurence Olivier—another "unlikely" match said the very magazine (*Life*) with the very word it had used to describe her marriage to Miller. The British newspapermen asked her what she wore to bed.

The picture was made, though not without friction among the principals. When it was done, Miss Monroe apologized to the acting company for having been "so beastly," writing: "I hope you will all forgive me. It wasn't my fault. I've been very sick all through the picture. Please, please don't hold it against me." To some commentators such a note, from a lady so wealthy, so famous, so well married, and with so little apparent reason to be difficult, had a whining sound.

Two miscarriages and gynecological surgery during the months that followed were perhaps more convincing. There were also two pictures—a lively comedy called *Some Like It Hot*; and *Let's Make Love*, with Yves Montand, whose expressions of admiration for her "professional conscience" tended to be lost among newspaper rumors that he and she were in love.

In Nevada, in the summer of 1960, she began *The Misfits*. It would be her last film. It was also Clark Gable's last film. In September her exhaustion forced an interruption, but the work was soon resumed and completed. The following February, divorced from Miller, she entered a clinic in New York for rest and psychiatric treatment. Fourteen months later she began work upon a film called *Something's Got to Give,* but she answered less than half her calls, and the shooting schedule fell impossibly behind. "She was sick, she insisted," according to *Life.* "She was reneging on her contract, said 20th Century-Fox. . . . Fox blew the whistle. They fired the star and filed a $750,000 lawsuit against her. . . ." To the cast and crew she had wired a message echoing her message to the company of *The Prince and the Showgirl* six years before: "Please believe me, it was not my doing. . . . I so looked forward to working with you." Four months later she was found dead in her bed.

Whatever it was that worked its poisons upon her—three dead marriages, two miscarriages, an absent father, an insane mother, a forlorn childhood, a devouring press, the revelations of psychiatry—disbelief in herself was an obvious fact and perhaps a first factor. It so deeply undercut her belief in her own potentiality that she was equally unable to believe in Miller's belief in her. Who was Arthur Miller that he knew more than the whole world knew? "You know, journalists," said Arthur Miller, "over the years that angle becomes the easiest thing to do, and it's gotten, in Marilyn's case, to be very fruitful in terms of copy. And they keep pounding her all the time until that thing becomes reality. By that time, it's impossible to imagine anything else."

First reports of the death of Marilyn Monroe said she died nude, later reports corrected the first, and a panting world knew at last what Marilyn Monroe wore to bed. But would anybody believe her, even now? "It can't be, it can't be," cried a Hollywood agent, "she couldn't have killed herself, she had three deals going."

Albert E. Schwabacher, Jr.

THE REPOSITORY OF WEALTH

A great many statisticians, economists, and miscellaneous writers and speakers have come forward in the last couple of years to proclaim that women are on the verge of taking over our economy. Very often these announcements sound like a call to the colors, because there is a message attached to them; we men are supposed to rise up and do something about this economic envelopment. On the one hand, we are invited to rally around the last preserve of male independence. On the other, we are urged to join a program for national economic reform that sounds at times like moral rearmament. It is implied that this new force in Wall Street is either made up of unregenerate moms who have done in their husbands and are looking for new worlds to conquer, or an entirely new species of human being—a kind of a cross between a den mother and a Cash McCall—who is nevertheless unmistakably female. It depends upon your point of view. Fortunately, neither side has come forward with a program specific enough to rally around, and hence bloodshed in the near future seems unlikely.

For the moment I am not disposed to argue with either point of view. However, it is perhaps well to remind ourselves that the relationship of women to property has always presented a kind of puzzle in our traditional patriarchal society. Years of devotion as wife and mother should count for something; a widow should have some sort of claim upon the property of her late husband, and a daughter should not be discriminated against because of her sex. But our ancestors always felt that the control of property was a serious affair, not to be turned over to just anyone.

The solution that the Middle Ages found for this real dilemma has always impressed me. According to medieval law, when there were no male heirs, widows and daughters had a right to inherit the property of their late husbands or fathers. But their feudal superior, the king or other liege lord, had a right to ensure sound management procedures. He was entitled to select a custodian whom the widow or daughter had to marry. If the table manners of a medieval baron are any indication of his general domestic behavior, this was not an unmixed blessing.

The Middle Ages provided an example, perhaps, of male callousness. But wait. In matriarchies, where the management of property was a female prerogative, a husband, upon the death of his wife, was frequently packed unceremoniously off to his mother with little more than the clothes on his back. And that is an example of female callousness. Perhaps we can preclude from both examples that we should not be too hasty with our moral judgments in these weighty matters.

The medieval example intrigues me. Perhaps this is male prejudice; however, it seems to me that their procedure manifests a kind of imagination that we need today. The requirements of both sides were met. The Middle Ages did not deprive either party of its rights; it added an element to make things come out—it added that hulking baron.

Our problem today, according to the concepts of the Middle Ages, is not enough barons. While men continue to be born at about the same rate as women, they do not have the staying power. In 1940, there were 500,000 more women than men in this country; in 1950, 1,000,000; in 1960, 2½ million. The number of women in excess of men has increased five times in a period in which the population has not quite doubled. Looked at in another way, the life expectancy of women has increased by 12½ years in the last three decades, while the life span of men has been lengthened about 8 years. This is the price we pay for medical progress, and while I do not for a moment suppose that those engaged in such research are plotting against the male, I do think that they have shown a lack of foresight and prudence which would be intolerable in the investment business.

A cynical friend has observed that the highest skyscraper on the the most prominent hill in any town in the United States is sure to be owned by a charming lady whose husband worked himself to death becoming wealthy, and who at the moment of her husband's death came into the secret of immortality—"Be a rich widow!" This is an exaggeration, and it shows a kind of partisan party spirit inappropriate to this gathering. The fact is, a woman marries earlier and dies later, and will probably outlive her husband by about ten years. I would guess that among the more prosperous classes men are apt to marry even later than in other classes and to die even sooner. This would account for the myth that rich widows are immortal.

In any case, it is this disparity that is chiefly responsible for the accumulation of wealth in the hands of women. There are, of course, other reasons. More women work today, and therefore more women save. But since their total income from wages has been estimated at 50 billion dollars in a 600-billion-dollar economy, this saving is minor in terms of the whole property of the nation. Tax laws encouraging joint property possession and various kinds of trusts have contributed to the wealth of women.

How much wealth do women, in fact, own? I have seen estimates running as high as 70 per cent. The figures at my disposal would suggest that women own about half the personal property—the stocks and bonds and so forth—in the United States and perhaps a smaller percentage of the real estate.

The title of this talk is [women as] "The Repository of Wealth," and I congratulate the committee on the ambiguity of that word "repository." I think I know why they chose it. They were forced to make women sound like a collection of old socks filled with dollar bills, because the relationship of women to money is not clear. In our present economy it is possible to own a lot of wealth, receive regular income, and enjoy any increase in the capital that may accrue, and still have very little or nothing to say about its management. To what degree women merely own property and to what degree they both own and control is a vital distinction. Where there is ownership without control, it is as though the husband or other benefactor merely arranged to pay a certain pension to his widow or other heir for a certain specified time. Neither the economy nor the beneficiary need be affected by the arrangement.

The fact is, a great deal of the wealth which is said to "repose" in women is only beneficially owned by them, or is otherwise held by, or under the management of, men for the protection of women. A lot of this wealth represents insurance policies where the beneficiary has no current control. Another substantial portion certainly is in trust funds. The widow may have some voice in the management of these funds, but almost always a male trustee is provided who has at least equal legal authority and even more practical authority. Even where property is owned outright by women, it is frequently in fact managed by professional managers. The male in this instance is clearly the modern version of the medieval baron. In my experience, brokers seldom fit this role, but perhaps there are other compensations.

A good deal more than half of the wealth that women own is actually managed for them by someone else. My own estimate is that they themselves manage not more than 15 or 20 per cent of our total national wealth. If women were so inclined, of course, this percentage could be substantially increased. Let us concern ourselves merely with this 20 per cent. Obviously, this constitutes a challenge to women. This amount of wealth is certainly large enough to be worth our attention, both from the standpoint of the economy, and because of its psychological effect upon the women who have undertaken its management.

How do women investors, in fact, manage their money? Does the way in which women at present do this suggest that money management is an appropriate feminine activity?

Let us preface what I am about to say now by an admission of ignorance on one or two points. I do not know what the nature of women, as distinct from men, is. I do not even know what the potential of women is. I do not know how much typically feminine behavior is innate, how much is due to their customary role as wife and mother, and how much is merely a response to masculine demands. I hope that women are fundamentally different from men in significant ways which are not purely biological, but this is perhaps mere wishful thinking. All I can speak of with authority is how women at the present time respond to problems of money management.

It seems to me I can distinguish three basic types of women among my customers: First, there is the charming woman who continually astonishes her broker by her real understanding of money and market. She is both thoroughly feminine and thoroughly knowledgeable in money matters, and these two capacities strangely enough do not interfere with each other. It would be a pleasure to sit across from her at a board of directors' meeting or a breakfast table, or anything in between. In my experience, this sort of woman is rare, and I do not personally think that this delightful combination of qualities is possible for very many women. Perhaps I am wrong.

The second type of woman customer is also—happily—rare. This type of woman is intelligent and at times alarmingly informed about matters financial. This competence is achieved at a certain cost. It is not merely that she is less feminine than I, personally, find desirable. These women are perhaps more shrewd than any man; they are definitely more inflexible and more ruthless. I have always remembered a passage on women written by the poet William Butler Yeats which I encountered years ago:

Women, because the main event of their lives has been a giving of themselves and giving birth, hold an opinion as if it were some terrible stone doll. Men take up an opinion lightly and are easily false to it, and when faithful keep the habit of many interests. We still see the world, if we are of strong mind and body, with considerate eyes, but to women opinions become as their children or their sweethearts, and the greater their emotional capacity the more they forget all other things. They grow cruel, as if in defense of lover or child, and all this is done for "something other than human life."

Mr. Yeats is too harsh, but we must admit that he points to a kind of development possible to women in the business world. As I have said, this sort of woman in finance is rare. Yet if we are going to urge women to take up the responsibility of the management of their own financial affairs—as many articles in various journals have suggested in the recent past—we must consider the possibility of a certain percentage of them developing in this fashion. Women of this sort are, of course, useful. Would they make fine corporate directors? Possibly. But across the breakfast table? No.

The great majority of women investors fall into a third category. They are often charming, and I take them to lunch as often as my wife or good judgment permits. But a discussion of investments with them is frequently a waste of time. I find myself putting off business in their company. We discuss the theater!

To put the distinctive characteristic of this sort of woman investor as fairly as possible, I would have to say that they do not think about investment and money in the same way that I do. Some of my colleagues have suggested, in moments of bitterness, that they do not think about business matters at all. This is not true. They do think. But I do not understand the principles which govern their thinking.

Sally Iselin, in a recent article in *Harper's* asserted that "Most women think that when they spend money, they are saving it." This was an astonishing notion when I first encountered it, but my own research has amply confirmed its truth. It was not too surprising to find that my wife heartily subscribed to Mrs. Iselin's thesis; I have long suspected that principles were at work in this area that I do not understand. But my secretary also agreed. Which goes to show that a man's feeling of confidence around the office is partly an illusion.

Mrs. Iselin explains this odd view of women toward the accumulation of money by the average woman's domestic experience. Being accustomed to shop for staples which will always be used ultimately, a bargain in these commodities is a bargain whether they satisfy an immediate need or not. Of course, this attitude readily extends to items they will never need.

The explanation is perhaps true, but I suspect that it not the whole truth. The motives that enter into women's management of money are much more subterranean than that; they are not to be explained so easily.

For instance, it is a common experience in investment brokerage houses to receive a call from a lady customer inquiring about a certain stock. Usually it is a sort of diffident inquiry: "What do you think about the stock of the Aunt Sally Candy Company?" Sometimes it is put more forcefully: "Why haven't you bought any stock for me in the Aunt Sally Candy Company?" Discreet inquiry usually establishes the fact that the lady customer has just had some Aunt Sally Candy and it was delicious.

So the broker must explain that the company is fortunate to still be in business. It spends too much time making fine candy and not enough time making a return on its stockholders' investments. Its managers are great candymakers but poor money makers, and therefore one ought to enjoy their candy but never buy their stock. But the same lady will be back shortly with another product: the principles of this distinction she finds difficult to grasp.

A new appliance generally leads to the same sort of inquiry. For some women any new project around the house can lead to a transformation of her securities portfolio.

I have been answering this sort of inquiry, made periodically by one customer, for over fifteen years. How many times I have explained the difference between a bargain in the stock market and a bargain in a supermarket, I do not know. Every pleasant experience with a new product inevitably leads to the same kind of inquiry. She has become very devious of late years, and cloaks the purpose of her visit—but she still has to inquire.

Of course, it works the other way. I had a customer a few years ago who insisted that I sell 500 shares of Safeway company stock that she owned. Now I think highly of Safeway stock, and in my opinion, it was the wrong time to sell. Furthermore, there was a very sizable capital gains tax to pay. But, finally, sell we did. A clerk at Safeway had been rude to her.

One frequently hears that women are particularly emotional in financial matters. This seems to me to miss the point. I can be as emotional about financial matters as any woman that ever lived. The fact is rather that women approach stocks and bonds in a personal way. To buy stock in a company is for them like a sentimental vote of approval, having nothing, or very little, to do with earning power. Similarly, to sell a stock may be an impulsive act. It is this personal relationship that women are apt to feel toward the stocks they hold which accounts for the frequent observation that widows are sentimentally reluctant to sell stock which their deceased husbands purchased. It is not that they develop a sudden respect for his judgment—a respect never manifest in his lifetime. It is that they loved him and his memory and are reluctant to go contrary to the decisions he made during his lifetime, some of which could have been made in error.

An example of this extreme attachment was a widow who told me that since her husband had picked out every one of the stocks that she had inherited, she did not wish to make any changes in her portfolio. This was sentiment at its best, but it was not a loyalty her late husband would have appreciated. The investment requirements for a married couple may be different than those for a widow. A widow with the same attitude in the 1920s, inheriting certain railroad and utility stocks, might have found the income from her husband's estate inadequate to pay her lodgings in an old ladies' home. Personal attachments in the stock market can be disastrous.

The feeling some women have for preferred stocks arises from a similar attachment. These women don't want something common around if they can buy something preferred. Most women like quality—brand merchandise. They like the bluest of the blue chips—A.T.&T.—so well that it could probably survive even rude long-distance operators and repairmen who track mud into the house.

A part of this affection for blue chips is simply that—affection. Blue chips have the same sort of prestige for women buyers as do preferred stocks. Also, women think about investment in terms of a secure income. Women like A.T.&T. because they have heard that it has paid a steady $9 dividend since 1922. (It has recently split 3 for 1 and now pays $3.30 a share.) They like Standard Oil of California for the same reason. If a stock pays $5 a share when they buy it, $5 a share is what they expect out of it. They are ordinarily not interested in a stock which might pay erratically $6, then $4, and perhaps $7, eventually.

Perhaps the difficulty is that the majority of women have only a very hazy notion about the fundamentals of investment, let alone an understanding of stocks and bonds. In any case, their conservatism is sometimes peculiarly ill-adapted to speculation.

I must be candid; my dealings with women investors entail, from time to time, a certain amount of professional distress. I frequently find myself engaged in transactions, upon behalf of these clients, that seems to me positively irrational, and the sale of that Safeway stock still causes me real pain. I feel, stubbornly, that many women have a disastrously inadequate conception of wealth and the responsibility attached to its management and its uses.

But the problem can be looked at somewhat differently. Why is this attitude toward money wrong? Or to put it another way, why is my own attitude right? These questions take us at least partly out of the realm of investment theory, because the answer isn't entirely economic. These questions also take me, obviously, outside my area of professional competence. Please forgive me.

One of my more traumatic experiences with women investors clearly illustrates this point. Some years ago a very pleasant, soft-spoken elderly woman came to my office to discuss investment. She wasn't sure she was interested, but her children felt that she should talk to someone. It turned out, finally, that my new client had 1½ million dollars in the bank, and that it had been in the bank, drawing 3 per cent per annum, for over ten years, ever since the death of her husband. I remember thinking that if she did decide to invest it she would probably present herself at my office carrying a large, knitted handbag and count it out in $20 bills. A million and a half dollars in a bank for over ten years! I didn't know where to begin. How much could I tell her? How much would she understand? A million dollars invested in tax-free bonds could easily bring a safe 3 per cent tax-free return—or double her income from that segment of her savings. Could she grasp this fact? What about conservative, well-run companies whose common stocks had paid uninterrupted dividends for over forty years?

But the passing years have permitted me to take a more serene view of this incident, and I have learned something from it. Such a sum of money invested in the stock market during that time would have earned perhaps $80,000 a year with very little risk (and would very nearly have doubled itself in the intervening years). And it was the idea of this money not earning at that rate that troubled me. But in the bank it was already making $45,000 a year; income taxes and charities would in either case have consumed a part of the income. And I wasn't really concerned about the lady's loss of income; I hardly knew the lady. I felt the way I should imagine a farmer feels when he sees a fallow field. The farmer's feeling would have little to do with considerations of the world's food supply, and my feeling had nothing to do with spendable income. Money ought to be properly invested—because money ought to be properly invested.

Aesthetics is not a term one hears frequently around a broker's office, but I think we need it to explain the difference between the way the average woman approaches the stock market and the way most men approach it. Investment is a kind of skill, and a good portfolio is a creative act. A good portfolio will, of course, earn money handsomely. But there is more to a good portfolio, in my feeling, than that. I could even admire Khrushchev's portfolio if it accomplishes its objectives economically, if it is nicely balanced—in short, if it has been creatively put together. I may not be Michelangelo, but in my own modest way I am a creator, and it troubles me to observe noncreators dabbling with my materials.

I am sure that my feelings are generally shared by men in my profession. This creative feeling toward one's occupation is not confined to investment brokers. I have observed the same sort of feeling toward their work in house painters contemplating the botched work of their predecessors, or by a breeder of thoroughbred horses. Any man who knows his business is something of an artist, because he derives some sort of deep and important satisfaction out of the activity itself.

If this is so, a good deal of what has been written about women in business, and particularly about women as investors, is misleading. We have descriptions about husbands teaching their wives to be good investors. First they show them how to balance a checkbook; then they turn over the household accounts to them (under supervision). Perhaps then the happy couple might make some "make believe" investments. Finally—the great day comes—she begins to understand investments, and they set off hand-in-hand for their broker.

I love domestic tranquility, and I trust this sort of campaign does not plague too many housewives. I can assure you that nothing of the sort goes on around my house. And, in my opinion, this has little to do with success in investment.

If we want to make women good investors, if we want them to exercise the degree of control of the nation's business that is presently available to them, we must teach them to be creative in their approach to substantial sums of money. They must be taught to engage in the management of money at least partially for its own sake, and they must be taught to experience the sort of aesthetic pleasure that can accompany such management.

Do we really want to do this on a large scale? If it were only a matter of adding another area of creative possibility for women, training in investment might be very useful. But I am skeptical. I do not think human beings are capable of being creative in very many areas. Creation requires too much sustained attention, for one thing. I think each person has to choose. I think that one of the questions which must be considered by this conference is whether we want to encourage women to be creative in heretofore masculine areas such as investment, at the expense of areas in which women are often brilliantly creative at the present time.

It seems to me, and I speak merely as a man, prejudiced perhaps, and not as an investment broker—that a primary difference between men and women today lies in their different approaches to human relationships.

Women pay great attention to, take great pleasure in, and are finally creative about the specific kind of connection they have with other human beings, and perhaps particularly with men. This is obviously a difficulty when it comes to investments, but it is also a field of genuine creation which we are apt to take for granted. Ordinarily, men have no gift for this sort of thing.

Few men, for instance, can or care to manage so simple a piece of female business as planning a formal dinner party. I could not, and I admire my wife's attention to, and pleasure in, the details of this process just as many of my women clients are apt to be inexperienced in the activities of an investment or brokerage office. Women think in terms of human relationships of much more importance than this, of course. I suspect that we men live in a human world that has been deliberately and tactfully created for us by women. I have a different understanding with each client. I have one kind of relationship with my wife and another, entirely different relationship with a woman colleague. I did not create these relationships. Rather, the women themselves created them, and I would be sorry to live in the impersonal world that men, left to their own devices, would create. I like my relationship with women and I trust they do, too, because they created them.

Are you surprised at what I've said?

I imagine that I was expected to extol the merits of women in business and business for women. I think the situation is not that simple. Some women, as I pointed out earlier, have managed to be both women and business women, even investment brokers, brilliantly. (Schwabacher & Co. has a registered representative in Salt Lake City who is happily married, raising six children, and is a professional in her chosen career. This is an unusual case.) Most women, I think, have to choose.

W.hat is the choice? What, exactly, does a woman gain by managing her own investments? Hopefully some additional profit, a certain satisfaction. An investment counselor, managing a woman's money, must act on the side of conservatism. This does not mean that her investments will diminish in real value as the gradual inflation which seems characteristic of our economy moves ahead. Managers of trust funds are particularly cautious at times. They sometimes fail to keep an estate up to its original value, considering shrinkage of the value of the dollar which may occur in a conservative portfolio consisting mainly of bonds. A woman who leaves her investments to others may well leave a smaller estate than the rare business woman who is able to manage her own investments effectively. Favorable economic conditions could also help the estate become larger than the one she inherited.

Furthermore, the nation's economy might well be strengthened by knowledgeable female investors in large numbers. The money which is managed for women is managed, on the whole, very conservatively. A substantial portion of insurance company funds, for instance, is invested in government bonds. The only "repository" that is more conservative is a hole in the ground. An investment counselor, insofar as he must assume the responsibility for other people's funds, must act on the side of conservatism. The money owned by women but controlled by men surely exercises an important force upon the economy.

This large amount of money being managed so negatively disturbs me. Capitalism needs risk capital and large amounts of it.

Consequently, there would be both personal and social gain if women became financiers on a large scale. But it would not be all gain. What might be lost if women plunged into financial theory, if they learned really to appreciate a good portfolio, if they became creative about money in the fashion I have described? I think a lot of the richness would depart from our society. To become adept in stock management, women would have to learn to think like men. The difference between men and women would become merely biological. I, for one, should not like that. I like my women clients. I am sometimes taken aback by their attitude toward finance, but I like their attitude toward me, and I would be sorry so see it change. I am sure that most men, in spite of their habitual complaints about women, would not really be happy with any major changes in them. After all, almost half the adult population at the present time are men. That is enough.

Whether the women might find themselves any better off I do not know. Women might find the investment banking business a very satisfying activity. I do not suppose that it is necessarily more satisfying than those activities in which women now express themselves creatively. It is at least possible that Mr. Yeats was right, that women in some very fundamental way are different from men. If we should really succeed in converting great numbers of women to masculine ways of thinking in order to enable them to undertake heretofore masculine kinds of activity, they might be, on balance, the losers. They might conclude that the arrangement with the medieval barons, shaggy bears, bad table manners, and all, was actually preferable. It was not an ideal arrangement, but at least it enabled the medieval heiress to take up once again the task of creating a satisfactory relationship—a kind of creation which is perhaps natural to woman, and which is certainly her special gift.

There is a kind of conflict in all this between the demands of the economy and personal demands. I believe that in such a situation the economic consideration must defer to the human one. I believe that society exists for man and not man for society, even in its economic aspects.

However, I think that we might, at very little cost, minimize this conflict. Women do not have to become stock market analysts for their own benefit or for the benefit of the economy. They need only apply to investment certain common-sense principles which they act upon in many other areas of life.

In the first place, there is no room for sentiment in financial matters. Affections are properly bestowed upon people; they can sometimes be bestowed upon boats, but they ought never be directed toward stocks and bonds.

Secondly, they need to recognize their nonprofessional status in this field. A very substantial amount of money is lost each year by women who try, in effect, to outsmart the male, financial world. They do this by looking for bargains outside the established financial channels, by buying land, oil stocks, and mining properties from independent, unknown operators. A few of these speculations might work out, but they are not for amateurs. The woman who is not making a career of investment should deal only in securities or real estate through established dealers, bankers, or investment counselors.

Thirdly, she needs to recognize that in money matters as elsewhere, a certain amount of risk adds spice to life, and furthermore, it is a necessary hedge against inflation. Risk, however, implies the possibility of losing. If the woman investor can learn to live with the idea that her stocks, as well as those of other people, go down as well as up, sooner or later her confidence will be communicated to her broker.

These are simple little rules, and they will not make women financial experts. They will make it possible for them to make effective use of people who spend their life in finance. If these principles were generally adopted by women investors, both the women and the economy would profit. And the majority of women could continue to do what they do best—be women.

Morton M. Hunt

THE DIRECTION OF FEMININE EVOLUTION

Those who are familiar with modern anthropological thinking may raise their eyebrows at the very title of this paper. Does womankind really "evolve" socially? Wouldn't "change" be a more neutral and therefore preferable word? For "evolution" involves natural selection, specialization, and increasing functional efficiency; it therefore implies that the direction of development is onward and upward. Anthropologists, however, prefer to discover and describe social patterns without permitting themselves to use such value judgments as are imbedded in "onward and upward," and without confessing to any philosophic or aesthetic preference for the civilized American way of life as compared to that of, say, the Tlingit of Alaska or the Mundugumor of New Guinea.

Happily for me, I am only an amateur behavioral scientist; I travel lightly, unburdened by a surfeit of objectivity, and therefore can find room in my mental baggage for value judgments. At the risk of displeasing all those whose taste runs to viewing-with-alarm and doom-crying, I intend to use the term "evolution" because I believe that the present direction of feminine development in this country will tend to increase the measure of fulfillment and satisfaction in the lives of women—and also of the men who are both exasperated and entranced by them, who complain of them and yet need them more than ever, who frequently fight with them and almost always love them.

Evolution in history, unlike that in biology, is an untidy process, full of zigzags, inconsistencies, and reversals. Neither the dinosaur nor Pithecanthropus ever reappeared on earth, once eliminated by evolutionary development, but in human history men have learned to read, and then forgotten how again; built great cities and then let them crumble; managed to compose music, think logically, and probe the secrets of the universe, and then reverted again to peasant ignorance.

Yet if one limits his view to the period of Western history between the Dark Ages and the present, there does seem to be a kind of evolutionary process at work, despite any number of contradictions and backward turnings. During the early Middle Ages, thousands of acres of swampy or marshy ground were drained in France, forests were nibbled away in Germany, and overall, the agricultural usage of land in Europe increased; generally speaking, this process continued and never has been reversed. Throughout the civilized West, villages grew into towns, and some towns grew into cities; very few have ever wasted away again, and the growth of cities has continued to this day. Barons once made war on each other from their individual strongholds, but counts and dukes, and then kings, slowly subdued them and forced them into ever larger political allegiances—another process which is continuing even today.

If, too, one were to chart the distribution of the ability to read, the right to vote, the possession of more than one pair of shoes, the per capita income, the average length of life, and the amount of mechanical energy available per person, the lines he would draw might prove irregular and full of dips but would nonetheless show a marked long-range rise. And unless one is being intransigently objective, these would all seem to be upward curves of social progress.

So would the curve or graph depicting the condition of woman seem to be upward-moving. A nineteenth-century writer on marriage once aptly observed that ". . . in all primitive races, woman was the first domestic animal of man." European society of the Dark Ages was no exception. Woman was a most useful creature—good for carrying water, building the fire, preparing the food, making clothing, concocting herbal infusions and poultices, rearing the children, and at night, though bone-weary from her labors, still available for the comfort of her mate and the relief of his natural tensions. The ninth-century *Leges Alamannorum* recognized her value in plain terms: if a man slew a young girl, he must pay her master 200 solidi, but if she were a mature woman and therefore fully useful, he must pay 600 solidi. She *was* a useful animal, but little more; at one ecumenical council the question was even debated as to whether she had a soul or not (the bishops reassuringly decided that she did). Medieval woman, soul or not, was in many respects a lifelong minor, ruled absolutely by her father and then by her husband. Even in the upper class, she was not taught to read, could not own property, or testify in court, or sue her husband for divorce, or make any decisions as to what to do with her person and her life. Typically, in many jurisdictions adultery was punishable by death, if she committed it; if her husband did so, there was no punishment whatever.

It was therefore a considerable upward step when the twelfth-century troubadours decided that woman (or at least woman of the castles and courts) was a goddess on earth and thereupon invented the moods and poetry of courtly love in order to celebrate her and to woo her. Not that this much altered the way she was treated by her husband; courtly love and the divinity of woman pertained only to extramarital relationships, and she was the guiding force in life only for a man who did not live with her. Not her husband, but some other knight, would fall on his knees before her all aquiver, begging for a handkerchief to carry into battle, or would risk his life in the lists to win the favor of a single kiss. The *reductio ad absurdum* of such love was a kind of life-long quasi-religious devotion in which the lover hardly ever even saw his lady; Dante, you will remember, never had so much as one conversation with Beatrice, much less one anything else. Still, he made her his guide to Paradise, which was quite a promotion; woman would never again be only a domestic animal.

The upper-class ideas of love and the idealization of woman filtered down slowly to the middle class, undergoing some changes on the way. The bourgeoisie, especially in those lands that swung over to Protestantism, were both too strait-laced and too thrifty to adopt courtly love per se; not only was it sinful to love outside marriage, but it took up too much time and cost too much money. They therefore borrowed bits and scraps of the fabric of romantic love and wove them into the pattern of marriage. Woman became less a goddess and more a human being, but the effect of romantic love was unmistakable; by Shakespeare's day, not only did the great dramas of love end in marriage or disaster, but on the level of literary trash one finds little manuals of advice on amorous conversation and wooing for young swains—the object being not licentious seduction but marriage.

Aside from the irregularities produced by wars and revolutions, this trend in the evolution of femininity continued, with woman's status and prestige growing slowly and yet almost inevitably. Why this should have been so is too complex a question to be answered here; in broadest terms, though, I think it reflects the growing complexity and urbanization of Western society, in which the idealization of courtly love had been amalgamated to the realities of marriage.

And then came steam. Nothing made so great or rapid a change in the meaning of femininity as the arrival of the Industrial Revolution. Woman, in her earlier indentured condition, had been a very useful person, if not one with much status; she had always been the primary producer of many of the goods needful to life, as well as the operator of the home. But the Industrial Revolution both relieved her of her labors and robbed her of functions. It became cheaper to buy nearly everything than to make it at home; concurrently, society began taking more of a hand in the education and regulation of the young, thereby decreasing woman's purposes in life still further. At one and the same time, woman was treated better—and left almost aimless—by the changes in society. She had only two alternatives—either to while away her time with knitting, culture, and attacks of the vapors, or to fight for her legal rights and to force her way into colleges, the professions, and the world of business. Some women did the one thing, some did the other—and you know which choice proved to be the evolutionary one.

When a woman ceases to make socks and plum puddings, and takes to quoting Milton or the stock market, she may not delight her man. As Dr. Johnson once opined, "A man is better pleased when he has a good dinner upon his table than when his wife talks Greek." More seriously, her changing interests and activities may alarm or anger him, since they seem to betoken an invasion of his lordly domain and symbolically are a challenge to his very sexuality. Accordingly, the early male reaction to feminists and woman's rights advocates was to call them sexless—a safe way to deal with the threat. Some of the early feminists, in truth, were pretty grim-looking old war horses, but others, like Victoria Woodhull, were voluptuous advocates of Free Love. Poor man! He couldn't decide whether the New Woman was a bloodless old hag or a passionate sybarite; and who can blame him if he was confused, since woman herself was just as confused?

In the key period of female emancipation—from the end of the nineteenth century to the 1930s—the image of woman was more contradictory and bewildering than ever. She was moving away from sexual passivity, for instance, toward greater participation and enjoyment of love making—but simultaneously was making of sex a "problem" for man, since he now had to woo her every time or else be considered a brute. Again, she was seeing ever greater opportunities for herself in the learned world and in business—and yet finding that when she chose this direction, it seemed to make her less womanly in the eyes of men, and even to condemn her to failure in her love life. Still again, in her home life she was finding that equality was a difficult boon: even while she had the right and desire to be her husband's equal in all major decisions, she was discovering that it often violated her husband's idea of how she should behave, offended his masculine pride, and sometimes even damaged his masculinity itself. And today this and many similar contradictions remain, being a part of the overall paradox of contemporary American woman: she has greater advantages, opportunities, and freedom than any woman in the past (except for a few queens, ladies, and such), yet seems to be more troubled, conscious of her problems, and perplexed as to her identity than women were in the past. Women in many other lands envy her and think her lucky; American woman herself, however, worries about the fact that she isn't as happy as she ought to be and wonders if it could mean there is something fundamentally wrong with her whole way of life.

Man reacts to this paradox with bewilderment and frustration, and with a variety of forms of revolt. One form is abdication: we have been told, *ad nauseam,* of the retreat of man from his masculine privileges, of his loss or voluntary cession of the right to run the family, establish the budget, choose the site and decor of the house, say who shall be his friends, or even select the times when he and his wife will make love. Abroad he may be an executive lion, but at home he is a marital mouse. Or so we have been told, until we believe it—until we accept Dagwood Bumstead as the image of modern man in reality as well as in the comic strips. And although the best recent sociological surveys lend little support to this view, it is at least true that many men, faced with the process of change away from the old patriarchal system, feel like Milquetoasts or fear that they are on the way.

Some men revolt by turning away from the contest altogether: homosexuality is either actually on the increase or emerging from its confines of suppression and repression. Other men choose adultery, either in hopes of finding compliant and passive women or by way of indirectly punishing their wives for alarming them and challenging their masculinity. (It is possible that more men are doing so today than formerly, but one cannot be sure; there simply were no Dr. Kinseys collecting data in the stews of Reformation London or the halls of Versailles.) Still other men react with impotence in the marital relation, although once again one cannot be sure whether this is more true today than formerly; it may be that the modern man shows up more readily in the doctor's office, whereas the Victorian man either suffered in silence or treated himself via visits to brothels or flagellation dens, or by taking a docile mistress.

The basic question is whether all these alleged and actual ills are merely the pains of transition, or whether they signify that the direction of feminine evolution today is fundamentally unhealthy, contravening the laws of nature and running counter to the timeless needs of male and female alike.

Those conservatives who take the latter view argue that the female is, and was meant forever to be, warm, tender, nurturant, yielding, lovable though a bit on the stupid side, willing to accept the rule and dominion of the male, a bit fractious but much improved by being beaten once in a while. Biology and psychoanalysis are usually summoned as evidence for the prosecution. Biology is said to show that this is how it is throughout the animal world and hence must be in the human realm. In actual fact, any good biologist can cite scores of instances in which the female of the species is stronger than, or dominant over, the male or in which she invites and excites him sexually rather than waits to be sought out and raped. In any case, to extrapolate from reflexive and instinctual animal patterns to the behavior of the human being is a risky business; we are not animals, and most of our conduct is not instinctual, but learned. It therefore need not be based on animal patterns.

As for the appeal to Freud, one should remember that as inspired and brilliant as he was, he derived most of his theories from the case material he had in front of him; the nature of woman as he sketched it is primarily that of late-Victorian neurotic woman, rather than of all women in all times and places. (It is not surprising to learn that he once told his friend, Marie Bonaparte, that after all his years of research he still could not answer the question *"Was will das Weib?"* —"What does woman want?"). Anthropology and history can lend the correction to this perspective. Women have been subjugated or controlled by men in nearly all societies—but the variations in the degree of control have been so wide that one cannot claim to see a natural law involved; it is likely that prosaic economics were more responsible, with emancipation of woman depending on the wealth and leisure man could afford to allow her. As for man's sexual nature, anthropologists have reported that in some societies women are sexually as aggressive as men and in a few societies have been far more passionate and active than the men; whatever the prevailing pattern, however, men brought up in that society consider it the right and proper state of affairs.

In some cultures women have done hard labor, while in others they have been thought of as fragile and weak. Sometimes they have been priestesses, but elsewhere they have been thought unclean and unfit for priestly duties. Sometimes they have designed or painted, done intellectual work, or engaged in trade; at other times they have been thought constitutionally unsuited to any of these activities. The moral is that what will offend, anger, or alarm a man in woman in one society will in another seem to be right, natural, and inevitable—and therefore feminine and attractive.

Even within recent centuries, in our own western world, we can find gross variations of this sort. A fourteenth-century Italian female, to judge from Boccaccio, was feminine to the degree that she was hot-blooded and overtly responsive; to a Victorian man, however, it seemed unnatural and disgusting for a woman to betray any evidence of passion. One such gentleman, introducing his bride to the rites of love on their wedding night, is said to have stopped short and sternly admonished her, *"Ladies,* my dear, do not move!"* Toward the end of the last century, one of the more widely used textbooks on the reproductive system written by the American physician William Acton stated flatly that any claim that woman had an appetite for sexual connection or took pleasure in it was a "vile aspersion" on the fair sex.

Again, one hears a great deal today about the "castrating effect" on a man of having a wife who is more successful than he or who earns a larger income. Yet in seventeenth- and eighteenth-century England, many an impecunious younger son of a good family would shop around for a wife, seeking one whose name and blood were at least adequate but who above all brought him land, house, and the maximum dowry with the minimum of jointure.[1] As any social historian will tell you, such men then spent their lives gambling, wenching, playing at politics or war, or managing their estates, giving no evidence whatever of being castrated by the fact that they were indebted to their wives for their income.

Or again, consider the brilliant, the accomplished, the intellectual woman today: how often have you not heard her described as cold, or unappealing, or seen her portrayed in movies and TV as a neurotic, driven nonwoman until, at last, she feels love and sees the light, abandons her career, and gives herself over gladly to diapers and mucus, rosebushes and PTA meetings. Yet during the Renaissance in Italy, the woman of many accomplishments was seen as highly desirable, attractive, and feminine; in the totality of her development, she was thought of as combining beauty with the best aspects of man himself and hence was given the sobriquet "virago"—a term which then conveyed great praise and only later, in the more cautious mouth of the middle-class man, came to convey reproach.

What all this indicates is that the larger share of those traits that are taken by men of any given era to be timeless components of femininity are, actually, only passing customs and manners. There are some essential aspects to femininity; there are, also, a great many nonessential or modifiable ones. To put it another way, femininity in any era is a whole cluster or set of roles which a woman plays toward the people around her; but some of these are biological roles and hence not changeable, while others are social roles and hence are subject to great variations. Biologically, woman will always be man's sexual lover (except in self-extinguishing societies) and will have to be at least coopera-

---

[1] The inheritance guaranteed to a widow from her husband's estate.

tive and accepting enough, despite enthusiasm and activity, to permit him to function in the essential and irreducible sense. Biologically, she will also harbor his seed, shelter the fetus, and bring forth the child —unless the nightmarish visions of babies in bottles in Aldous Huxley's *Brave New World* ever come true. She is also always going to be smaller, weaker, softer, and warmer than man, and to some extent she may always therefore make a better caretaker of small children. These experiences affect her outlook and a thousand details of her behavior, as is only reasonable for them to do; but whether these effects are drastic or moderate is determined by her society.

But what else is absolutely determined by biology? In the past, the biology of the flowing breast determined her role as the giver of nourishment, but in the present state of technology breast feeding has become a social role—and what woman will dare to say that her husband cannot convey warmth and love while giving a baby the bottle? What of the female roles of housewife, cook, nurse, hostess, clinging vine, dizzy dame, ball and chain, battle-ax, and instiller of morality into the childish bosom? Viewed from anthropological and historical perspectives, which of these has any roots in biology? Which are essential elements of femininity? None, I submit. And what of the roles of intellectual, thinker, artist, executive, companion, friend, inventor, passionate lover, and sage counselor? Which of these is fundamentally incompatible with biological femininity? None, I submit.

I am not offering a precise prescription at this point; do not cancel out all of the first list, or include all of the second, and think you have any answer. I am only trying to suggest that according to the needs and the institutions of a society, the traits that seem acceptable in woman and the aspects of her nature can vary very widely, and that in trying to choose freely among her potentialities, she runs into conflicts, not with her innate nature or man's, but with the social roles expected of her in her own time and place. What seems to alarm many men today, and to cause discontent and uncertainty in women, is not a departure from sound biological femininity—mass homosexuality, or chastity, or childless marriage would be real examples of that—but rather the dislocations and jars of the transition in woman's social roles, which both she and man confuse with her essential biological femininity. And confusing the acquired and learned with the innate and essential, woman

feels uneasy and discontented at the changes, while man feels his maleness threatened.

Most of the masculine protest and fear today is, therefore, oc-
casioned by changes in social behavior rather than by any repudiation,
on woman's part, of her quintessential femininity. Woman's suffrage
was once regarded as a pseudo-masculine desire in her, and grossly inappropriate; smoking was once thought hideously unfeminine; even the
use of anesthesia during childbirth was regarded by the Anglican
Church, for a time, as a violation of basic femininity, for did not the
Bible say that she should bring forth her children in sorrow? Any
illustrated history of costume ought to prove the point: time after time,
new styles for women have been the cause of howls of protest on the
grounds that they were unfeminine, but some years or decades later,
the new styles have become the very embodiment of femininity, while
the old ones look bizarre and sexless in retrospect. And yet despite this
obvious truth, men continue to struggle against social change in
woman's nature, fearing it and resenting it; most men will tell you,
for instance, that women bosses are domineering and difficult, but when
sociologist Margaret Cussler interviewed men who worked under
women, she found most of them admitting that their own bosses were
"different." Which didn't change their opinion on the subject in general.

Modern woman vacillates, all her life, in her conception of herself,
largely because of her fear of alarming or losing man. For above all else
she wants to be loved and to attain a normal family life; and in order
to gain these ends, she tries to minimize the seeming conflicts between
her diminished roles as mother and housekeeper and the multiple new
roles available to her today. There being no clear and approved pattern,
as yet, for the integration of all the things she wants to be, she fum-
blingly seeks any one of a variety of adaptations, some of which are
wholesome and some of which are not.

As an example of the latter, let me point out how many a female
unwittingly denies her own brain power. It begins somewhere in grade
school, when she first gets the idea that it isn't girlish to be too smart
about science, mathematics, or mechanical things; from here on, she
starts muffing or being indifferent toward these subjects, until, as a mature young woman, she can never get it straight whether the solar system is a galaxy or not, regularly makes mistakes in adding and

subtracting in her checkbook, and seems unable to grasp the theory of parking a car in a tight spot. Yet we have abundant evidence that woman's innate intellectual abilities are, on the average, so close to those of man—a little lower in some areas, a little higher in others— that these and other failures must be self-imposed rather than inescapable.

Other women, who do not fool themselves into believing they are unapt at certain kinds of thinking, try to fool the men in their lives into believing so. In the words of one bright fourteen-year-old girl who had just discovered the grand stratagem of this type of woman, "A girl has to be smart about it—if she likes a boy, she has to let him beat her at games and arguments. And if he's a creep and she wants to get rid of him, she tries her best to show him up." Professor Mirra Komarovsky of Barnard College reports that 40 per cent of the girl undergraduates on two different campuses admit "playing dumb" on dates in order not to frighten off the male or acquire a reputation for being unfeminine.

A third form of maladaptation is the pattern of the all-out career woman—the claw-and-fang type who is so bent on success that she has no time for love and marriage. Or if she has longings for those things, she frustrates herself by continually finding them in conflict with her more urgent purpose in life. These days she is not likely to be a virgin spinster but a divorcee or a bachelor girl with bed companions; nevertheless, you see her alone more often than not, and her quick bright flashing smile is often replaced, in thoughtful moments, by the tight, discontented mouth of the woman who has missed out, somehow, on the fullness of life. Woe to the man who works under such a woman; he had better be made of tough material, or she will chew him into a pulp to relieve her own feelings.

A fourth and more serious form of maladaptive accommodation is the embracing of neodomesticity. Many a bright college girl, after spending $15,000 to $25,000 of her parents' money to gain a degree and a set of skills badly needed by her society, abruptly junks the whole thing as soon as a man offers her the chance to "prove" her biological femininity. Instead of waiting for real marital adjustment, a little maturity, and a good toehold on a career, she opts for Instant Motherhood and Total Domesticity—usually in a suburban setting remote from hired help, relatives, or day nurseries. Shortly, therefore, she discovers to her dismay that she is a "trapped housewife," that she is "rusting away" or "becoming a vegetable," or even, as one twenty-one-year-old correspondent wrote me, that "her real life is ended." If these feelings do not produce an explosion of some sort, she may gradually adjust to it all and fill up her life with these roles—but at what cost to herself, and what cost to her husband and children, who must provide her with all her satisfactions in life, an awesome burden for them to bear! Even so, if her choice were stable and long-lasting, there might be some argument in favor of it; but by the time she is forty this synthesis is beginning to disintegrate—the children are escaping, she is not as necessary as she used to be, no one outside wants to hire her, and club and community activities are, for the most part, a pallid substitute for some truly engaging purpose in life.

At this juncture, many women begin to suffer from minor undiagnosable ailments that take them to the office of a sympathetic, but silently exasperated, doctor; hypochondria and psychosomatic symptoms become a purpose in life. Others try adultery, which reaches its peak among middle-class women at this time of life; as compared to hypochondria, it would seem the more enjoyable choice, but it is a good deal more dangerous and, moreover, offers no long-term solution to the loss of identity, the sense of aimlessness, or the lack of a feeling of value. Like alcohol, it works superbly on a short-term basis and then yields a fearful hangover.

The more functional direction of adaptation, I suggest, is for modern woman to envision herself as a highly complex creature whose potential role-set is unlike that of almost any woman in the past except the Renaissance virago. If from childhood on she is encouraged to conceive of herself as capable of many things—and to recognize that in the modern context she will need many new forms of fulfillment—she will not vacillate in her self-concept throughout her school years, nor play the game of pretended dumbness, nor abandon the many cherished aspects of herself in favor of the simplicity of marriage and motherhood. There are enough men who enjoy the brainy girl and who need a complex woman in their lives to make it come out all right; this might not have been true a couple of generations ago, when most women who used their intellectual gifts ended up as spinsters, but men are changing and women no longer face an either-or choice.

By "the complex woman" I mean a female who no longer is a primary producer of domestic goods but who, in place of that role, has become the mental equal and closest friend of her husband—a situation nearly unprecedented in history.

I mean a female who is no longer the passive receptacle of man's passion but in place of that role has become his lover—his married mistress—whose sexual and emotional relationship with him remains as intense and aesthetic as familiarity and habit will allow.

I mean a female who is neither man's indentured servant nor sharp-tongued tyrant but his friendly collaborator and equal, who, moreover, uses up her aggressive energies not upon him and the children but sublimates them into creative activities or work and so competes only with the outside world.

I mean a female who realizes in advance how short a span of her life, in today's world, can be filled and fulfilled by domesticity and motherhood, and who therefore diligently cultivates the other aspects of herself also, in order to make herself a happier and more purposeful human being after motherhood is done.

I do not suggest that all this is easy—but neither is it easy to be frustrated, hypochondriacal, and continually simmering over the low flame of discontent. But if it is not easy to be a complex woman, it is not impossible. To minimize conflict among her many roles, the modern woman of many parts has to experiment and to seek out a number of compromises. She need not be all things at the same moment—and she must discover the time and place in which to play each of her roles, and to hide or lay aside briefly certain others. She may find, for instance, that it is frequently wise to play the pursued—and captured—in the game of love; she may find it needful to the male ego for her to simulate the appearance of desire, when he desires and she herself does not, and to follow his lead on many an occasion when she would rather not. Again, though a husband and wife may consider themselves to have substantially equal voice in all major decisions, many a wise woman allows her husband to rule over certain traditionally masculine areas—what kind of car to buy, how much to spend on vacation, what restaurant to visit on their night out, when to undertake major repairs on the house, and so on. And the adaptive woman may find it good to temper her outspokenness in front of other people in order not to give the appearance of belittling or competing with her husband; a male friend of his would not have to do so, but many a wife still needs to practice this much deceptive giving-in for the good of her man, and thus of herself.

Perhaps the most significant adaptation of all is in the area of work. There is a clear trend for modern young women to desire careers in ever-larger numbers—and to temper that desire and settle for a great deal less achievement than the feminists formerly sought. Women's Bureau statistics show that a larger proportion of married women work than ever before—and this is true even of middle-class women who still have young children. But there is a difference. Today's career-minded girl is not passionately dedicated to maximum advancement; she is willing to put her career on ice for a few years when she marries and is ready to have children. Yet she does not "retire"; instead, she plans on an early return and makes arrangements that permit her to go back on at least a part-time basis within a few years. Still, if her children or her husband's career runs into a conflict with her work, it is she who generally drops out again or who yields rank and seniority in order to move with her husband to some new city where larger opportunities await him. She rarely rises as high or accomplishes as much as her talents warrant—and she accepts this as the best compromise arrangement and achievement that life presents her with.

I don't argue that all this is ideal but only that since the world is never perfect, this represents the optimum solution available at the present time. For an increasing number of educated and career-minded women, it seems that this compromise plan is currently proving more workable and satisfying than either total domesticity or all-out careerism. At the same time, this choice of the complicated life and the broadened role-choice, though it calls for many adjustments and maneuverings, is also proving more capable than other schemes of meeting the needs of a growing proportion of educated middle-class men.

For one thing, ours is an era when men move too fast, geographically and socially, to maintain important and intimate friendships as they once did. Who, then, can a man depend on to be his lifelong

friend, adviser, and confidant? Why, his wife—that is, if she is intellectually furnished for the job. American life and mores do not favor
the comfortable European practice of keeping a mistress for one's romantic and passionate needs. Who, then, will be mistress to the American male? Why, once again, his wife—that is, if she does not identify
herself so completely with housekeeping and mothering as to lose her
identity as a lover, or to bore her husband, or if she does not compete
with him so hotly as to unman him or send him off looking for less
tough-minded company.

The American male is able to live and survive without a helpmeet
to make his clothes, grow his food, and fix his meals, for he can get all
these services and goods for cash; but what he cannot buy, in our
strangely alienated and disjoined age, is that constant assurance of be-
longing that his grandfathers got from their more stable and intimate
community life. Who, then, will be his surety that he is not alone in
the world, that he is tied to some other part of humanity by a thousand
invisible bonds? Why, inevitably, his wife—that is, if she is not so
frustrated, bitchy, bored, or aimless as to be incapable of being all this
to him.

One last task remains for me: namely, to indicate the direction that
feminine evolution will take in the future. This, of course, is sheer
folly: nearly all the detailed long-range forecasts men have ever made
about such things have proved wrong except, perhaps, for such sure-
fire predictions as "This, too, shall pass away."

Still, what I have already said virtually states my guesses as to the
near future, if not the far one. For one thing, ever more American
girls are going to college, and they are learning something about their
own capacities—and developing a taste for the activities and rewards of
the larger world outside the home. Again, the attrition of woman's
traditional roles will continue for a host of reasons that are deep-rooted
in the nature of our modern society; and despite well-meant advice to
return to canning, baking, and other "womanly" activities, as the road
to happiness, history tells us all too plainly that deliberate efforts to turn
time backward—whether proposed by Metternich, Ruskin, or Gandhi—
have never worked. Thirdly, alienation and personal loneliness seem to
be endemic in modern life, and to be on the increase rather than the
decrease; that being so, there is all the more reason for the husband-wife

relationship to need all the richness, interplay, and complexity it can derive; it is the one and only lastingly concentric or ego-identifying relationship we have today.

And statistics seem to stand in solid support of all this: I think that the Women's Bureau data on changing patterns in female employment make it seem very likely that more and more educated young women will hold jobs both before and after the infancy of their children, absenting themselves from the labor market only a few years rather than fifteen or twenty. I think it very likely that teaching, since it offers opportunities for part-time work, will continue to be the major choice of profession for college women; but at the same time more and more women will aim at middle-level executive posts as their goal in business, or will select certain professions that require less than a maximum amount of training and continuous effort. Already, for instance, the percentage growth of women among accountants, auditors, chemists, draftsmen, and various kinds of laboratory assistants is most striking. Some women, to be sure, will continue to prefer the most demanding professions, but this does not seem to be the direction in which feminine evolution is moving. The percentage of women among physicians, for example, is no greater in this country now than it was in 1910, and although women earned one out of every six doctorates granted in the various learned fields in 1920, they earn only one in ten today.

And one more prediction. We hear a great deal these days about the broad premarital experience of single girls and about the rampant adultery of married women. But in contrast to rumor, fiction, and wishful thinking, the best data available indicate that although American girls are gathering experience earlier than their mothers did, there is no real revolution in mores. They still seem to feel that sex should go only hand-in-hand with serious emotional involvement and not be a purely carnal pleasure; accordingly, the most reliable figures I know of—Kinsey's—indicate that only about a fourth of American college girls give up their virgin status before they marry, though admittedly many of them are virgins only in a technical sense.

Similarly, despite all the blather about adultery, the Kinsey data indicate that even in the thirty-six-to-forty-year age group—the peak years for female adultery—only one out of five married women ever sleeps with a man other than her husband, and most of these do so only once or a few times. Adultery may be a fling for a certain number of American women, but for almost none of them is it a way of life.

And my rash prediction is that to the extent that American women more and more find fulfillment in a multiplicity of satisfactions in their lives, and to the extent that they and their husbands develop a more complicated and total set of interactions with each other, adultery will not markedly increase, despite the growing permissiveness of our attitudes toward sex. I predict that the complex woman will, by and large, remain a faithful wife despite her exposure to other men, and that American marriage will accordingly become not more fragile, but perhaps a little less so, because of this direction of feminine evolution.

This is an unduly hopeful note on which to close, and I quite realize that it is not fashionable these days to speak with optimism and good cheer about the future. For this I apologize, pleading as my excuse only that I have let my thinking go where the facts seemed to lead me.

CONTROL OF TRANSITION

This is an actual transcription of the formal but spontaneous panel discussion of the papers immediately preceding. Only minor editing has been done where continuity and clarity required it. The editors feel that the spontaneity of the actual discussion gives a particular value to the panel in this form, since it amplifies questions arising from the formal presentations of the participants as well as answering questions from the audience.

Moderator: David G. Mandelbaum
Panel Members: Mark Harris, Morton M. Hunt, Albert E. Schwabacher, Jr.

Dr. Mandelbaum The subject for this panel, "Control of Transition," assumes that there is a transition, and I think there has been an implicit assumption that in this transition it is the women who had better change and the men who better do the controlling. We might begin by asking: Is there a male revolt? And if so, what is this male revolt about?

Dr. Harris Is there a male revolt? Is there transition? We often don't recognize that there are about as many worlds as there are people looking at it. The best complaints, I think, are all justified as far as women on the whole are concerned. But there are wide areas in our civilization where some of this has been fulfilled, the complaints answered, and the transition accomplished. The male revolt does not exist because the men in a particular situation accept, like, encourage, and welcome the fact of women's accomplishments in whatever areas. I more and more discover for myself that the world I live in is somewhat special. I also more and more discover that people think when you say you live in a college environment or that you have such and such a degree, that you are flaunting your status.

The fact is there is a different quality of life at different intellectual levels, just as there is a different quality of life at different economic levels. Among people I know, after dinner the men do not segregate themselves from the women; the men do not think that the women have less intelligence. I just want to refer back to something that Mr. Schwabacher said this morning, that women do not pretend to be able to add the checkbook. I don't want to get personal about this, but this is not a very safe generalization and does not fall within my experience.

Dr. Mandelbaum You are really saying there is no revolt and no necessity for it among your friends and people whom you know.

Mr. Hunt As far as the separation of men and women after dinner, we are in transition. I went recently to a very elegant dinner given in a town house in New York by the distinguished head of a publishing firm; to my utter amazement, I found the ladies drifting over into the drawing room and the men off to a library, where we had cigars and brandy, and in thirty minutes we rejoined the ladies. It was sort of a token defiance, and that is about all.

Dr. Mandelbaum Let us come to the other tough point, namely, the control of transition. Did I detect in Mr. Hunt's paper the note that it is really the women who are changing and must change, and it is the men who have to control this?

Mr. Hunt I don't know whether they have to control it, and I don't even know what mechanism they would use, but the whole thought of the control of this transition seems to be an elusive one. I can't think of a mechanism by which to do this, but I am sure men are changing in response to these changes. One very good example is that less than fifty years ago, a woman who pursued an intellectual career was very likely to wind up being a spinster and to get most of her satisfactions out of her career. Today, women pursue careers and you also find them married. Evidently although there was once no supply of men who wanted such a woman, there is such today. I think this is an important proof that we are passing through a transition period, but I don't know who controls whom. I don't think any of the men whom I know who married career women were caught by women, and therefore I just don't really understand the question. But I will rescue you from limbo and say that I think there were some very excellent suggestions put forth earlier in the symposium. The attitude of colleges and employers toward women is tremendously important, and where states and the Federal government can actually legislate to assure a woman the right for maternity leave for her return to the job, or to require universities to admit women on the same basis as men, this is the kind of control that can be exerted by transition.

Dr. Mandelbaum In this transition obviously men have changed, society has changed, we are all moving along on this problem at about the same pace. I see no enormous resistances to that kind of legislation.

Mr. Hunt I will give you an example of an awful resistance that may be widespread. I heard from a young woman with a Ph.D. in literature in New York in a system whereby she gets no tenure until she has six consecutive semesters. In her sixth semester she became pregnant, which is not permitted. Therefore she lost five semesters of seniority and had to start all over. This is written into the constitution of that particular university, and I think very well deserves changing.

Dr. Mandelbaum If indeed they said that a pregnant person can't teach.

Mr. Schwabacher hinted at several things that he did not amplify. One was the place of the secretary and the administrative assistant in the business world. It is quite well known that in government and university bureaucracies the steel frame of the administration is comprised of the secretaries and administrative assistants, the people who really know both the rules and the ropes, know how you get something through and how to get something done which needs to be done. Now this in the bureaucracies with which I am familiar is in itself not only a very useful function but a truly creative one. Is the same sort of thing happening in your experience?

Mr. Schwabacher In many instances, yes.

Dr. Mandelbaum Let me toss you another, then. You said something which I am going to use in my lectures for several years, I am sure. You showed a stockbroker as a truly creative person or a potentially creative person, and that there is room for real creativity in being a stockbroker. Now I think the public image of a stockbroker does not include that dimension; he may be a great golfer, great something else, but not a creative person. But the other side of the coin was that with the exception of a few gifted women, the women who have money to invest and are not professionals are kinds of economic Philistines and this is a sphere of activity for which they are not suited and in which, with a rare few happy exceptions, they cannot be creative and should not be creative. Did I get you right?

Mr. Schwabacher   I would like to correct one thing you said. Let us define the difference between an investment banker and a broker. A broker generally in our concept is a person who sits at a desk and takes orders and engages in trading activities. An investment banker is the one who does the creative work. They don't all do it, but they would like to do it; it depends again on the individual. There are certain professors who give classes. They are able to get the message across right now. There are certain authors who have a way of putting forth words that pack a real wallop. I don't have to talk about the others. We are talking about someone who is a sincere and devoted full professional who spends his time on it.

Dr. Mandelbaum   I am glad you corrected me on that, because I can correct you on something quite different. There were several mentions of anthropologists, and since I am an anthropologist, I can't let the opportunity go by without putting in the proper correction. First of all, you mentioned that a man, at least in our society, can't manage a formal dinner party. This very well may be true; however, I have lived with people who worked in societies where no woman would ever be entrusted to the management of a formal dinner party; it is much too crucial for a woman to take care of. I am thinking of certain village societies in India, where the people are ranked and get their food in order of caste status, and this is to delegate a matter that only the most prestigious men can handle.

Dr. Harris   Thinking of the bankbook business or the preparation of the dinner party—I first became acquainted with the word "confidence" in this sense in connection with baseball. Baseball people use the word frequently to mean that a man isn't doing something, but when he gets the confidence, he will do it. In other words, he really can do it but doesn't know he can. This seems to be an immense reality in our society. In all kinds of ways we do things that we didn't know we could do. Keeping the bankbook is part of what I tried to say about Marilyn Monroe. The innocent believes in his own guilt if he is brainwashed enough. Society does brainwash us about women on the whole, about women's role and what they do. My little girl is in junior high school, and her common complaint is that she is given certain domestic science courses; the school has defined the nature of her activity, since the boys are given different courses. On the question of confidence, I would say that when both men and women believe that women can do things that they do not now do, they will begin to do them.

Dr. Mandelbaum   Dr. Harris, let me ask how you came to choose the topic of writing about Marilyn Monroe? It is a sensitive piece and speaks for itself. We should not ask this question of a novelist or writer, but we can ask this question of a professor, and in that capacity, how did you happen to choose it, and do you think a woman could have written this sort of piece?

Dr. Harris   It seemed to me that for a symposium on woman, that the history of any woman is the history, or would be in part, of the present situation of women. Every woman is a symbol of womanhood, but the cases are different. Mr. Schwabacher and I see woman quite differently, perhaps because of the different ways we see our wives or the different kinds of wives. We make generalizations from our experience. So I was casting about for a topic, and her death had just occurred. I thought if I wrote with some detail about her, it would be a good symbol and would tell us something.

Dr. Mandelbaum   Let me then ask you an unfair question: do you think a woman could have written this piece with as much compassion?

Dr. Harris   I would say with certain few humorous exceptions that women can do anything men can do.

Dr. Mandelbaum   This is the point of my question.

Dr. Harris   They can have the same composition.

Dr. Mandelbaum   But, after all, a woman does take a different role than a man. In certain respects she must see things differently, and although she can do anything a man can within certain limits, can she see the world in exactly the same way? Every writer sees the world in a different way, but is there still a sex difference?

Dr. Harris I think I could write feelingly about a man in that situation and, in fact, I have tried to do so. It was not just because she was a woman that I could feel sympathetic. I don't see why writing feelingly, movingly, or sympathetically is only man's activity.

Dr. Mandelbaum There are several questions for Mr. Schwabacher.

Mr. Schwabacher "To what extent would you educate a daughter in the management of her own finances (not everyone marries her investment counselor)?"

Let us choose a company: Wrigley pays a monthly dividend, and if you were to buy X number of shares of Wrigley when your daughter is ten, eleven, or twelve, whatever time you think is right, the dividends from the Wrigley's could be her monthly allowance. Wrigley also pays a quarterly extra, and the money should go in the bank and you should match it dollar for dollar. So what are you doing? You are teaching her about a monthly dividend, which is her allowance; you are teaching her how to save; and you are also partly teaching her how to chew gum.

I am also asked: "Do women with small amounts to invest have more business sense than wealthy widows?"

I think that women with small amounts to invest should be, but are not necessarily, very careful. The most important thing in investing is to find someone who has a sincere interest in you, who is a professional, and then tell him everything you can about your financial condition. When you go to a doctor, it isn't long before he knows all about you physically. When you go to a financial man, you should treat him the same way. Give him the facts, give him a chance to tell you what might be done, then go home and think about it and come back and make a decision, and follow the plan.

Dr. Mandelbaum Apparently the great room for creativity in investing for a woman, at any rate—I suppose for a man also—is in choosing the investment banker, and if she does that wisely, all good things will follow.

Dr. Harris I really can't restrain myself any longer on this. The idea is like Aunt Sally's Candy again; she buys the candy because it is good candy, and so she wants to invest in that company. She is being wise as to the quality of the product but not wise economically and financially. I would hate to see investment brokers or bankers or any other group try to exorcise out of women this generally female impulse to yearn for the good quality of the object, never minding the profit and the loss involved, even at some economic risk. Otherwise Aunt Sally's good candy will disappear, and we won't have any good candy.

Mr. Schwabacher   Dr. Harris, I hope you don't put your money where your mouth was today. But seriously, when people do come in with something like that, and that was a figment of the imagination, we do our best to placate them and say, "If you have got $5,000 to invest, let us put $50 or $100 in Aunt Sally's Candy." We end up putting in $300 or $500, so we try to give them something they want or think they want. They are like children, generally, because they don't know what they want. That is the problem.

Dr. Harris   The movie company said the same thing to Marilyn Monroe: "We can't put our money where your mouth is," and this was her destruction.

Mr. Schwabacher   Yes, but for every Marilyn Monroe, there are another 10,000 girls who are disillusioned, disappointed, and never make the big time.

Dr. Mandelbaum   And they should not buy stock in Aunt Sally's Candy.

Mr. Schwabacher   I think we are going too fast here. We see very many who cannot afford the luxury of buying stock, long before we get to Aunt Sally or anything like that. They would better take care of their home, insurance, and the fundamental things, and have some money in the bank before they expose themselves to this possibility of appreciation or depreciation.

I have also been asked to comment on women as investors and speculators in common stocks and bonds.

This is very difficult, because there is just no single person. No two of us have the same needs financially. A survey in our office gave a general inference that women are better investors and more interested in investing than men. They are more reluctant to speculate unwisely and are slow about taking a loss but get very attached to something whether it is good or bad. With the main emphasis on common stocks today, people do not talk about fixed income bonds perhaps as much as they should.

Dr. *Mandelbaum* Mr. Schwabacher mentioned that women investors are a conservative force generally in the market. Isn't this a good thing because if they were not that kind of conservative investors, the government would have to pay much more for its money?

Mr. *Schwabacher* This is one discussion point, but when you realize the tremendous amount of money that is in pension funds, investment trusts, and in trust departments of banks, this far, far overshadows women's conservatism..

Dr. *Mandelbaum* A question for Mr. Hunt: "At what point does the wife's catering to her husband and making him feel important and strong result in apathy, abdication, indignity, and loss of her self-respect? Isn't this deceitful and demoralizing in a relationship?"

Mr. *Hunt* Well, I think if we were all utterly honest with each other, we would be in an awful lot of trouble. I don't think it would be any more deceitful for a woman to flatter her husband and cater to him and make him feel important in noncritical areas of their lives than for him to tell her she looks beautiful when she looks only moderately nice or to say that she is as slender as he would possibly want her when she is really 15 pounds too much. As it is in all the rest of our human relationships, we have a cloak of manners and of kindnesses that we do. I didn't say that she should be a nineteenth-century woman, in order that her man should continue to cohere and not fall apart, but simply that she adapt herself in these fashions. Wouldn't she be sorry if he ever stopped being a hypocrite and were absolutely possessed by integrity? What would he say, for instance, in the morning, when he took one look?

Dr. *Mandelbaum* Another one: "How can husbands be educated to accept the evolved woman as you see her?"

Mr. *Hunt* I think it is something like saying, "Now that the chicken is hatched, how could we have had a puppy instead?" It may be too late by the time she got him; maybe she should choose better. Nevertheless, there are some interesting answers to this. One of my questionnaire respondents wanted to teach. She had done some teaching, had had a child, and wanted to resume her work, but she found that her husband very much resisted it, wanting her to play the real womanly role and to stay at home. Over a period of time she realized and felt the resistance decreasing as his income increased. When it became absolutely clear to him that he could support the family totally without any help by her, he not only allowed her to go back to teaching but encouraged her to go to graduate school and get a higher degree. There is a woman who recognized that she had a man who inherited a leftover threat but that the threat would pass away in time if she simply watched carefully. I don't know whether that comes under the heading of education by the evolved woman.

Dr. Harris I have a question here that I think relates to the business of education of husbands, and I agree with Mr. Hunt that education begins probably very young.

"Will men in revolt act to protect such fragile persons as Marilyn Monroe, not by protecting one's own individual family life but by assuring social conditions in which no child must suffer as this one did?"

I think men's attitudes toward women are very proportionate to men's general sympathies. I think, without making any studies of it, that we could guess at the fact that men who believe in expansion of equality for Negroes or immigrants or any other deprived class would also extend these sympathies to women insofar as they are a group seeking the opportunity.

Mr. Hunt I have a question here which says, "What about female equality and feminism abroad?"

Women in many foreign lands are changing rapidly now, and wherever the country is becoming a productive, highly urban, highly mechanized country, the changes in the family tend to go much in the same direction. This does not mean that women all over the world are becoming American women or replicas of them, but they are beginning to want the same things: education, a vote, an end to concubinage, and all of the man, not just a little part of him. They want a whole interaction of the man they are married to, and this is what to me is significant about it; it shows that the direction of feminine evolution is not a peculiarly American happenstance or accident but is in the very nature of the changes in society. The sad thing here is that a certain number of men still wish they could have a traditional woman of the old type and believe they are to be found elsewhere. They go abroad and come back with a European wife, and she suffers a strange sea change; after she has been here two or three years, she suddenly gets wised up just like my French housekeeper. We lost a French housekeeper, and he may lose a French wife, unless he yields and gives her a parrot.

Dr. Mandelbaum This question applies to all of us: "Very little has been said about the burden of guilt that society has placed upon the working mother, especially those who work because of the wish to do so rather than a financial need." In most school problems, behavioral problems, delinquency discussions, the mother is the villain, and the absent mother is doubly blamed. What do you think?

Mr. Hunt I think it has been historically true that women have been scolded and made to feel guilty, and the mass media still to some extent do this, but I don't think the professionals are that silly any more. I read recently a report from the Women's Bureau or Children's Bureau, summarizing the recent sociological studies with working mothers and indicating, as we already heard from the symposium, that children of working mothers don't suffer unless the mothers are grossly neglectful or dislike their work and everything and therefore are just generally bitchy to everybody. To the extent that government agencies and psychologists are now finding this and disseminating such findings, they are going to reduce these guilt feelings somewhat.

Dr. Harris One of the previous speakers touched on the hero of the magazine story and the hero of the advertisements, too; there is always a mother who is home with the children while the father is working. Whenever we depart from the official image (and we do tend to think of magazines and TV as official), we worry about ourselves unless a society, group of friends, or somebody tells us differently. In my paper, I tried to say who in Hollywood could have corroborated her skepticism, who could have told her, "That's right, you are smart, even though you are a beautiful blonde girl." She didn't know the right people, and so many mothers feel guilty in their isolation.

Mr. Hunt I remember a paper which dealt with the children of women who have a career or part-time job. It said that young girls growing up in such a home are much better able to incorporate these various roles in their image of themselves; they see themselves as doing the same thing. When those girls grow up, they will very likely suffer less guilt, because they won't be violating some internal image of themselves, and since the number of women who work and have children is on the increase, we can take a guess that within a generation the guilt feeling will be reduced.

Dr. Mandelbaum The next question is directed to Mr. Hunt: "Why should asking your husband to fix the toaster plug, which you can do much better than he, do more to inflate this man's ego than asking him to prepare the main dish at dinner because he is a much better cook than you are?"

Mr. Hunt Well, if he is a much better cook than you are, I don't think you will have to ask him to prepare the main dish. I think you will have an awful time trying to stop him. And one final personal note, my male ego is served perfectly well by having the housekeeper prepare the main dish for company, and my wife's female ego likewise, because neither of us are good cooks and neither of us is harmed by having a housekeeper or threatened. Each of us has other things which seem more to flatter our ego.

Dr. Mandelbaum I think the next topic for discussion at a forthcoming symposium should be "The Potential of the Housekeeper."

I think this question is fitting as a final note, "Do you see people rather than women as the center of the discussion of the kind of topics we have discussed?"

That, I believe, is certainly true. Whenever we talk about the potential of woman, we are really discussing the potential of people, of men, of women, of children, and so all our discussions so far about the potential of woman or women have really dealt as well with the nature of potential, and the promise that our society and other societies in our civilization hold for men and women in this country and everywhere.

PART SIX

THE PRIVATE WORLDS
OF MR. AND MRS. MITTY

Chairmen: Alice K. Leopold
Enoch Callaway, III

The final session consisted of two panels, alternately of the male speakers and the women, entitled "The Private Worlds of Mr. and Mrs. Mitty." These panels gave the speakers a chance to intermingle in the light of what had already been discussed, re-edit previous comments, and introduce concepts and questions that had been aroused. The panel of "Mr. Mitty" concerned itself chiefly with the concept of woman as a person and yet as the love object of men. The panel of women which followed discussed the stereotyping of roles and the lack of reality with which both men and women regard themselves in the present age.

THE PRIVATE WORLD OF MR. MITTY

This is an actual transcription of the formal but spontaneous panel discussion of the papers in this book. Only minor editing has been done where continuity and clarity required it. The editors feel that the spontaneity of the actual discussion gives a particular value to the panel in this form, since it amplifies questions arising from the formal presentations of the participants as well as answering questions from the audience.

Moderator: Alice K. Leopold
Panel Members: Mark Harris, Thomas Carr Howe, Morton M. Hunt, Peter Koestenbaum, John Money, Edmund W. Overstreet, Albert E. Schwabacher, Jr., Alan Watts

Mrs. Leopold After 2½ days of deep and thoughtful exploration of the subject of the potential of women, I hesitate to tell you how much I enjoy the role of being the mediator for eight men. Perhaps this is a clue to my femininity; perhaps it is just the opposite.

To remind you of the story of James Thurber's Walter Mitty: Walter Mitty drives his wife to town one Saturday afternoon to have her hair done. While she is at the beauty parlor, he is given a couple of errands. In spite of these, he goes off into the dream world of Commander Mitty, in charge of a famous hydroplane; the great surgeon, Dr. Mitty, who solves the most difficult problems in operations; and the ace pilot Mitty.

But he has these two errands to do. One is to get a pair of overshoes, which he is perfectly certain he doesn't need but which he remembers; the second one escapes him, but he finally recalls that he is supposed to buy puppy biscuit. He buys these things and goes back and waits for Mrs. Mitty in the hotel lobby. She comes in to find him dozing in one of the dreams, and she says, "You just have not been in good health lately. I am worried about you. You are going to have to go to the doctor tomorrow." As they leave she goes into the drugstore to buy a thermometer, because the first thing she is going to do when she gets home is to take his temperature. While she is in the drugstore, Mr. Mitty leans in the rain against the wall of the drugstore, patiently waiting again. In a dream he is facing a firing squad with that last fleeting smile playing about his lips. "He faced the firing squad, erect, motionless, proud and disdainful. Walter Mitty, the undefeated; inscrutable to the last."

Now the question is: how do we relate the distinguished men on this panel to Walter Mitty? I think we are going to identify this panel as a symbol of all men whose private dreams are broken into now and then by women: secretaries, wives, sisters, or daughters.

I would like first to ask Dr. Overstreet whether he believes that men understand the characteristics of women and whether he thinks that men in general know how to cope with these characteristics.

Dr. Overstreet   I think that is probably one of the problems of our time. We physicians are discovering more and more biologically about women very rapidly, but psychologically we are probably far behind in really understanding the gamut of female responses. With the rapid moving of the revolution in female functions, it seems to me that one of the big problems is the understanding of men keeping up with this knowledge in relation to women.

Mrs. Leopold   In the light of our discussions are we any further in understanding that, despite the large number of women who have been supporters of the arts, everyone is so hard pressed to find a list of artists themselves who happen to be females?

Mr. Howe   I think it is now a little simpler for me to try to answer this. The discrepancy may be due, at least in part, up to the present century, to the fact that women did not have the freedom of action and the intellectual development to the degree that they have it now. Certainly there is evidence in today's roster of artists that an enormous number of women practice art in every community; it is true of the Bay Area region.

Dr. Overstreet   Do not women turn to the arts, first of all, because they have been traditionally thought of as aesthetic and artistic and, secondly, because our male club, so to speak, has tended to exclude them from other pursuits, leaving this as one of the open avenues for expression?

Mr. Hunt   I am much perplexed by the fact that women do demonstrably have abilities in these areas but that few of them have actually made major achievements. I can't think of any major woman symphony conductor, although there are some minor ones; there are no women composers of any great rank. I can't understand why this is so; this is a mystery. Women have written very good novels, but I don't know of a symphony by a woman that I would like to hear. I would like somebody to explain that.

Mr. Schwabacher   Yesterday I was asked the name of a woman who had done an outstanding job in business, and I couldn't do it. But last night I did remember one lady who made a fantastic contribution. She and her husband (and she is at the creative end of it) are the management of probably the fastest-growing and perhaps one of the two most successful toy companies in America. It is just amazing, but there are very few and they are far between.

Dr. Harris   I object to the restriction of success in life to the kind of success which is identifiable in the production of a symphony. It seems to me the extent that women modify, refine, curb, restrain, and limit man's arrogance, power thrusts, and his warlike tendencies, or to put it in another way, the extent that women keep investing in Aunt Sally's candy instead of the other candy is an index of success.

Dr. Overstreet   I would like to support that. I got the feeling during the course of the symposium that an undue emphasis has been placed upon creativity for women. I much prefer Dr. Koestenbaum's term, "fulfillment." This has a much broader range of implication than the term "creativity" alone.

Actually one of the problems that arises is that in all humans the peak of creativity is probably between the ages of twenty-five and forty. We then have the conflict with reproduction in females at just that peak age range in creativity and productiveness in other fashions. One of the big problems in the emergence of the potentiality of woman is how to reconcile the conflicts between her necessity for reproduction and her necessity for other kinds of fulfillment.

Mr. Watts I subscribe very much to what Dr. Harris and Dr. Overstreet just said, and I want to add that there is another side to it. It isn't only that women restrain the aggressive tendencies of men, but that they immensely encourage the creative tendencies of men. Most men who have done something creative have done it very largely to please and interest a woman who is one source of inspiration in this matter, and this is to me a tremendously valuable function.

It takes us back to what I was saying about the pseudo-event. Very often people who get reported about as creators and to whom the public's attention is drawn are only figureheads. Their creation is not necessarily all that important; it is just that they get noticed. Certain saints are canonized by the church, but probably many holier saints were not recognized at all just because they were self-effacing and unrecognized. That was the measure of their holiness, and so it can be with creativity.

Dr. Overstreet There is a difference between fulfillment and notoriety.

Mr. Hunt I begin to perceive that I am something of a minority on this panel and may go down as the Quisling of this symposium. In fact, Walter Mitty himself would have liked nothing better than to imagine himself one of the troubadours or knights of the thirteenth century, which is where you have all put him because you wish woman to be an inspiration once again, and to exert her kindly and ennobling influence on our character while keeping her nose out of our business. Those who are about to swallow this sugar-coated pill whole should see what is inside and reconsider how they would enjoy it.

No man wrote about the ennobling influence of woman in his life any better, even in the thirteenth century, than Ullrich von Liechtenstein. He worshiped a woman; she was a princess above him in rank, which made it very appropriate. He could therefore really worship her and strive to win her. He worshiped her for five years, during which time the extent of his devotion, since he could never speak to her, was to wait until she washed her hands, then steal away with the basin of dirty water and in his own room drink it. If you think that is going to fulfill, you are welcome to it.

Dr. Overstreet   As a matter of fact, I am not at all sure we all agree with Mr. Watts. Certainly I do not believe that man's creativity always springs from the need to satisfy woman or even springs from her stimulus. I think creativity in men is an inner type of thing, just as it is in any human individual, male or female.

Mr. Schwabacher   Let us go a step further, what about some of the great electronic scientists who try to stay ahead of their competition? Does that come from some female? It is a hard, cold, business fact, or they are out of business.

Mr. Watts   What is one in business for?

Mr. Schwabacher   For fun.

Mr. Watts   That does not sound very practical; therefore I will move into the dimension of something feminine, like the dance, which is done for its own sake, not for gain. If you are in business for fun, I congratulate you.

Mrs. Leopold   We heard earlier about the cluster of roles of women, and this is partly connected with what we were just talking about. The question occurs: is there time for this cluster of roles in the life span of a woman?

Dr. Money   As Dr. Overstreet said, the creative age is widely accepted now to be in the young adult period, which is the reproductive age of women. I think in a way our discussions and papers here over the last 2½ days can be crystallized out as the theme of the problem of career versus motherhood, because in times past the career of a woman and her activities in motherhood were closely bound together and well defined by tradition. It is in our recent day and age that new perspectives have opened up for new careers for women, and many of them trespass on what used to be exclusively the careers of men. Now I make it a problem of career versus motherhood, because to make it a problem of career versus sexual eroticism would be too wide. I mention in passing that we have been a little fearful of talking about the facts of sexual life and the new dimension that has been brought out by the restriction of motherhood by family planning and birth control. This makes a very great difference in our whole problem, because it leaves a woman with more time for a career while she does not have to abandon all possibilities of motherhood.

If a career is going to be something outstandingly creative, the demands are all-consuming. We have the saying of being married to medicine or to the church, and those who are really that way are intensely devoted and often, in fact, are unmarried or postpone their marriage. Sir William Osler, when he started the service in medicine at Johns Hopkins, forbade the young men to be married until they finished their training. Woman's role in motherhood cannot be in any way equated with man's role in fatherhood because of the very nature of the feelings, activities, and often the instinct itself of motherhood. Many times I have heard women in my office spontaneously talking about whether they wanted to have another baby, perhaps because of some genetic defect, and in a very spontaneous way they compare their feelings now with the feelings they have when they see someone holding a little baby. It is immediately demonstrable how they feel about having something tiny to hold, cuddle, and cherish. I have never seen any evidence of this sort of thing to such a degree in men. Therefore, it is the very act of personally caring for, and being close to, young babies that is very important to a mother in her experience of motherhood. Of course, she could take the maiden aunt's role and be the breadwinner or take care of someone else's children, but that is not true mothering. It is the substitute motherhood of religious women, schoolteachers, or nurses, who have never been married, but it is really maiden-auntism.

Another possibility often seen today is that a woman could have her own children and work on a full-time or part-time basis by having servants to take care of them. She thereby relinquishes part of her motherhood. That would not be possible on a universal scale; there are not enough servants to go around for everyone, since someone has to be the servant. This Pandora's box has been released on us by our age of technology and machinery, which has been a source of power releasing women for all these possibilities by giving her enough time for a career.

Dr. Koestenbaum   I would like to express a general feeling of uneasiness about some of the things that have been said, including Dr. Money's very wise comments.

It is much easier, more palatable, and amusing to deal with the relatively superficial issues of the problem of women and at the same time ignore the truly fundamental, basic, and ultimate first issues. If the premises are found to be faulty or false, an argument itself is invalid. In a system of geometry if you find some fault with either your methods of procedure or the axiom, the conclusion is invalid. Similarly, unless we can answer and think of really and truly fundamental issues, all these problems of home versus career, sexual abstinence versus sexual passion, and things of this sort become quite superficial and meaningless questions.

To understand the potential of woman from the true philosophical beginning is to understand what it means to be a woman as a person. In other words, the differentiation between man and woman is secondary; we have first to understand what it means to be a person, and after we have understood that, we can then worry about the relatively minor differentials between men and women. This point has not been brought out sufficiently, and the reason for this is that it is probably one of the most difficult problems we know of but at the same time possibly the most important one with which we could be confronted. Let us start by asking, "What is man?"

Mr. Watts   Do you think we can solve it at all?

Dr. Koestenbaum   I think you can work in that direction, although I suspect you cannot dedicate yourself to anything without some hope of an answer. But this problem, which can be codified well for some and not so well for others, is the problem of the meaning of life. What is its ultimate meaning? What does it mean to be really and truly fulfilled? Without these answers, nothing can be solved.

Dr. Overstreet   In speaking of that word "fulfillment," let us go back to Dr. Money's statement. He talks about career versus motherhood as if they were mutually exclusive and as if a woman had to have a career. We are talking about fulfillment of the individual, and in that sense really very few people have careers. I wonder whether a better way of thinking about it is in terms of the combination of motherhood and reproduction with other types of fulfillment for women. We heard a good deal about how women have to suppress their intellectual functions and abilities in order to catch a man. This intellectual function is one method of fulfillment which has nothing to do with motherhood, and I wonder if it isn't a question of whether other types of fulfillment fit into reproduction.

Mr. Watts This is very difficult to generalize about, because everybody's way is his own. I think we are all blocked in fulfillment, particularly in our culture, by a method of education in which everything we do is for the future. This is a perpetual blocking of fulfillment just like inducing a donkey to run along by dangling a carrot by his own harness in front of him. People constantly seek fulfillment by this kind of grade-step method. You put a child in kindergarten and say, "Come on now; in another year you will be in the first grade—then second grade—high school, college, business." This is pure sales talk, and at the age of forty-five you suddenly say, "By God, I am there, and I feel just as if I were not." So I think fulfillment is an impossible goal but a possible realization so long as you know it's here.

Mr. Hunt. I have a feeling that Dr. Koestenbaum and perhaps Mr. Watts are speaking of fulfillment as though it were absolute and timeless, just as so many discussions assume that woman's nature is also a timeless thing unchanging over the centuries or between cultures. We cannot be Aristotelian in this discussion, because much of our fulfillment is in terms of the goal which our society has set for it. Neither our grandmothers nor our grandchildren may want what we wish ourselves. To tell women that they can be fulfilled by being a restraining, modifying, and gentling influence on men is inadequate under present circumstances. It may be fun in part, but I don't think it is adequate, since they are reared and schooled in the same way men are. Therefore they learn to prize many of the things that men prize and want the same kinds of prestige and accomplishment as men. This is not a violation of some kind of perennial, unchanging femininity; I don't think there is an eternal femininity in that sense. Wherever woman is eternal, it is in some part that I am perfectly delighted about, but I think fulfillment is very important to women and today it must be in terms of participating in the masculine world to a greater or lesser extent.

Dr. Koestenbaum All this assumes that fulfillment is a thing, a state of mind, and, above all, something that perhaps we know. I submit that we ought to begin by understanding and realizing that we know very little about the nature of human fulfillment and that the beginning of our research and inquiry into the fundamental problem of human potential and fulfillment is to understand exactly what the problem is. What is it that we want out of life?

We have representatives in this symposium of many areas which throughout the history of ideas have concerned themselves with the effort to solve the problem of the meaning of life, including physicians, psychologists, men of letters, and philosophers. However, there is no representative of the theological tradition. Much of religion can be construed to be an effort to meet this special problem in this particular way, and this is perhaps a significant gap in the things we have discussed. While not proposing either favorable or unfavorable views on it, I think it is certainly one of the efforts men have engaged in to try to solve this particular problem.

Mrs. Leopold Does the culture and education of males today make this finding a way of life more difficult? Do we make it easy for a woman to find her way of life?

Dr. Harris We are trained, I think, to the wrong kinds of dreams. By success we mean something immediately; we all have an image, rather than a theological or philosophical idea, of the *moment* of success. We are all going to the future—the next grade. I think Mr. Mitty is unfulfilled and his wife is such a terrible nag because she is unfulfilled. They are both unfulfilled, because they have the wrong kind of ambition. Ambition is a function of our education, which teaches us, among other things, the importance of financial responsibility and economic success rather than theological and philosophical success.

Dr. Overstreet There is an added factor in that the male, starting out with a necessity for dominance in a wild state, has a long background tradition of vested interest in maintaining the superiority of this club. Fortunately we have gotten a little away in this symposium from that thought, and as Professor Higgins in "My Fair Lady" asks, "Why can't a woman be like a man?" That we are just beginning to think in terms of what a woman should be like and how well a man should understand her is a long step forward.

Mrs. Leopold Would Mr. Hunt tell us what he thinks the average husband thinks of his wife's participation in work, in social activities, or in making herself an interesting companion? Are women born bores, or do they work hard to make themselves into bores?

Mr. Hunt   I wish I could give a simple answer, but there are a variety of kinds of men, and some men really don't want an interesting wife. For all I spoke before about the process of transition and evolution, I know of some men who are mortally offended when their wives speak up and have opinions of merit or perhaps have something of substance to say. In fact, one such man I know is now in his third marriage; he is fatally addicted to intelligent women and can't stand them. Some day or other he will find out that Rousseau had the good sense to be in love with a brilliant woman whom he rarely saw and had the better sense to live with an ignorant woman who couldn't even tell time. He lived with her for twenty-five years and finally married her. That is one kind of sense; I don't think that it is the dominant but rather the disappearing mode. The kind of people I have met, middle-class men, businessmen, and particularly men in all sorts of professional life, deeply appreciate a woman who can not only listen but actually respond in an intelligent way and who knows what they are doing. One of the worst things about modern life is the specialization that makes a man spend his whole day in the physics laboratory and then go home and be totally unable to tell his wife anything about it. No wonder if he runs off to Atlantic City with a lady physicist who is helping him on the project. You do have to talk before and after, whatever else it is you do.

Mr. Schwabacher   There are several areas here we have not touched on: one is the environmental background; the second is timing, which is probably the most important thing nobody has mentioned; and the third one, which has really upset the entire discussion, is the difference between people living in Europe and this country; there are a few more.

Environment is something that has gone on for years, for ages. When you start tying fulfillment and objectives in, it may be partly the fault of men in this country, but what about the differences between American and European or Oriental women?

Dr. Overstreet   Obviously, the variation is extreme, and it must be taken into account in thinking about the nature of woman. We are trying to get down to basic aspects; as we have gone along through this symposium, we have recognized the major importance of cultural and sociological aspects, rather than the biological ones, although the biological ones cannot be ignored as basic factors.

Mr. Watts   Mr. Hunt a while ago made a great point in the social determination of our individual ideas of fulfillment. I do think that is important, only I am afraid it is fashionable in sociological thinking today to overdo it, and that it is the combination of individual differences that make up the social attitudes. Both sides of this are true; it is an egg and hen thing. But we must agree with Mr. Hunt in the question of a relationship between men and women in which there is not in the long run real intellectual compatibility, and the possibility of conversation which is the desideratum for any cultured person. It is all very well to have a beautiful dunderhead around, but it becomes exceedingly boring. All sorts of things stand in the way of that kind of communication, and it is a real problem that we have discussed in many ways already in this symposium that the educated woman will very often be conditioned to become a bit more of a bluestocking than the man likes and therefore be the kind of person of whom one can say, "You know all the words, but you don't know the music."

Mrs. Leopold   There was one thing that was said by Mr. Schwabacher about environment that I will comment on. I have had to deal with men in politics, business, and government, and it has always seemed to me that I could tell a man whose mother was interested in the world around him from one whose mother was house-centered.

Do you men feel that more husbands are ready today to respect the potential of women?

Mr. Hunt   I will reiterate, at the risk of repeating myself, that the intellectual and mentally active woman was very likely to be a spinster thirty, forty, or fifty years ago, and today she is not at all likely to remain unmarried. She gets married because there are enough men who have come to like that kind of woman, appreciate that kind of woman.

Dr. Money   I have been asked two questions which fit together: One of them says, "How about social solutions to motherhood combined with a career, that is, more day child-care centers and nurseries?" And the other question says, "Is not the idea of a cluster of roles for women the same situation that Miss Mannes called 'having to be feminine, charming, and twice as confident at the same time'? What about clusters of roles for males?"

If one looks back beyond the time when woman was emancipated for more roles than just motherhood, weaving, and making dinner parties, it is possible to see that there were really two roles that could be sorted out which were allocated for women. One was the role of a young woman, a sort of debutante, which was highly developed in the upper classes; the other, after she was married, the role of a matron. It is easy to recall the historical anecdotes of matrons who developed their roles to extremely high degrees of efficiency. In the South, the woman often was the person who really ran the plantation; but before she reached that age and dignity, she had to play another game, the role of the charming debutante. Much of our problem today is for men to know what role to attribute to women when they are, let us say, working, and for women to know what role to attribute to men. Instead of working together in a workaday kind of role, as two men or two women would work together, it often breaks down, especially at a moment of stress and crisis, so that the girl begins to play the debutante role and an older woman a domineering matriarch.

There is the real question in this symposium of what it is to adapt in the 1960s to the role of the woman who has bigger horizons before her.

Child centers and nurseries will solve the problem for some, but a woman cannot be a man, because she is a mother. Unless she is a rather unusual woman, motherhood is her great satisfaction and fulfillment, her first role; the other must be adopted as secondary.

Mrs. Leopold   So far we have not mentioned "the divine nature of women," and have completely passed by the spiritual side of woman and what this means to her own life and home life. These are facets many hold as most important.

Dr. Koestenbaum   One of the fundamental principles that must govern in satisfactory relationship between a man and a woman is that of mutual respect for the dignity of a human person.

There are no good theoretical reasons why we should think of people as dignified or why we should think of, in this case, women as particularly sacred or divine individuals. This is what is missing and also applies to our whole foundation of democracy. It is essential for the theoretical understanding of the democratic principles that govern us to have a good solid foundation for the dignity of man, and the foundations that we have are based on some antiquated philosophical positions.

If we understand what it means to be a human subject, to have to make decisions and to face death, we will find in ourselves a replica of the image of God. Whatever you think of God, you will either be an image of God or some sort of projected idea of God as a symbol for ourselves. This is a necessary foundation for appreciating and revering the divinity of any human being including, of course, the divinity of woman. The proper philosophic understanding of what it means to be a human being will almost automatically lead us to revere humanity, human subjectivity, and human inwardness as something sacred, as the most important thing in the world and something that ought to be cultivated, respected, and preserved. This is the fundamental basis for any human relationship.

Mr. Hunt   I would like to get a little bit mundane, however, about the divinity of women. To stress the divinity of woman is to get into a very dangerous area, at least historically. If you look to the Middle Ages, you find that it was there that woman was most considered a divine creature, but at the very same time she was also a minion of Satan and a witch. There was a very peculiar schizoid feeling about a woman. A man was unable to synthesize his feeling about her, and in that tremendous separation of woman into Lady or Madonna, she was semidivine and honored, and at the same time she could be the source of man's temptation and fall.

If you stress the divine in woman along these lines, you run that same risk of being incapable of having in one human being a whole rounded person. As man came to accept the fact that woman could be sexual and that this was not necessarily evil, he had to degrade her a little less divine. In consequence, he was able to marry her and live with her more happily than before. So don't stress your divinity too much; be a little earthbound.

Mr. Watts   This is a terrible conception of divinity; it means antithetical to the earth. It means I have a mission in life to point out that we need a synthesis of spirituality and sensuality. That was the original meaning of Christianity in the doctrine of the incarnation that the

word was made flesh. But Christianity is also the history of the resistance
to that idea, so we developed a concept of divinity which was ethereal
and emasculated. God was the Father and the Son, both male, and the
Holy Spirit was a dove, and nobody could make out what sex it was.
The only woman admitted to the hierarchy of Heaven so far is a virgin;
this won't do at all.

Professor Koestenbaum said that it is important in the philosophical
basis of democracy to regard all human beings as dignified, but he said
it in a way which made it look as if we need to drag philosophy into
this. What needs to be added is that everybody is a philosopher willy-
nilly. You cannot help but have some metaphysical assumptions about
the meaning of life and the value of life, and if you don't know what
they are, they are liable to be bad ones.

Dr. Overstreet   I would like to correct a question which seems
to have been implicit in some of the discussion that has gone before.
Briefly it seems to have been said that I implied that women live too
long, both physically and mentally.

What I was talking about was a biological and physiological span
of life, as seen in nature, which has been extended by civilization and
medical science, and my contention was that it is up to the medical
sciences to keep women functioning productively, creatively, and ful-
fillingly even after they have outlived their physiological span.

I have been asked, "When is childbearing going to be taken out
of the realm of the pathological?"

No obstetrician considers childbearing as pathological but as a
physiological process which is very quickly subject to pathologic change.
Walking across the street is not pathological, but it is changed when
you get hit by an automobile. Obstetricians guide women through the
best possible physiology of childbirth in order to avoid the pathological.

And the second question was, "Do you see an evolution to a
marriageless society?"

Prior to the knowledge of the origin of offspring there was some
tendency to this, but I like best Margaret Mead's description of what
marriage means in all cultures and all societies; that marriage is simply
the public acknowledgment of the responsibility for offspring. That
being the case, it seems rather unlikely that we shall get away to
marriageless society, Hollywood antics to the contrary notwithstanding.

What will be interesting and perhaps may occur in our lifetime and I think certainly in our children's will be sex determination by choice of offspring. When we can choose whether we are going to have a boy or girl as an offspring, then we really have a revolution comparable to which the population explosion, I think, is probably mild.

Mr. Hunt I have a question here which says, "It has been mentioned that women feel trapped by suburban life. Do you think the negative or destructive activities they engage in are a reaction against this? By destructive, I refer to such things as the committees who fight to ban books which they would never corrupt their minds by reading."

There are many examples of destructive activities on the part of suburban housewives, and these are not all of them. Some are self-destructive, as in women who develop symptoms of various sorts and haunt doctors' offices. Women are destructive of their husbands when they become nags or discontented, or forever spend his money on changing the living room, when it is perfectly fine the way it is. They are destructive in a sense when they overmother the children. Everyone has a certain amount of natural aggressive drive. When aggressive energy is sublimated in a highly constructive fashion, it ceases to be expended on the nearest objects at hand, the husband, children, and themselves. This is one of the best possible arguments for modern woman either having a part-time or full-time career or important activities outside the home. Even if these do not earn money, they are outlets into which she can channel those energies and not necessarily to the detriment of the outside world, because when sublimated they are no longer sheer aggression but what has happened with aggression.

Dr. Harris One of the early things I began to be aware of in this symposium concerned the numerous ways in which sexual characteristics of a biologic and genetic nature overlap. This clear social division between male and female in so many of our activities gives many difficult moments—certain jobs men won't do, others women won't do; they feel it too feminine for a man or too masculine for a woman. Something central to these problems lies in relating social sensitivity and skill to the concept of success. In the arts, for example, so much of what we learn we do because it was taught to us because we were either male or female.

To trap woman in the suburbs in which book banning is only a symptom of her aggressive release may derive from the fact that her role has been assigned most of all by herself. What she does and how she entraps herself are due to her not having major confidence to try to do other things.

Mr. Watts Aren't you saying we are all making the enormous semantic mistake of talking about men and women instead of people? There are six kinds of men and six kinds of women, at the very least.

Dr. Harris Somebody here used the phrase "that kind of woman." Everyone is different. I used to be very upset on the subject of Negroes many years ago when I was a kid, and I first learned lots of phrases to answer people when they said bad things. So many of them are applicable again as when people talk about "the Negro." When they used to say "the Negro," we said, "Which Negro?" Which woman?

Mr. Howe This ties in with what Dr. Harris just said. The question is, "If all creative women go into careers, what kind of woman will enter the home and 'mold' the child while the mother is at work, as her time with the children is limited and harried while at home?"

Isn't that best answered by a question, "Since there are so many different types of women, with the different kinds of interests they have, is there any reason to think that every woman is suddenly going to turn into a madly harried, creative type who wants to abandon the things associated with home life?" It seems to me it all averages out.

Dr. Harris Also the madly harried, creative types lead a home life, too. When one is free to do some of the things that have been traditionally thought of as the job of the other sex, then one is freer than we now are.

Mr. Hunt Moreover, when it is stressed that behind every successful man is a woman, this might imply that women have a greater capacity than men for vicarious satisfactions.

The first part has already been disposed of.

The second was a favorite idea of the late Victorians and Edwardians. It actually was a very comforting notion to women who were relatively powerless, and it seems that in fact the hand that rocked the cradle did rule the world. That was a vicarious satisfaction, and in some sense women who are behind a successful man today have vicarious satisfactions. But a vicarious satisfaction is what you accept if you can't have the real commodity, so I don't think that women have innately great capacity for vicarious satisfaction but that a lot more of them have to put up with it.

Mr. Hunt I have a question here: "Isn't the woman who is molding the child performing a creative activity?"

I suspect that anybody who uses such terms as molding a child may have a slight power complex. I would like to help my child grow and to point out useful avenues and interesting things, but I think it is a dangerous thing to mold him.

In the second place, even if we grant that doing a good job of bringing up a child and helping him flourish as a human being is a highly creative activity, it is still an activity limited to a short span of years in modern woman's life, and she may find herself with some thirty-five years ahead of her in which she may have very little to do. The only children around to "mold" will be her grandchildren, and her daughter won't let her do that and may move 1,500 miles away to develop new career and family. In any case grandmothers are notoriously poor molders; they are better as flatterers who let the child do whatever he likes. If you are content to pin your whole life to a fifteen-year period which is diminishing because the child is in school so much of the time once he is six or seven, I think it is rather poor judgment.

Mr. Howe From a limited but concentrated experience in this, I believe that my daughter, beginning at the age of about three up to the time she was about fifteen, was developing excellent material for a book on educating one's parents, and I think the "molding" had worked the other way around.

Mr. Hunt I thought I ought to mold my son into liking good music, and the more I wanted him to listen to music I like, the more he retreated into his room and turned on rock and roll, which he knew I detest. When I stopped pushing him and let him have all the rock and roll he wanted, he came in and started to play chess with me. One day he said, "Put on some of that organ music," by which he meant some Bach that I had been trying to foist on him for half a year. I think the unmolded child grows best.

Mr. Watts The hand that rules the cradle wrecks the world.

Dr. Harris The state of poets as the unacknowledged legislators of the world is similar. By whom are we all acknowledged if we want some critic? In American success terms, it really isn't sufficient for the lady to know that she is the unacknowledged cradle rocker.

Mrs. Leopold   I have a question: "What do these charming, intelligent men consider an ideal feminine woman?"

Mr. Hunt   There was a poet who was trying to describe what he loved in woman; he really adored a tall woman, but then he liked a short one, too; he liked a plump one, and some of the skinny ones were great. Our culture allows me to marry one woman, but I enjoy an awful lot of women, and I think it should stay that way.

Mr. Schwabacher   I think the first prerequisite with me is to have a sense of humor; my wife has one and keeps reminding me she has to have to live with me.

Mr. Howe   I think Mr. Schwabacher made a fundamental comment when he spoke about the necessity for a sense of humor; I think that the cornerstone.

Mr. Hunt   I don't remember that Isolde was funny, and she was pretty desirable.

Mrs. Leopold   Did it last?

Mr. Hunt   She wouldn't have worked out too well in Levittown, would she?

Dr. Overstreet   One of the objections to Isolde was that she had no sense of humor. But to go a little farther, a sense of proportion, of what is important and not important in life, is imperative in a good mate.

Mrs. Leopold   Any others?

Dr. Harris   I wish Dr. Koestenbaum had said what essentially he said in the larger sense. There seems to be for myself the ideal woman who would be one who is always a pleasing person and has all these good things, such as humor, proportion, intelligence with a sense of security and confidence.

Dr. Koestenbaum   One prevalent hypothesis as to what the problem of fulfillment really is—is the fact that man is mortal. Whether we believe in immortality or that there is a God or not, all of us know that we are going to die and are somewhat anxious about this anticipation. This is a dramatic way of calling attention to the fact that we are limited and that in one way or another this is the fundamental problem underlying the entire discussion.

Dr. Money   One of the most classic remarks I ever obtained from a woman who really hated her husband was that she prayed to God for only one thing, that is she might survive her husband by at least twenty-four hours, so she would know what it was like to be at least one day without him. One could turn that around the other way and have her praying to live for another twenty-four hours, because it would be so good to be one more day with him.

I have been asked: "Do you see any indication that in the future women can be less obsessed with their own children and tend less to identify with their own children, so that public nurseries could take the place, to some extent, of their mothers?"

I don't see any contraindications to that; let me say I would imagine that the more it becomes an acceptable practice for wives on a widespread basis, the easier it is for people to go along with it without feeling guilty. I have seen quite a number of instances in which children, in fact, benefit in having another mother or a mother substitute to escape to when their own mother gets to be too much of a nuisance. Perhaps there has been much too much emphasis on the personal responsibilities that a mother has for her own children, and she is left with too much of a feeling of guilt if she does not give close personal attention all the time.

Dr. Harris   That question is asked of this panel because this is a discussion of women; but men also have these very severe anxieties about their children, are concerned, and in many cases are less relaxed than their wives about them. This seems to me again an artificial separation here of the sexes.

Mr. Howe   I remember, at the end of our panel discussion Friday, that the final $64 question was, "What is a woman?" And it came to me first, and thank God I had at least an answer, and I said a woman is a man's wife. Dr. Money said a woman is a man's mother, and Mr. Watts said the cleverest of all.

Mr. Watts   I answered the question in that way because it was stylistically appropriate, and I just had to fall into the trap. But I really did demur when I thought of a great many women who are not a man's mother, nor his wife, nor his mistress, but are still women. They're all men's daughters and cannot be categorized in these very formal relationships.

Dr. Harris   Miss Mannes touched in her talk on that, too, and would Dr. Koestenbaum add the parallel construction that a woman is a human being.

Mrs. Leopold   This is an interesting question: "If a woman earns eight to nine times as much as her husband because he is employed and has definite hours while she has a career, why shouldn't he do all she cannot, if he does not object, such as care for the children, shopping, and housework? Is she to be expected to be a perfect lover if she is too tied up with her work evenings and the family is used to living on a high standard based on her earnings?"

Mr. Hunt   It seems to me this is a kind of peculiar nonconforming marriage that is being portrayed here. We should all be relatively tolerant of it. The people who are involved are the ones who matter. If they are comfortable in that kind of life, I don't see how any of us can call it abnormal or improper. There is a whole range of character traits. Some people are very dependent and others very strong; it is possible for a strong woman to have a man who very much enjoys playing the opposite role with her, even though it violates the usual norms in our society. If she earns eight to nine times as much as he, though, and wants him to do the housework and also is too tired evenings, I would like to know why he is hanging around.

Mr. Howe   Wouldn't it be possible to have a high-powered housekeeper sharing some of the burdens?

Dr. Harris   Someone said here that that man needs a marriage counselor, and Mr. Hunt said he didn't know why he is hanging around. If they feel more comfortable with it this way, then he should hang around, since that would be more widespread and acceptable and might be a possible way of working out a relationship. People have very odd relationships.

Mrs. Leopold   As you recognize, this panel has been made up of men of singular differences in their backgrounds, attitudes, and interests. It is almost impossible that we would reach a conclusion, but I had hoped we might agree that neither men nor women understood either men or women, but I don't think we quite brought that out.

However, from what has been said here, we reached the feeling that this is a better climate for the development of the potential of women; we should be happy to have achieved this even in part.

THE PRIVATE WORLD OF MRS. MITTY

This is an actual transcription of the formal but spontaneous panel discussion of the papers in this book. Only minor editing has been done where continuity and clarity required it. The editors feel that the spontaneity of the actual discussion gives a particular value to the panel in this form, since it amplifies questions arising from the formal presentations of the participants as well as answering questions from the audience.

Moderator: Enoch Callaway, III
Panel Members: Ethel M. Albert, Barbara Bates Gunderson, Phyllis C. Jay, Adrienne Koch, Marya Mannes, Esther Peterson

Dr. Callaway The things implicit in this final portion of the conference seem to be a chance for our speakers to add, rephrase, and edit. The explicit title of this panel suggests a stereotype, the timid, unproductive dreamer and his officious wife, a potential that has little chance of being translated into reality. The notion of a stereotype is the antithesis of this conference. If I had to label the most dominant theme that emerged, it would be the value of differences both among and between men and women which make a vital reservoir of wide talent. Such a reservoir is our only hedge against the challenge of the unforeseen. As a psychiatrist I know that repetitive and stereotyped behavior is one of the stigmata of all mental illnesses whereas variety is the hallmark of health. I suspect the same holds for society. Some variety is not only the spice of life but may well be the essence of survival. If I wanted to exhibit the delights of diversity, I could pick no better exhibit than this panel.

I would like to ask each one of them if they would be willing to speculate on just how practically and actively to go about translating dreams and developing diversity in women and in men. What are the substrates of reality which define the limits to which the potential of women, in particular, but also of mankind in general, can be developed today?

Mrs. Peterson First we must wake up to the fact of what is reality and maybe come out of the dream world that I am afraid our whole society is in.

We still think so much in unrealistic terms of what the situation really is. This is because we read in journals and we see on television this lovely dream world in which the woman wakes up in the morning with her hair in place wearing a lovely chiffon robe and she is on the pedestal. Everything is quite rosy; the children are all well, husband gets up and brings her the coffee in the morning; she has time to whisk through the house, hear a little chamber music meanwhile with it, lunch with a lovely friend, buy things quickly instead of taking hours in the department stores, come home, make the Martinis correctly, and everything is all right.

The reality is that the woman has small children who don't want peanut-butter sandwiches that morning, and her husband says, "We're spending too much." The reality is that families live on incomes of less than $5,000 and that the average earnings are not so much higher. Most women who work do so to bring home a pay check.

During the last panel, we heard that this dream world is a woman's world of the fifteen years when she is having her children, when there is much more to it. There is the time before, when she is getting ready, and there is the wonderful reproductive period for many but not all women, and there is a longer period afterward. Let us have some reality in our view and what we as a society can do about this.

There is the reality where a girl doesn't get as much pay for the same job or an equal opportunity for advancement always. Perhaps she wants to be a truck driver, but there are few women truck drivers. There may be many ways in which she can fulfill this creative role. I would like to direct ourselves a bit to what can be done, and to come down out of the cloud onto the basis of where we really are as a society. I am convinced that we can dream and set our dreams high but by dreaming from a practical base we can solve many of these things on a basis which is real.

Dr. Callaway Let us pretend that you had a good fairy who would come to Washington, part of the New Frontier, and say, "I will give you one wish. Go ahead."

Mrs. Peterson I have a lot of wishes; I would say that I hope, as I used to as a child, that I would have that one wish to be that all my wishes would come true, and if I may say it, the true life of this Mrs. Peterson is this that I have to leave in a few minutes.

There are many things I can see. I don't think we have begun to think of the way that we can help remove a lot of these barriers. I am thinking of practical things, like the equal-pay bill, of community planning, of community centers where women and men can go where there will be opportunities for the day care of children, not to get rid of the children but where the professional woman can have the opportunity to have her children; new kinds of services. Why can't we have a wardrobe center that could come and get my kids' clothes all fixed? Look what happened to our society when they put their minds to developing drip-dry clothes. Weren't they good, ladies, so you don't have to iron!

There are many, many kinds of services: the specialist that comes into a home when there is an emergency, a mother substitute that could be called in—all these kinds of services that are possible when we put our minds to it, and I think that men and women can do this, and those are just a few.

Dr. Callaway I know that Dr. Koch has some thought on this matter of just what things might be and what things are in the woman who faces really developing an original career.

Dr. Koch I will go back to Dr. Callaway's original formulation on how you translate dreams into reality. The best method I can advocate is that advocated by William James, who said that when somebody tells you he wants to commit suicide, never argue with him rationally about it,'but say to him, "Wait for the next mail." That is the strategy which I think we have to keep as a primordial pattern governing all the recommendations that we make.

A very good project for a woman who doesn't want to leave the home would be to create a lexicon of illogical reasonings that have been advanced about woman's role and woman's position and of all the stereotypes, poisoned-well arguments that flourish.

And a second project for anybody who is looking for self-employment is a semantic task of trying to purify the language of its unconscious male orientation. When you talk about "every man is entitled to his right," some people really think that means the male of the species and not the woman, the female.

Dr. Albert   Having no strictly practical background and being one of these true career types who thinks only in terms of professional interest, I can't propose anything very practical, but it seems to me that we ought to take quite seriously something that has been said by at least half of the people who have delivered papers and that in spite of the repetition is not yet really believed, namely, that women are people.

It has been said in various forms. Even as I look up at the audience, I see people; I guess this is because I have been trained to see people. I am reminded of the curious experience I had when I got back from Africa. I had lived for a year and a half in the Bush, and when I got back home, after being away for a while, I was talking to my brother who was walking about the airport, and I said, "Good heavens, all these Americans look alike." Now being able to perceive women as people is not the easy kind of procedure. It is something that women and men have to learn to do, and it is connected with the semantic problem that Dr. Koch suggested, of finding ways in language to make real an awareness that "everybody is people." Perhaps the fundamental issue that has arisen is that the male and female real difference is not enough to stop us from being necessarily interdependent and to give us a common interest in whatever does happen to either the male or the female.

Dr. Callaway   This very nicely leads me into a question which I have been saving for Mrs. Gunderson: Mr. Watts earlier gave away one of the secrets of the program committee, that there had been some thought of entitling this symposium "The Control of Woman." He properly interpreted the term, however, as it had been considered, as the control that an artist exercises over a line, something that does not restrict freedom but improves smoothness. There was another subtitle to this that also hit the wastebasket with a slightly damp thump, and that was "The Control of Woman: subtitle—Mutual Coexistence." I am not sure that is not implicit a bit in what you say, except that it still implies that men are men and women are women.

Mrs. Gunderson spoke on the problem that mutual coexistence implies competition. I wonder if you would care to comment on just in what ways competition can practicably lead to the development of individuality?

Mrs. Gunderson I prefer the word "rivalry," although I admit they get mixed up in our minds.

The ideal I really hope may be achieved sometimes is the idea of loving rivalry where individuals, man to man, woman to woman, and most interesting of all, woman to man, would achieve full potential. It is a lot harder right now for women to be objective about themselves than for men. I get more and more puzzled at the push button, the frozen dinner, the polish that says it polishes itself—all the easy things which have not done very much, to make quite what we are after here.

We would like women competing with men at full stature, happy, competent, maybe delightfully arrogant creatures who say, "This is me. Look at my muscles. See what I have done. Can you do as well? Can you do the other half of this thing?" So I think this has very little to do with ease. Was it John Adams who said, "I seem always to have to go after ore that has never been mined before, with no tools made for it, and I end up by scratching everything up with my bare fingers." He was writing about the work of a writer as well as maker of history, but I think that is the thing that women were particularly meant to do; to work hard, not to always be comfortable.

I am not at all sure that we are not all secretly miserable; aren't you fascinated to know that we won't buy a cake mix unless it calls for one real egg that we put in and thereby prove that we, too, are creative in doing something? What we don't want is any mental foot binding for this big job of coming to full stature. Competition is not going to be the better for common humanity if we think only for services and conveniences for the female half of this world.

Dr. Callaway   I asked Mrs. Jay in advance if I could be so impertinent as to ask just what advantages and disadvantages does such a pretty girl have in becoming an anthropologist?

Dr. Jay   Well, I might say that anthropology is one of probable fields where women, I think, enjoy a great deal more equality of opportunity and in the variety of work which they can do in contrast to biological fields or medical fields, where I think the competition—if you want to call it that—is a great deal stronger. There are several things I would like to say as an anthropologist and as a person who has gotten into something quite deeply in the last few years.

There are many problems in being a female in a graduate school as well as a female trying to become a professional woman, because of the obviously great percentage of females who leave school and professions to get married long before they pursue the careers for which they acquire training. Those who do go on to follow the profession that they have chosen may find it harder to demonstrate their intentions or their seriousness. Females are so often conditioned by the folklore that surrounds them that perhaps the first step is to stop letting society tell them what they are. This applies equally to the housewife watching a soap opera or hearing any kind of commercial. Indoctrination is quite effective.

In anthropology, as in many fields, there are very strong selective factors which would tend to operate on the female in the field. Whereas a woman may be able to do very well in the study of a primitive culture—and many women do this, there are peripheral factors as a strong selection against a great many temperaments among women, such as getting train tickets in a country where you can't speak the language, and if you go to the Far East, the attitude makes it extremely difficult for you. In my field it helps if you can climb a tree; if you can't, you can use binoculars. It is really quite a delightful task and quite a delightful field, and I realize that is a little atypical.

Miss Mannes   I think it is the climate that has to be changed and have been interested in two phrases by the other panelists—foot binding and indoctrination. I think both of these exist to a fantastically large extent, and I blame the stereotyped and rigid thinking about men and women on two things: one, I think, is the Puritan basis of our society, which has done us inestimable harm in my view, and the second is the effect of mass communications as a whole.

I have been very interested in the reporting of this symposium. It is quite different for a television station like KQED to give the public the entire proceedings so that they can themselves decide what they accept and reject; this is really in essence one function of journalism which a great newspaper like *The New York Times* attempts to perform but which very few others do. It is another thing to report the proceedings of a conference like this with such angles as "Career Girl Forlorn."

Now I personally think this is a very unforlorn group. Most of us are married, many of us have children, and we live comparatively normal lives as women in spite of what we do. But the reports would leave the public at large with the impression that we are complaining, griping, militant, hostile battle-axes who don't believe women should have children or stay home and who are disruptive of the basis of American life. All this quietly pervades accounts in the poorer newspapers. I exempt about six in the United States, but in the poorer local newspapers these things do not enlighten and inform, but they indoctrinate, condition, warp, and obscure, and they perform, I think, a major public disservice.

This is not confined to newspapers; it is, as various others said, in fiction, in magazines, and certainly in soap operas. It is in all things that reach most people and that make a woman and a man stereotypes. Until the masters of communication realize what they are doing, our practical steps for an enlargement of ourselves will not be possible. But I also wish to say—and I should have really said it in the beginning— that it is marvelous to have this conference on the subject of women on the front page of any newspaper. It is in itself a great compliment when the usual procedure is to put anything to do with the woman on the woman's page, a form of segregation which I strenuously resist.

Dr. Albert I fully agree with Miss Mannes that the quality of all mass-medium communications leaves much to be desired, but it is probably because I have a good, solid New England background that I prefer to interpret the reactions to such poor-quality materials in a somewhat different fashion. It is a problem I confront as a teacher, as an adviser to young people, and as a human being—that is the problem of accepting responsibility. It is true that the public is fed a lot of garbage; that does not mean we have to eat it. It seems to me that ultimately change can occur only if individuals make it occur. Today there is a widespread tendency, not merely in our culture and certainly not merely in one or the other sex, to look for something or somebody to blame when something is wrong. The mass media are to be criticized, but they do not explain; what explains things going wrong is our failure to correct them.

I am perfectly well aware that there are certain conditions, legal and otherwise, that can actually keep you from doing something. For example, when slavery was permitted in this country, the slaves could not help themselves, and they needed help; but they needed help and got help from people who assumed responsibility. One of the things that distresses me endlessly about most of the young people I know is that they feel like helpless victims. Nobody has ever given them the notion that something they do can make a difference. They learn to think in terms of putting the blame on something. They block, so they ought to get a psychologist because they can't do a term paper; or they have been molded to this image or that; or else you can always find somebody to blame. We will begin to get out of this fix if we put the blame where it belongs: squarely on ourselves.

Dr. Koch   In adding just one sort of historical note to support what Miss Mannes said about the image which is constantly put before us, I think there is so much richness in terms of historical continuities in America. Somehow we have not used these and seized upon them as a power against the stereotype image of the last phase of our existence. I was thinking of the richness in the private lives and creative desires and aspirations of women like Anne Bradstreet, the Puritan poetess, who was a wife and mother of, I think, seven or more children. The Puritans were very fecund despite all the usual stereotypes about themselves, and she wrote very good poetry in which she struggled very hard to subdue properly the great sense of natural love for her husband, which nevertheless had to be assimilated under a properly religious set and dutiful pattern. The excitement of the New World that was opened to the first settlers in the seventeenth century was a constant challenge to them, and an environment that really made them become individuals no matter how much they were structured in their thought, and they happened to be more structured in their thought for many reasons, having much to do with the power of religion, than we are in our own. We are not structured in thought. We tend to be reflexive to immediate habit and stimuli. How things get started we don't even know, like pointed shoes, which suddenly became necessary for all women to wear, even though they are very uncomfortable, and which little children have to wear when they are eleven or twelve years old. When I went to Japan in 1959, I went down the Ginza the first night I got to Tokyo, and to my horror there were in the windows the same pointed shoes.

I talked about Abigail Adams last time. This remarkable woman is an unbelievable source of richness. She never left the home, and the entire education of her children really depended upon herself, because John Adams had to be away at the Continental Congress and then he went to Europe. Abigail Adams was a most learned woman. Her letters are remarkable and will soon be published; they read exceedingly well today. She is part of a group of women in New England, including Mercy Warren, the historian, who were friends of Miss Katherine Macaulay, the English historian who came to visit for a brief while. These women were remarkably different; self-motivated, in a wilderness, a relatively rough colonial environment in which there were few books and few opportunities of easy sort to achieve education. They made the richest possible mental life for themselves with no nonsense about the fact that it is easy, but that it takes a great deal of hard work to do anything meaningful with your life. The continuity to this, the suffragettes (I prefer the term "feminists"), themselves, are rich in this same sense. We have imposed a stereotype upon them out of laziness and laxness and out of a desire to accept a slogan for the much more complicated human and individual realities. We are murderers of the richnesses which other people's lives contained and which could form part of a continuing human community in which we are the last or the most recent members. We destroy that when we are too superficial to have a sense of history, too lacking in inquiry to open ourselves to the arts and literature, and then we settle for all the junk that is thrown at us and then have to live with it.

Miss Mannes But did Mrs. Adams have a lot of junk thrown at her?

Dr. Koch Well, yes, she had junk thrown at her; I mean the junk that she had to put up with in the letter I read yesterday, that woman should be a clinging vine, and so on. On the other hand, recalling Mr. Hunt's comments, it is curious that the eighteenth-century woman in America was supposed to be clearly dependent upon her husband, when her husband was really in trouble and was deeply involved in the revolutionary movement; the first thing he did was to say, "You pitch in, take over for me; take over the task of education and business management of our farms; take over even in terms of seeing to it that various kinds of economic sanctions are visited against the British at Boston," and Mrs. Adams proved competent for all this. He then became a diplomat, and when Mrs. Adams was asked to come over and join him, she said, "Oh dear, I don't know if I can do it; I am just an American woman in those great courts of Europe and I will cut an awkward figure." But she went there, and even her awkwardness had integrity, and she did not become overcome by the blaze of royalty and glory. What I am trying to say is that very often men who use stereotypes about women and what they want of women don't know what they do want or what to ask.

Think of the widows who suddenly prove themselves capable of carrying on a man's business. This is not a twentieth-century development; this was true in colonial times. They are quite able to do things if they really must, and if we know that in advance, we may be more ready to give women the chance to do whatever they can as fully as possible.

Mrs. Gunderson The thing you might have been saying is very much like "Should I be buying this dress, Emily? Would my husband like it?" We all know very well he will, if I with my taste like it. The dear girl at forty-five who is still dressing as if she were still on her honeymoon is making that awful mistake. The very rigors of the demands made on Abigail and her wonderful breed seem to me to have given a starch to what they did.

Miss Mannes But what I object to is not the honest, pure Puritanism of those days but its residue coupled with a real, monstrous hypocrisy. On the one hand, from every pulpit in the country there is intoned the usual thing about spiritual and moral values, and chastity, and all the rest. On the other hand, there is no country that I know of wherein the volumes of filth are so widely distributed, where the naked female is a selling device, and where grown men have to go to Bunny Clubs in order to get vicarious kicks which they should be able to have in other ways with less money. This is where I return to the hetaera. At a certain time in Greece they were a recognized class. We have nothing like it; we have nothing, in fact, between the call girl and the housewife, as far as I can see. These ladies combined a great many arts of the mind and the body to use for the delectation of intelligent men and themselves. As I understand it, ideally the relationship between that kind of woman and the man who benefited from her was a quite remarkable one on quite a high level. It had nothing to do with marriage or childbearing, but it had a valid and very stimulating place in the life of Athens. A great many things flourished then, and I am sure that was possibly one reason.

All I am saying is that we should consider a number of different ways in which a woman can be useful as well as an adornment. That is just one of them. I think we should revise our thinking about the woman who chooses simply not to marry. This is not necessarily a tragedy. There have been some marvelous single women, I know, who obviously are not always happy—who is? Here again is this stereotype that one thing makes for happiness and the other does not; it depends entirely on the person. I know a number of distinguished single women who for one reason or another have not married or had children, who have yet contributed a great deal to society. I think we may even some-day realize that the mother may want a child without a husband; I know this is a horrible thought, but some women are intensely maternal but profoundly unwifely.

I am not saying that we are going to have these things or that they will ever come about, but if we look at people honestly we should at least be prepared to accept that the wide variation and diversity that Dr. Callaway talked about is our salvation.

Dr. Callaway   There is something bothering me, and it may have the elements of at least some controversy on the podium here. We face a society then that does mold people, whether they like it or not, and molds them in ways that we, who know much better, don't particularly approve of.

Mrs. Gunderson, do you think that loving rivalry is going to be enough to shake the shackles off the slave that loves the shackles?

Mrs. Gunderson   I think it will be very difficult. I believe if there is any single golden thought, it will be as Mr. Hunt said, that men will get just about the women they like, and frankly this annoys me. Why instead aren't we saying women will be as good as they intend to be? But all of us have been aware of intensely able people bent out of shape by parents who loved them in the wrong way too much, and we have seen splendid men become very tragic nonentities because of a certain type of love they felt for a woman or she felt for them, and certainly we have seen good fathers, brothers, and husbands ruin women.

Loving rivalry seems to me rivalry in its real sense. If you are playing a hard game of tennis or bridge, it means you give no quarter; you give the very best you have and compete with them. Frankly, I am not sure, though, that those who love being delightfully mediocre are going to like this kind of petty business.

Dr. Koch   I think anything that is worth doing, even a game that one is playing, sets up its own requirements and demands. It is an objective commitment outside the self, and I think that there is such a thing; it used to be called the instinct for workmanship, but it has got a much longer history than Veblen's name for it. It goes all the way back to the sense of aesthetic perfection of giving yourself to some object, perfecting it, and studying it as something beyond yourself. It can be the appreciation, or it can start as simply enjoying the quality of light on trees; it can then become weaving or shoemaking or the greatest game of all, the game of minds, of testing ideas against ideas, the birth really of dialectic in the Socratic sense of the term. Anything that can bring richness to the personality is something to which that personality gives itself in the most ultimate sense possible.

If you are playing a game of chess, you play it as well as you can, and therefore I support Miss Gunderson totally in terms of what she says on the much more fundamental question of the relationship between men and women. Of course, there has to be rivalry, because anything else implies that you are not dealing with persons but something less than persons.

It is like losing the game to a child, to an inferior being, possibly to an animal; to an inferior being, to a thing but not another person. If two persons are involved, then it must be two persons essentially, however unequal they are; because they are unequal, they must be given every chance to do what they can with themselves and create their own destiny.

So I would say that personhood means this kind of rivalry that Barbara Gunderson has been talking about, and it means more than that. It means that to be a person you must be more than a person; you must have objective interests which compellingly involve you in other things than simply yourself. In tailoring yourself to somebody else, you give yourself to something, but the human person wants to be more than simply a series of floating impressions, adaptations, and stereotypes; he wants to live in the largest sense that he possibly can. To make an automatic compromise, because the male expectations are that the female is going to be so big but not so big as a Procrustean bed which destroys individuality.

Dr. Callaway   We hear a somewhat closer view of our culture, and I would like to turn back to the anthropologist now and see if from a little greater vantage point you have anything to clarify for us in this.

Dr. Jay   I think our concept of woman in this entire symposium has obviously been Western woman, with the exception of Dr. Albert, who dealt with other cultures. There are so many things that we need to know about woman as a mother, a female, and a wife that we know only one end of the spectrum of the possibilities of her roles.

Woman as a female Homo sapiens has evolved to adjust to being a mother. She is a primate, and we can perhaps understand her a little bit better as a New Yorker, Chicagoan, or Parisienne, if we understand basically the kind of thing that she is and that her behavior has been adapted to in the past. The behavior she displays now is no longer adaptive to the situation in which she finds herself, as witnessed by the high incidence of a great many physical disorders such as heart troubles, ulcers, and psychosomatic disease. Not that monkeys cannot get ulcers; we can frustrate them deliberately in the laboratory and reproduce modern society very easily in terms of the pathology of the situation.

Perhaps we are asking some of the wrong questions. I said earlier to stop letting society tell her how to act. Women in American culture have a great deal more freedom than women in other cultures. What are they doing with it? The problem seems to be the constructive use of the freedom we do have.

A monkey mother is a mother 70 per cent of her life. A modern female mother is not a mother 70 per cent of her life, and many females are never mothers at all. The suggestion that Dr. Maccoby made that we ought to train women and define roles more realistically because of the things that we see on TV and so forth really refers only to a very small percentage of a female's life, and we're not at all realistic in facing the problem.

Dr. Koch   I am sure Dr. Jay recognizes as fully as anybody does that there is a certain sense in which studies of rat behavior or ape behavior worry one in the sense in which they are extrapolated as the kind of "norm" for human behavior. I have no intention of discouraging the empirical research that this wonderfully fertile world of ours can possibly create, but there is a dangerous sense where sometimes we put alongside the role of the female primate and then say, "Woman is really a female primate," and then what? We are highly complicated, highly evolved, very troubled people with our own natural sources of developing ulcers. Nobody has to structure us with pellets or reward situations, because we figured out how to get these for ourselves. So very often the result of animal experimental testing is very important in learning about the animal, but it adds up to absolutely nix about the human species.

Dr. Jay   That is quite true: a rat is a rat and a monkey is a monkey; but a human being—don't forget—still is a primate.

Dr. Koch   May I just add to that with *"Vive la différence"* even here.

Dr. Callaway   I have one last anthropological question that is gnawing at me that has to do with this enormous emphasis on love. As a man I think we should stand against this tender instinct and call attention to the ethological studies which show that the wolves will not kill an injured wolf if he turns his neck; this is behavior that allows the survival of the extremely hostile and predatory species. When we come, however, to the gentle dove, we find a most wretched behavior toward the vanquished. Now can we make any inferences about the effect of insisting that one segment of the population be "gentle" and the other portion rough, in terms of failing to develop in the gentle species the necessary protective devices that present roughness from becoming destructive to the species? How is that?

Dr. Jay   Actually when you look at forms of aggression in animals, such as wolves or any other predator, the aggression within the species, that is aggression wolf to wolf, is usually minimal, and there are many ways, factors, and patterns of social behavior which are developed expressly to control this aggression when it is turned to other members of the same species. Man being an essentially domesticated animal compared to his fossil ancestors, in the sense that he has domesticated his own animals, is not at all basically an aggressive animal. In the course of his evolution he has had to learn to live in social groups and has done so successfully, as all the primates have. But in any patterns of behavior within a species usually there are a lot of gestures and vocalizations to channel aggressiveness, to minimize actual physical harm from fighting per se. If you look at antlers on deer, these things seem to be very formidable and capable of doing immense destruction, but if you watch these animals fighting, you see they are indeed buffers to prevent real harm, because they match perfectly the antlers of the same species, and it is the animal with the broken antler who does the real damage. Perhaps we could look at a lot of patterns of social behavior in our own society from this point of view.

Dr. Albert   I apparently didn't make a sufficiently strong impression when I presented the data in my paper or took advantage of the opportunity to speak. Any notion that women are biologically or otherwise sweet, gentle types is, as all of us girls know, by and large a figment of the imagination of males and of some females. Again, as is best and proper for us, we are being conned into being gentle and sweet when we are just as tough as anybody. Observing real behavior, not simply looking at stereotypes, is hardly likely to give us the notion that there is a sex-linked difference, excepting perhaps in the behavior of new babies; even my type likes new babies. I am reminded almost irrelevantly of a trip I took in France last year to see the cave paintings at Lascaux, and because I am more or less French-speaking, I was dumped in with a bunch of French women, all about the same age, and I was the only one still wearing size 12. In terms of their sentiment and behavior—which explained their ample figures—and in terms of what I learned about their careers, they were about as soft and gentle as their husbands, who were not the least bit soft and gentle, who were also too fat but, by some of our elegant standards, too much interested in money. So the difference between the husbands and the wives were of the *"Vive la différence"* variety, and, of course, age does make a difference.

It is difficult, unless you are really kidding yourself, when you are past forty to be a sweet young thing. In any event, the behavior of mature women in any society I know tends to manifest a great deal of toughness, and some of it has this kind of survival value. I don't know anything about direct motherhood, but I know about being a big sister. When my kid brother fell off a fire escape, I didn't have the right to faint. I had to put his face back together again, and many, many mothers have to be tough in that respect. Any practical woman has to be inherently tough, tough enough to do her job. There are times and places for this cute little business of how sweet and tender we are; let's not overlook that. But the generalization that men are or should be tough bruisers and ladies should be sweet, tender, and soothing has nothing to do with the realities of life in any human society, ours included.

Miss Mannes   I am asked, "Is the Lesbian type of woman, present panel of course excepted, apt to be more successful in a man's competitive business or a creative field?"

I don't think you can generalize here, since there are some Lesbians who have gone quite high in creative and cultural fields and just as many who have not. I don't think this is a guarantee of anything. A Lesbian has her own problems and frustrations, and can be as much an enemy of herself as a "normal" woman.

Dr. Albert   We are asked the same question as the last panel. This is a question from a gentleman who says, "Since the panel is discussing Mr. and Mrs. Mitty, why has the panel not included representatives of the common man and the common woman?" Indeed we cannot use the exceptional or extraordinary as the criterion for everybody. In any group talking about the values of individuality, respect for the individual means not respect for some kind of ideal maximum but respect for each human individual, as he or she actually is, and the establishment of norms and ideals which are realizable by human beings as they happen to be. It would be utterly absurd for us to insist that every girl become a Ph.D. in philosophy, just as it would be as absurd for me that I become a mom just like some of you. The respect for individuality includes the respect for individual differences along every axis we know.

Now what stands between the panel and the question is the plain fact that the kinds of studies that have so far been made have not been adequate. What clearly needs to be done, which I think is the whole purpose of this panel, is to point out that in studying the potential of woman we have to get much more adequate data on the realities of woman and the inseparable question of the realities of men. So the question is of great value in helping us to focus all the additional realistic information about all of us.

There is an interesting question here. "In a three-day symposium on the potential of woman, why have none of the speakers discussed the life of Eleanor Roosevelt?"

I would say that I would certainly consider this an omission if we had been trying to talk specifically about the great women of the twentieth century. I think Eleanor Roosevelt's life surely has become internalized deeply in the consciousness of men and women in America and that it would indeed be a fitting subject for study in terms of a very remarkably skillful adaptation of a woman with great intelligence and creative imagination who nevertheless carried out her role of wife and First Lady with much becomingness, although there was much of the country that resented Mrs. Roosevelt's efforts in behalf of civil liberties and all her other causes. Her life is an answer to some of the women who have raised the questions of what happens to women after they are forty-five, because it seemed to me that she became intensely more human, humane, and richer in depth, the older she became; she must have been of exquisite transcendent sweetness just before she died.

Mrs. Gunderson   I quite agree with your answer; I think we didn't come to eulogize the already established, but there are parts, particularly in my convictions, that are illustrated in Mrs. Roosevelt admirably. I said that one of the wicked weapons that kept us grandmothers, teachers, mamas, and mothers of misguided girls was the weapon of ridicule. It is most magnificent to contemplate that America was not ready for such a unique woman, who was vulnerable because she didn't look like the lady on the candy box and because her children were so full of life and excitement. She had a very dominant and selfcontained mother-in law in the house, and her dental structure and everything was used against her, but she went on sweetly being herself. She didn't suddenly disappear and come out of a charm school; she just went on being Mrs. Roosevelt until we got the hang of her.

Dr. Albert Another question that has been presented that I am rather evading but will do my best to answer is, "Does a woman who takes advantage of educational opportunities offered her by society have a real obligation to repay society above and beyond any contributions she might make as a wife and mother?"

I suppose so. I don't know how we measure our obligation, but I make the assumption that in some sense making our contribution to society involves doing something that we ourselves like to do. My utopia would be one in which everybody, male, female, in-between, or both, would have the liberty to do what best suited him, her, or it and would at the same time by virtue of this be able to make a contribution to society. This is utopian, but I wouldn't like to have to set up a measure of invidious comparison to decide between these ideas and those other women give to their children, and what our individual obligations are.

Miss Mannes The question here is "Career women attain independence financially, intellectually, and sexually, but is it possible for women to attain emotional independence as well as men?"

I think we get back here into the generalization: is anyone emotionally independent? It is virtually impossible to answer this. I don't think that any living, breathing human being, male or female, who is fundamentally healthy, can live without emotional involvement. There is a great difference between involvement and dependence, and they are necessary to both sexes in varying degrees.

Dr. Callaway That is perhaps a more important question than it may seem at first glance, and I would like to hear some other thoughts about it. Clinically the problem of dependence and independence is today more evident in psychopathology than sexual phases, for example, and the problem of dependence and independence in relationships is a very crucial thing that perhaps could stand a little more scrutiny. I think you spelled out the role of individual difference sufficiently. I think you have also spelled out the fact that people are dependent one upon another, and particularly when a man and a woman live together in a culture that sets up certain roles for each one, the business of dependence and independence becomes a good deal more thick. The sum of what Miss Mannes has been saying has to do with how one deals with dependence without losing independence. The fact that a woman and a man can have certain differing needs might cause them to turn to one another for these needs and in so doing be dependent upon one another, but this does not necessarily involve them in some lifetime sticky web. On the other hand, again I think that there is a wide range of possibilities in the dependence-independence scheme of things.

Miss Mannes Could I put this into a sort of wider frame, because the whole business of sovereignty and dependence or independence in the world is terribly important now. The world was going in the only possible direction of the abandonment of total sovereignty in favor of interdependence. I think that it is the hope of mankind that in order to achieve a unity of thought and prevent self-destruction, we of necessity have to give a little of our sovereignty. This is essentially what happens in a male-female relationship but in equal part. For many hundreds of years the male sovereignty did not give; it was the female who had to abdicate to a certain degree. The revolution happening now in sexual, emotional, and intellectual relationships between a man and a woman is very much a parallel to what is happening or what must happen in the world at large.

Dr. Koch It is a very intriguing idea to think of the relationship between men and women as that of the Federal republic; I am going to play with this one.

We have rehearsed this in the matter of dependence and independence in Western civilization. There was the sect of the Stoics in ancient Greece who maintained that in order to be independent man must root out all desires man gives as hostage to fortune—wife or children, and so on—to stay clear of these in order to lead a life of great equanimity and lack of perturbation and endure and renounce. The pattern is very clear that if you want no dependence at all and the kind of total independence in which you have given no hostage to fortune, you end up with a very severely restricted life in which you have nothing except some sort of dedication to reason. It is, as Mrs. Gunderson says, a pretty dismal independence that you get, and if you want it, you can have it.

Dr. Callaway I seem to remember—and I may be entirely wrong—that the Stoics did, of course, go off and deny all their earthly attachments, but didn't they come back once they had divested themselves of the emotional bondage and marry and raise families?

Dr. Koch The Stoics, just as most theoreticians, were not quite able to live up to their theory. I don't want to lampoon the Stoics, for whom I have really great affection; we stand in rather great obligation to them, because it was the Stoic conception of the brotherhood of man and of a natural law which was more fundamental than municipal and civil law, which is the origin of what we talk about as natural rights in our environment.

Dr. Albert I think Phyllis Jay and anyone else who has done anthropological field work will understand my proposal that we make a distinction between independence and simply being alone for some sort of time. Those of us who do field work go out for weeks or months, and I was asked when I got back from a year and a half in the Bush, "Weren't you lonely?" Of course, my chief problem was nobody would leave me alone. My surveyor, steward, chauffeur, and clerk all felt responsible for me. This is alone in the sense that one does not have one's usual circle of acquaintances or family. But there is a more or less normal or natural love of being really lonely and alone, and there are some very interesting representations in literature of the most tragic kinds of loneliness, that the individual surrounded by family and friends still feels alone. If we take the word of some of the French existentialists, it is *the* illness of our times that one can be in the midst of so many people and still be alone. But there is a distinction between being alone, in the sense of not being in a crowd or not being pressed upon by individuals all the time, and being in that kind of constructive and religious solitude in which you can think a little bit clearly. Sound dependence upon others has to be based on enough trust so that you cannot feel lonely or afraid when that man is away; you don't have to be afraid that that cute blonde secretary is really going to get in there and spoil your show. The notion that people have to be together all the time to be interdependent is a bad one more than a good one, and in our culture mothers and children and husbands and wives are too intensely together. We have got to learn to be alone without being lonely.

Miss Mannes I am extremely glad Dr. Albert brought up this business of solitude, because if I were the usual fairy godmother and wished something for every single woman in the world, it would be a period of total solitude during the day. I think this is the terrible deprivation of most woman who are never, never alone.

Dr. Albert Curiously enough my awareness of the importance of being alone did not come out of my own experience or my awareness of what other people had as problems, but rather from problems of one of my dearest friends, one of my own brothers, who has never been alone. He has paid a fortune for an immense house, which is loaded with children, television, wife, and so forth. He has not been alone in his own home at all, and his only rest is to go to the office on Sunday to be alone for a quarter of an hour. So it is for all of us this terrible need to have a little recovery time.

Dr. Koch I think we are beating a drum which has already entered into American folklore. Was it not the most lovely woman on the silent screen and later the speaking screen who said, "I want to be alone"?

Mrs. Gunderson I believe that the dependence that a child or subordinate has is the wrong kind. It is a necessary, unchosen dependence. The active love and selection to which we are privileged as free American women is that we choose this interrelation with nations in which we say, "I will become dependent on you; you may trust me and be dependent on me." This is a very selective kind of emotional dependency and is where the definition of passionate teen-age love is so wistful to be so absolutely pole axed that dependence is quite beyond choice.

Dr. Callaway This puts me very much in mind of one of the most gifted women that I ever had the opportunity to come in contact with, Frieda Fromm-Reichmann, who was quite famous for her work with psychotherapy with schizophrenics. She spent a great deal of time talking and teaching about the difference between aloneness and loneliness, that aloneness is something that is absolutely essential and loneliness is something that is so terrible people can't speak rationally about it.

Miss Mannes The equal inability of men and women to be alone starts very early through what I consider a really dangerous or harmful childhood of the same quality.

Our children are accounted for and with people every hour of the day. Their time is organized so that they move from one group to another; if they're not with their family, they are with a den group, or if not with a den group, they are with somebody else. How a child who has never been alone can learn to be alone productively is a great question, and we ought to insist that our children have two hours a day entirely alone by themselves. I don't mean by locking them in a room, but by making it possible, for no organization is a training.

Dr. Koch Unfortunately they are getting that two hours alone but it is spent doing homework, and we all believe that it should be spent in that way, but on the adult level you can do much more about it, because we can really test how serious we are about whether we really want to be alone. To want to be alone means to be able to refuse a meaningless social invitation or to read a book rather than to go out and play cards. The choices one makes daily on my old technique of waiting for the next mail before you commit suicide are really a proof of what we mean in terms of behavior rather than what we say we want. Many people do a great many things which give them diminishing returns in terms of pleasure, but because they are expected of them, because they think they must be popular, they do them. You test popularity by how many cocktail parties you attend or how many dinner parties you are invited to, even though you know you are going to be terribly bored if you go and you can give yourself the guest list and the agenda of conversation before you ever participate. Nevertheless you feel you are in some sense a pariah if you choose to stay home to read or write a little; but we will find the time when we care enough about being alone.

Miss Mannes How does a woman with four small children manage to be alone?

Mrs. Gunderson   My favorite mother is my own who had six children. A friend asked her, "Where were you all day Tuesday?" This was in a town of 3,500, so she knew she wasn't down at the bowling alley. Mother said, "What day was Tuesday?" "It was the day that the pipes broke in the schoolhouse and all the children were let out." "Oh yes, I had a great crowd of children at my house, and I took a detective story and a bag of peanuts and drove out to the cemetery for the afternoon."

Dr. Callaway   Mrs. Jay, you raised your eyebrows there? This is perhaps not the warm mothering terry cloth of Harlow.

Dr. Jay   A mature monkey mother has to cope with only one at a time. When she weans hers, there is nothing socially unacceptable in saying, "Okay, Junior, you are thirteen months old and you have got to pick your own leaves now."

Dr. Callaway   I understood Miss Mannes to say that our children should have two hours by themselves. Do you think our children should be imbued with this sort of training?

Miss Mannes   They can use it in any way they choose; that is where diversity comes in. I think it is a valuable training which can be of great benefit to them individually later in life. Here we come to the independence that is the necessary core of the human spirit, the ability to be one's self alone, to look into one's self to choose without perpetual outside pressure or interference.

Dr. Albert   For those of us who want to do anything, you have got to be alone; you can't have things popping all around you.

Dr. Callaway   We have one last rather terrible question which I have been asked to pass among the panel: "Inasmuch as the men who preceded you were asked their opinion of what constitutes the ideal woman, it is only fair and just to ask your opinion on the ideal man. Let us hope that you can answer more imaginatively than the men, who seemed terribly inhibited." This question is asked by a man.

Dr. Jay   My man is certainly adaptable and willing to put up with my going off and doing what I want to and still keep things going; but I sort of like most men.

Miss Mannes   The ideal man is the man who thinks I am divine.

Dr. Albert   We have only expressed a disapproval of negative discrimination; I just like men.

Dr. Koch I think the ideal man is the man who creates a world which I cannot see without his creation.

Mrs. Gunderson I think the ideal man saves some part of his observance of life for my ears alone and is at least partly spellbound when I tell him my secret world story.